Everyday Theology

cultural exegesis

William A. Dyrness
and **Robert K. Johnston**, series editors

The Cultural Exegesis series is designed to complement the Engaging Culture series by providing methodological and foundational studies that address the way to engage culture theologically. Each volume works within a specific cultural discipline, illustrating and embodying the theory behind cultural engagement. By providing the appropriate tools, these books equip the reader to engage and interpret the surrounding culture responsibly.

Everyday Theology

How to Read Cultural Texts and Interpret Trends

Edited by

Kevin J. Vanhoozer

Charles A. Anderson
Michael J. Sleasman

Baker Academic
Grand Rapids, Michigan

Published by Baker Academic
a division of Baker Publishing Group
P.O. Box 6287, Grand Rapids, MI 49516-6287
www.bakeracademic.com

Printed in the United States of America

Library of Congress Cataloging-in-Publication Data
Everyday theology : how to read cultural texts and interpret trends cultural exegesis / Kevin J. Vanhoozer, Charles A. Anderson, Michael J. Sleasman, editors.
    p. cm. — (Cultural exegesis)
    Includes bibliographical references and index.
    ISBN 10: 0-8010-3167-2 (pbk.)
    ISBN 978-0-8010-3167-0 (pbk.)
    1. Christianity and culture. 2. Theology, Practical. 3. Theology. I. Vanhoozer, Kevin J. II. Anderson, Charles A., 1975– III. Sleasman, Michael J., 1976
    BR115.C8E94 2007
    261—dc22   2006030278

16 17 18   10 9 8 7 6

Contents

Part 3 Interpreting Cultural Trends

Part 4 Concluding Untheoretical Postscript

A Reader's Guide

How to Use This Book

This is a book about everyday theology, written by everyday theologians for everyday theologians.

Everyday theology is the reflective and practical task of living each day as faithful disciples of Jesus Christ. Theology is not for Sundays only. Disciples must walk the Christian way the whole weekend and throughout the workweek. Theology is an everyday affair: to live to the glory of God is a full-time privilege and pursuit. Everyday theology is the mandate of every Christian who is actively trying to walk the way of truth and life.

Theology serves the church by directing the people of God in ways of speaking and acting that embody the love of God, the reconciliation won by Jesus Christ, and the fellowship of the Holy Spirit. Theology not only articulates beliefs but suggests "designs for living." Precisely what form our life together takes, however, depends on where (and when) we are: the house churches in first-century Palestine are a far cry from medieval monasteries or modern megachurches. The gospel gets worked out somewhat differently in diverse cultural settings. The gospel—the power of God unto salvation—can transform culture; culture, however, is only too happy to return the compliment. Everyday Christians have to learn to negotiate their way carefully, following the one way of Jesus Christ through a variety of cultural byways.

The purpose of this book is to teach Christians to get the theological lay of the cultural land. It is less a matter of spying out some new land than of becoming conscious of the land in which one already dwells. What the apostle Paul says to the Athenians about God is also true of culture: "In [it] we live and move and have our being" (Acts 17:28). Faithful disciples need to understand the biblical text, but they also need to understand their cultural context; they need to become bilingual.

If theology is the ministry of the Word to the world, it follows that theologians must know something about the world to which they are ministering. What should have been common sense, however, has for various reasons been something of a blind spot, at least until the advent of postmodernity. Indeed, one way of viewing postmodernity is as a "turn to culture." Postmoderns have criticized modern myths about universality precisely because postmoderns have a keen sense of our situatedness in race, gender, class, history, tradition—and culture.

Christian missionaries have always been aware of the need to engage culture. Yet only recently has it been suggested that the West has become a mission field. Lesslie Newbigin points out that the West presents a special challenge to Christian missions, for this is the first time the church has had to mount a mission to a culture that was previously Christian.[1] How does one evangelize cultures that have already received the gospel only to revise or to reject it? For these and other reasons, Christian colleges and seminaries are increasingly coming to see that the study of culture is part and parcel of the prospective minister's theological training.

Where This Book Began

The genesis of this book lies in a course that I first taught in 2001 and have taught annually since then at Trinity Evangelical Divinity School: "Cultural Hermeneutics" (my two co-editors were student guinea pigs in that original class). The name of the course is significant. Most seminary students are well acquainted with biblical hermeneutics: the study of the principles and methods for interpreting the Bible. Similarly, cultural hermeneutics is the study of principles and methods for interpreting culture.

Devising the name—and of course the aims and objectives—of the course was the easy part. I quickly discovered that the plethora of textbooks in biblical hermeneutics stood in stark contrast to what I was able to find for my new course. While there were books in specific disciplines (e.g., anthropology, sociology) that dealt with interpreting culture, there were no textbooks that dealt with how to interpret culture theologically. I therefore have devised my own approach, a distillation of which may be found in the first essay of the present book. I also developed a number of case studies of cultural phenomena—ranging from body piercing and gardens to John Ford's film *Stagecoach* and Levi's ads—that served as catalysts to my students' imaginations.

The chapters that comprise this book were originally submitted as term papers for my course. My co-editors and I have selected a representative sampling from the one hundred and forty-five term papers written over the past five years. Other papers deserve to be included here but could not be due to considerations of space, balance, and so forth. Honorable mention goes to those students (you know who you are) who wrote on such diverse trends as makeovers, Starbucks (a very popular topic), masculinity, femininity, magazines for teenage girls, free-market dating, Internet dating, professional football, Notre Dame football (a world unto itself), extreme sports, bumper stickers, cell phones, lifestyle centers, worship styles, procrastination, facebook.com, Slam poetry, rap, hip-hop, literary genres (e.g., cyberpunk), radio shows (e.g., *This American Life*), television shows, and films like *Memento*, *The Matrix*, *Moulin Rouge*, and *Minority Report* (and that's just the "M-list").

Some may wonder what these topics have in common or what seminary students are doing writing on these issues. Good question! My opening essay serves as the long answer. The short answer is that each chapter is an exercise in "reading" culture theologically, that is, with a view to achieving Christian understanding of what is going on in our part of the world, why it is going on, and how we should respond.

What This Book Is About

It is appropriate that the subtitle of our book is a subtle allusion to a cultural icon: Dale Carnegie's *How to Win Friends and Influence People*. First published in 1937, the book was an overnight sensation, eventually selling more than fifteen million copies. Carnegie believed that the secret to financial success has less to do with specialized knowledge than it does with people skills. *How to Win Friends* is really a book about how to "read" men and women: *people* hermeneutics.

Everyday Theology is also a how-to book, as its subtitle—*How to Read Cultural Texts and Interpret Trends*—indicates, though the success for which it aims is measured not in terms of money but of understanding. I set forth the principles for understanding—"cultural hermeneutics"—in my introductory essay: "What Is Everyday Theology? How and Why Christians Should Read Culture." I call these principles for interpreting culture "the Method," but what I actually propose is somewhat less formal than the kind of methodology one finds in the natural sciences. Cultural interpretation is, after all, a study of the human creature and as such is concerned with comprehension, not computation.

While some readers may find themselves tempted to go straight to the illustrative exercises to find out about Eminem or blogging, that would be a mistake. While those essays may be more immediately attractive, skipping the first essay runs the risk of missing the main point of the book. The chapters on busyness, blogging, fantasy funerals, and so forth are primarily intended to show how the Method plays out when applied to a whole range of cultural expressions. It is important, therefore, to begin with the first essay because it presents the Method used in the rest of the book. The essays in part 2 employ the Method to interpret specific cultural texts; those in part 3 use the same Method in an attempt to make sense of more complex trends and movements.

One theme that pops up in both parts is the question of what it means to be human. A second, closely related theme pertains to the good life: how to define it, where to find it, and at what cost to pursue it. A third theme, which emerges from the first two and takes us to the threshold of religion, is the notion of hope and human flourishing. In sum, this book is about some rather fundamental questions: Who are we and why are we here? What should we be doing? Where are we heading? Yet we approach these questions indirectly, turning not to philosophers for abstract answers but to discern what concrete answers and guidance culture offers, if only implicitly.

How to Use This Book

Everyday Theology is not an encyclopedia of contemporary culture, nor is it a full-blown textbook of cultural hermeneutics. What it provides instead is a model for "reading" culture theologically as well as a number of illustrative exercises. Again, it is important that readers begin with the methodological overture that sets forth the Method used in the rest of the essays because the main purpose of the book is to help Christian readers—college and seminary students, lay readers, and clergy alike—learn from these concrete examples what is involved in interpreting any cultural phenomenon.

Our authors are, for the most part, "everyday" rather than expert theologians. Some are still students, others have entered the workplace, and still others are engaged in Christian ministry. While some may see the lack of professional qualifications on the part of the authors as a weakness, I view it as a strength. If each of us had to acquire specialized knowledge before making any judgments about what was going on in our world and what it means, we would forever be agnostics. The whole point is that *all* Christians can and should achieve some degree of cultural literacy, that is, the ability to read or interpret the world we live in through the lens of the Bible and Christian faith. This book is for all kinds of people: for shoppers surveying racks of magazines in the checkout line at the grocery store, for friends discussing Oscar nominees for Best Picture, for couples planning their weddings. Most of all, it is for any person trying as a Christian to understand his or her culture in order therein to embody the life of a faithful disciple.

The present book serves as a Christian primer for cultural literacy. As I argue in the methodological overture, every Christian needs to be aware of what is happening in our everyday environment, of how it affects us, and of how we can affect it. Accordingly, we hope the book will be used as a text in Christian colleges and adult Sunday School classes, or wherever two or three gather together as disciples.

Each of the essays in parts 1 and 2 has been shaped to follow the same basic pattern: (1) a respectful assessment of a particular cultural text or trend on its own terms, (2) an analysis of that text or trend in light of the biblical story line and Christian doctrine, and (3) a suggestion for responding to that text or trend so as to become what I refer to in the opening essay as a "cultural agent." Each of these interpretations works to produce a "thick description"—a rounded picture of the cultural phenomenon that integrates different disciplines and sources, including theology—in order to say what that text or trend means. The essays therefore display a unity in aim and overall method while respecting the variety inherent in the texts and trends themselves. Of course, the cultural texts and trends our authors survey continue to develop. These essays are not meant to be the definitive word on, say, Eminem's life and music; they are illustrative, not comprehensive.

In order to enhance the pedagogical value of each essay, three additional editorial vehicles have been deployed. First, each essay includes editorial sidebars designed to highlight how the author is actually employing the Method. Second, several longer "book links" engage significant works from cultural studies and other fields that touch on particular texts and trends and assess their adequacy or contribution vis-à-vis a Christian theological hermeneutic of culture. Third, a glossary provides brief definitions of certain key concepts that figure prominently in the Method.

The book concludes with a final case study—on weddings—that takes a behind-the-scenes look at how one actually goes about employing the Method advocated in this book. As such, it serves both as a review of what the other chapters have done and as an invitation to readers to begin to interpret culture theologically for themselves. So take, read, and become an everyday theologian.

Whom to Thank for This Book

I wish to thank all the students who have enrolled in my Cultural Hermeneutics class over the years for teaching me so much. I am particularly grateful to those who have contributed essays to this volume for their willingness to revisit and revise their essays with a view to their publication. Most of them did so while still pursuing academic degrees and thus coping with other papers and exams. My co-editors, Charles Anderson and Michael Sleasman, deserve special mention. This book is their brainchild, and they have done the lion's share of the nitty-gritty editorial work while simultaneously pursuing doctoral studies in New Testament (at Cambridge University) and systematic theology (here at Trinity, with me), respectively.

The three of us are delighted to be part of Baker Academic's series in "Cultural Exegesis" and wish to thank William Dyrness and Robert Johnson, the series editors, for going the extra academic mile by being open to a volume of student essays, and Robert Hosack, our editor at Baker, for believing in this project enough to make it happen.

Kevin J. Vanhoozer

Part I: Introduction

Toward a Theory of Cultural Interpretation

1

What Is Everyday Theology?

How and Why Christians Should Read Culture

KEVIN J. VANHOOZER

Theology, my professor said, is the ministry of the Word to the world: the application of the Bible to all areas of life.[1] Theological educators have typically tended to gravitate toward the first element of my professor's definition: the Bible. Those training for the ministry have been traditionally required to study the history and theology of Scripture with attention to the original languages. Even schools that no longer require Hebrew and Greek continue to equip their students to interpret and to preach the text.

As to the second element of the definition—the *application* to *all areas of life*—students were left pretty much on their own. Yet life is complex; "all areas" is so comprehensive as to be intimidating, and "application" is as much art as it is science. No wonder, then, that people in the pews are so often left wanting to know how the Bible relates to the rough and tumble of daily life.

There is another way to think about theology that, while not contradicting the first, makes it relevant both to prospective preachers and to lay people. Theology, according to Anselm's celebrated eleventh-century definition, is "faith seeking understanding" (*fides quaerens intellectum*): the attempt to grasp conceptually the nature of God, Jesus Christ, and humanity in light of the significance of God's acts. Anselm himself produced two treatises that continue to serve as aids in understanding the nature of God and the necessity and significance of Jesus' death respectively.[2]

What might "faith seeking understanding" mean when applied not only to the biblical text (the Word) but to everyday life (the world)? That is the key question this essay sets out to explore. Everyday theology is simply faith seeking everyday understanding: a grasp of what is going on in ordinary situations (and why), an attempt to make sense of one's surroundings. Understanding is the operative concept. *The ultimate purpose of this chapter is to help readers make Christian sense of everyday life, especially of cultural texts and cultural trends.* The two definitions of theology—bringing the Bible to bear on all areas of life, and faith seeking understanding—converge, for the way we make sense of everyday life is by reading it in light of the Scriptures.

Everyday theology, as presented here, is both old and new. The Reformers were well acquainted with the concept, if not the exact terminology. Luther believed that it was the privilege and responsibility of all Christians to interpret the Bible to gain understanding.[3] And Calvin believed that the way to gain understanding was to view (read) the world through the Bible, our "spectacles of faith." What is new in the present proposal is its way of suggesting that faith should seek understanding not only of the Word but of our everyday world.

Why not restrict theology to clarifying what the Bible says? Do we really need to go messing about in culture? Giving reasons for answering yes to this latter query is the main burden of the present chapter. For the moment, suffice it to say that theology and understanding alike are short-circuited if we are not able to discern (1) how our faith is affected by the world we live in and (2) how we are to embody our faith in shapes of everyday life. The reason why theology must study God *and* contemporary culture is the same reason why preaching must connect both with the biblical text and the listener's context: because disciples do not follow the gospel in a vacuum but wend their Christian way through particular times and places, each with its own problems and possibilities. We can follow God's word only if we know where we are and if we have a sense of where various ways lead. Doing theology is part and parcel of one's daily walk and is too important to leave solely to the professionals.[4]

Introduction: What Is Everyday Theology?

Everyday theology is faith seeking understanding of everyday life. Nothing should be easier to understand than the notion of "the everyday" for the simple reason that it is so commonplace. What is most familiar to us, however, is often the hardest thing to understand. Augustine expresses this irony perfectly with regard to our everyday experience of time: "What is time? I know when nobody asks me. But when asked to explain it, I no longer know."[5] What time, the everyday, and culture have in common is that they are so familiar, so close to us—our social "skin," as it were—that we have a hard time stepping back and examining them at a distance. We can hardly distance ourselves from the very media of our existence. Nevertheless, I shall argue that we can still seek understanding of these things even if such understanding falls short of scientific explanation. Everyday theologians are readers, not scientists, of the everyday.

Interpreting "Signs of the Times"

If everyday theology had a biblical "proof text," it would have to be Matthew 16:1–3:

> The Pharisees and Sadducees came to Jesus and tested him by asking him to show them a sign from heaven. He replied, "When evening comes, you say, 'It will be fair weather, for the sky is red,' and in the morning, 'Today it will be stormy, for the sky is red and overcast.' You know how to interpret the appearance of the sky, but you cannot interpret the signs of the times."

It's all about interpreting signs: natural signs (the weather), the signs of our (cultural) times, and theological signs (e.g., Jesus' deeds as signs [*semeia*] of the kingdom of God, and Jesus himself as the sign or "Word" of God).

Jesus' words were probably directed at the Jewish leaders' willful refusal to see what God was doing in Israel through his own person. Yet it is reasonable to extrapolate from this that Christians today should similarly be alive and awake to what God is doing in our own time through the Spirit of Jesus Christ. Indeed, there is more than a verbal similarity between the "signs of the times" and the *Zeitgeist* or "spirit of the age," for to interpret the signs of the times *is* to discern the mode of the Spirit's presence in the spirit of the age. An inability to interpret the signs of the times is, conversely, to be guilty of what we might call the "Great Omission."

There are signs everywhere. Some, like traffic signs, are easy to read: green means go, smoke usually means fire, a red rash with small blisters often indicates chicken pox. Yet in a fast-paced, multimedia world, there are so many signs of various types that the sheer complexity of the task of discerning what it all means is overwhelming. It is tempting to let others—the meteorologist, the news anchor—distill, reduce, and package the raw chaos of life into a pristine sound bite. Data, data everywhere and not a drop to drink. Life is more than information-processing, as T. S. Eliot well knew:

> Where is the wisdom we have lost in knowledge?
> Where is the knowledge we have lost in information? (Choruses
>   from "The Rock," I)

Christians must learn to read the signs of the times. To that end, this book advocates a special kind of literacy. Literacy is the ability to read and write and, on one level, is not a problem for most Westerners. Most of us learn to read and write English in school. What we do not learn, however, is *cultural literacy*: how to "read" and "write" *culture*. This book provides basic tools and a method for achieving cultural literacy. The focus is on reading culture and involves critical engagement, not merely passive consumption. Yet we also should learn how to *write* culture: how to make *one's own mark* in our everyday world as an active participant.[6] Cultural literacy is crucial for those who are not content simply to be carried along by cultural winds and waves (cf. Eph. 4:14) but who want critically and constructively to engage culture for the sake of the gospel. The watchword, again, is everyday theology: faith seeking understanding of our everyday world.

The Everyday World

To speak of the everyday world is to refer to our environment, in the broadest sense of the term, or that which surrounds and sustains our everyday life. This includes not only our physical location but the moral, intellectual, and spiritual atmosphere in which we live and breathe as well. It is the ordinary practices that fill our days, the songs and messages that fill our minds, and the products that fill our homes and offices. Everyday theology is about making sense of the world we live in, its shape and its stuff.

While most of the authors in this book live in North America, the method they employ is applicable more generally—anytime, anyplace. After all, *my* everyday world is not the same as my neighbor's. My everyday world includes Dostoyevsky, Brahms, PBS, conversation around the dinner table, doctoral students, philosophical problems, and Christian doctrine, as well as grocery shopping, getting gas, going to movies, and balancing the checkbook. My neighbor's everyday world, however, seems to me like a planet far, far away that orbits around American idols, football players, and fast-food, as well as playing the lottery, surfing the Internet, and watching porn.[7] One need not travel far to enter other worlds.

Yet my neighbor is not really an alien from another planet for we share a context that is not only geographic but cultural. We are both white Americans, males, taxpayers, and suburbanites in our forties. We share a similar situation but we inhabit it differently. Though his property is adjacent to mine, his world is miles away. He is ultimately "other" to me. If I am to love my neighbor as myself and thus fulfill what Jesus calls the second greatest commandment (Matt. 22:39), then I will have to work hard to understand him. For I cannot love my neighbor unless I understand him and the cultural world he inhabits. Cultural literacy—the ability to understand patterns and products of everyday life—is thus an integral aspect of obeying the law of love.

Some readers may find my tendency to speak of "worlds" in the plural somewhat confusing. Yes, there are other planets but, with the exception of the odd cosmonaut, don't all human beings live on earth? Moreover, there is only one universe, and in this sense we all live in the same world. When I speak of "worlds" in the plural, therefore, I mean what the *Concise Oxford English Dictionary* lists as its seventh definition: "all that concerns [those] who belong to a specified class, time, domain, or sphere of activity (*the medieval world, the world of sport*)." The operative term is *concern*. Martin Heidegger, the existentialist philosopher, believed that concern or care (*Sorge*) is what makes us distinctly human; you shall know them by their concerns, we could say. Paul Tillich, a leading theologian of culture, said that the best way to understand a particular culture or even epoch is to discover its greatest anxiety (i.e., the focus of a negative concern) and its greatest hope (i.e., the focus of what Tillich called "ultimate concern," or simply "religion"). We begin to understand others and groups of others, then, when we begin to understand what concerns them and why.

Everyday Meteorology

Everyday theology seeks understanding of the everyday world, the pattern of people's everyday concerns whether trivial or ultimate. To sharpen our distinction between the physical world and the world of people's concerns, consider the weather report. No everyday reality concerns more people or is more often talked about than the weather: "You know how to interpret the appearance of the sky." Weather, of course, is a phenomenon of nature and as such belongs to the physical world. Human concern with nature and the way this concern is expressed, by contrast, varies from time to time and place to place.

Here, then, is a first puzzle: What does our culture's fascination with weather reports say about who we are and what concerns us? Whence our fascination with this page of the newspaper? When did it come to be a fixture on the evening news? How has the role of the meteorologist on television news shows in the mornings evolved, and what do these changes mean? And why is there a cable channel devoted to this subject?

One clue is that weather reports not only report but predict: they tell us what the day's high and low *were*, what the current temperature *is*, and what the weather for the next five days (probably) *will be*. This latter aspect, the forecast, has been improved considerably over the years thanks to radar, satellite technology, and the like, yet everyone knows that foretelling the future is still not an entirely reliable affair. Nevertheless, predicting the weather scientifically gives us the comforting illusion that, though we may not be able to rebuke the wind and the waves (cf. Matt. 8:26), we may nevertheless have a modicum of control over nature if to be forewarned is to be forearmed.

Perhaps our obsession with weather reports stems from anxiety over our helplessness before the world of nature. Or perhaps it is simply a matter of practicality and convenience, of wanting to know what one should wear outside on a given day. Neither of these suggestions explains the peculiar role that television meteorologists now play—something between reporter and entertainer—nor the typically quirky persona many weathercasters project.[8] It is not my purpose here to advance a specific thesis, only to raise the question and to begin to distinguish the everyday world of physical phenomena (e.g., weather) from the everyday world of cultural phenomena (e.g., weather reports).

It is this latter world—the world of everyday culture—that Christians urgently need to understand. This opening chapter introduces the project of understanding culture. The aim is to encourage and equip everyday Christians not only to achieve but to demonstrate their understanding by embodying gospel truth in compelling ways in contemporary contexts. My hope is that readers will recognize the importance of this destination and thus persevere in the journey to get there (no pain, no gain!). Here,

Toward a Theory of Cultural Interpretation

then, is the itinerary: the first section focuses on culture, the second on understanding (hermeneutics), and the conclusion on the response of the church. The goal in all three sections is to encourage theological thinking for the sake of Christian living.

Why Should Christians Read Culture?

We begin with culture as the object of faith seeking understanding. In order to read culture theologically, we must first come to know what culture is, what culture does, and what culture has to do with Christianity.

What Culture Is

What are we reading? Initially it is easier to say what culture is not rather than what it is. We therefore begin with some contrasts (culture versus nature; culture versus society) that help to sharpen the concept. We will then be in a better position to appreciate my proposed definition of culture as made up of "works and worlds of meaning."

Culture versus nature. The "appearance of the sky" to which Jesus refers in Matthew 16 is a natural phenomenon, not the result of human work. The so-called "state of nature" is the world untouched by the presence and activity of human beings.[9] Modern science views nature as a self-enclosed, impersonal, physical system ruled, yes, by tooth and claw, but even more so by causal law. The Enlightenment philosopher Immanuel Kant ratified this view by sharply distinguishing the realms of nature and freedom. Nature (*physis*) is explicable in terms of scientific law. Everything that happens in the realm of nature can ultimately be explained in terms of causes and effects: force always equals mass times acceleration, whether one is in Samoa or San Diego. Because human life is embodied, humans also exist in the realm of nature and are subject to nature's laws (e.g., gravity). Yet Kant realized that not everything that humans do can be explained in terms of causal laws. If it could, there would be no room for morality. Kant believed that ought (morality) implies can (freedom).[10] The salient point for our purposes is that culture proceeds from freedom alone. Indeed, in its broadest sense, culture refers to everything that humans do voluntarily as opposed to involuntarily (e.g., by nature, reflex, or instinct).[11]

Given the success of modern science in explaining the realm of nature, it is tempting to want the same kind of knowledge of human beings. The problem, however, is that instrumental rationality is unable to account for the particularity of individuals or to make room for human freedom. Consequently, it fell to Wilhelm Dilthey (1833–1911), the father of the human sciences, to come up with a principle that would do for the study of humanity what causal law had done for the study of nature. Dilthey coined the term *Geisteswissenschaften* ("sciences of the mind" or "spirit") to refer to those academic disciplines that have as their object human historical and social reality.

Dilthey's genius was to identify both the object and the method of the human sciences.[12] The object of the human sciences is, appropriately enough, human existence: the lived expression of human life, freedom, mind, or spirit.[13] Such expressions of life are not susceptible to explanation by causal law. That was precisely Dilthey's point. Whereas the natural sciences seek explanation by law, the human sciences seek understanding. To be sure, we cannot study freedom or mind or spirit directly, but we can do so indirectly. Humans "objectify" their "spirits" (e.g., their thoughts, values, beliefs) through concrete objects and works (e.g., poems, buildings, games) that call not for explanation but interpretation.

Culture is the realm of these objectified expressions of human freedom. Dilthey thought that specific cultures were the expressions or objectifications of the peculiar "spirit" of a people or a civilization (e.g., the medieval world). The spirit of the age is not so ethereal after all, for it is expressed in concrete, "bodily" forms (e.g., cathedrals, cinemas, cash machines, etc.).

Culture is closely related to history, for history is the field in which humans do things freely rather than by nature. History is for Dilthey the document of humanity. What is it to understand a historical event, which is an expression of freedom? Dilthey's answer is also decisive for faith's search for understanding. To understand the meaning of an event or an action, he says, we must look not to its causes but to its context, that is, its place in the larger whole. The goal of the human sciences—understanding meaningful expressions of life—ultimately relies not on the logic of cause and effect, but on the logic of part and whole. Just as a word makes sense only in the context of its sentence and a sentence only in the context of the larger discourse of which it is a part, so we understand what humans do in terms of the larger wholes—projects and narratives—of which their actions are a part.

Understanding culture is thus a matter of discerning patterns, especially as these involve the relation between embedded parts and their larger meaningful wholes. Culture, then, is that meaningful relation, or that complex meaningful whole.[14]

Culture versus society. By culture, then, we mean the distinctly human world that persons create by doing things not by reflex but freely as expressions of desire, duty, and determination.[15] While social studies and the other human sciences have existed in the university for about a century, cultural studies as an academic discipline is a relatively new development.[16] It is therefore important to understand the distinction, and the relation, between culture and society.

"Society" refers primarily to the institutional forms of organization within which and the norms or conventions by which a group of people live. Sociology, the study of society, began in the nineteenth century. Though it is a human science, its preoccupation with institutions and laws gives it a somewhat impersonal focus. Sociology studies the *system* and the institutional structures of our common life. The special focus of sociology is the connection between the everyday life of individuals and the social structures that form the context of everyday life.[17] Whereas psychology studies individual behavior, sociology studies the influence of society on individual behavior and belief. In other words, whereas psychology focuses on what goes on *within* people, sociology tries to get at what goes on *between* people, especially when these people have different social identities (e.g., worker and manager, white and black, etc.).

Culture and society are distinct yet closely related. Culture may be the atmosphere we breathe, but society is the building we inhabit.[18] Think of social institutions—banks, police, schools, etc.—as the physical body of which culture is the personality. For example, the British *do* police differently than Americans; the same institution exists, but policemen in Britain do not carry guns. Individuals relate differently to the American "cop" than they do to the British "bobby."

Computer operating systems provide an even better analogy. Think of social institutions as the "hardware" for which culture provides the "software" or programming.[19] Without the social hardware, the programming would have nothing to run on. Conversely, without the programming the hardware does not function. Everyday theology is a matter of coming to understand the cultural programming that runs our social institutions. On occasion it also involves deprogramming and reprogramming what we could call the cultural matrix.[20]

"Culture": Toward a definition. The term "culture" is "one of the two or three most complicated words in the English language."[21] It comes from the Latin *cultura*, which had to do with cultivating or tending animals and crops. We still speak of agriculture and horticulture and we even "cultivate" bacteria—a biological culture—in the lab. The idea of tend-

ing natural growth extended metaphorically to cover the idea of human development as well, so much so that by the eighteenth century culture came to refer to the process of civilization, or the cultivation of the mind. The term came to stand for all those institutions, practices, and objects that nurture the human spirit. While some were tempted to define late eighteenth-century European civilization as the apogee of human culture, others were keenly aware of the way people lived at different periods and in different places. The nineteenth-century voyages of discovery supported Johann Herder's revolutionary practice of speaking of "culture" in the plural: cultures were organic unities whereby land, language, and tradition converge to shape a people's "spirit."[22]

A new human science and academic discipline—anthropology—was charged with studying these diverse cultures, especially those outside the reach of European civilization. One of the oldest and most influential definitions of culture is that of the first professor of anthropology, Edward Tylor, given in his 1871 work *Primitive Culture*. According to Tylor, culture is "that complex whole which includes knowledge, belief, art, law, morals, custom, and any other capacities and habits acquired by man as a member of society."[23] Thus from anthropology we learn that culture is a way of life—everything that people say, do, have, make, and think—that is learned and shared by members of a particular society.

Cultural anthropology proceeds from the insight that humans live in worlds they create for themselves, worlds in which they invent and discover meaning. One of the most sophisticated cultural tools for making meaning is *language*, though there are many nonverbal ways of creating systems of meaning as well (e.g., traffic signals).

Culture, therefore, can be understood as "the meaning dimension of social life."[24] Modern anthropologists view cultures as complex, bounded wholes that are structured like languages and thus analogous to texts. To understand one piece of culture one needs to place it, like a sentence, in the context of the whole. Every part of life signifies something about the values and beliefs that shape culture. Therefore, every part of culture communicates something about the meaning of the whole. Everyday theology is about trying to read bits of culture that communicate not only explicit messages but implicit moods—basic orientations to life, or one's sense of one's being-in-the-world, to use Heidegger's phrase.[25]

Everyday theology has not only a "proof text" (Matt. 16:1–3) but also a virtual patron saint. Clifford Geertz is a leading social and cultural anthropologist whose seminal collection of essays, *The Interpretation of Cultures*,[26] has exercised a formative role in my own thinking, not least

Toward a Theory of Cultural Interpretation

because he, like Jesus, is interested in interpreting the signs of the times.[27] Indeed, a culture is a "web of significance," an interconnected system of meaningful signs that cry out for interpretation and understanding. Doing anthropology, says Geertz, is "like trying to read,"[28] and what we are trying to read is symbolic action—action that signifies or means something.

The real patron saint of everyday theology, however, is Augustine. Long before any anthropologist defined culture as a signifying system, Augustine had already written the book *On Christian Doctrine*. This is a profound treatise on the relation of signs, things, and minds.[29] The most common signs are spoken and written words, so Augustine devotes most of his discussion to reading the Bible in order to infer things about the mind of God. For our purposes, Augustine makes two important moves. First, he distinguishes literal from figurative signs. Signs are figurative when they refer to things that themselves signify something else (e.g., "Jerusalem" and "Athens" are signs that signify cities, yet these two cities have themselves come to signify faith and reason, respectively). Second, for Augustine everything in creation is ultimately a sign pointing to the goodness of its Creator. Only God is to be enjoyed (*frui*) as an end in himself; everything else—music, cathedrals, literature, married love—is to be used (*uti*) to point us to the source and destiny of our meaning and existence.

On Christian Doctrine was one of the first works in semiotics, which is the science of signs and their meaning. Semiotics has become prominent in the study of culture because it recognizes meaningful patterns in a vast array of cultural products from cars to clothing, all of which it treats as signs.[30] Modern semiotics is the study of the conventions and operations by which a system of signs—a signifying system (e.g., words, traffic lights, hairdos, Morse code, etc.)—produces its effects.[31] Combining Dilthey, Geertz, and Augustine produces what we might call a semiotics of "spiritual" culture. We can look at everything in culture as part of a system of signs that together express in concrete forms the "spirit" of the times, or culture's embodied "soul."

Modern semiotics differs from Augustine in one important respect. In modern semiotics meaning is determined not by seeing what "thing" a sign refers to but by seeing how a sign *differs* from other signs.[32] "Man," for example, takes on meaning thanks to its contrast with what is not-man: "woman," "boy," "ape," etc. Similarly, in the sign-system of automobiles, the meaning of "Ford" is partly determined by its contrast with "Chevy," "Honda," and "BMW." The denotation of "Ford" is the car that it refers to, but its connotations reveal its meaning in our culture (i.e., its place in a particular sign-system).

To speak of culture as a signifying "system" is, however, somewhat misleading. Contrary to what modern anthropologists have often suggested, cultures are not closed boxes in time and space; they are neither static nor monolithic. Culture is a way of life, and what is living changes and develops. It is only a slight exaggeration to say that one cannot step into the same culture twice. Further, in these days of multiculturalism where people from different cultures inhabit the same space, it is often hard to know where one culture ends and another begins. Cultures have "porous boundaries."[33] While the snapshot approach that views culture as a frozen system is helpful, we also need to remember that the people who inhabit culture are always on the move. Academics who study culture are divided with regard to the direction of influence: does the cultural system determine those who indwell it or can the actions and practices of cultural agents affect the system? My own take on this variation of the determinism versus free will question is that it is both, as it is for language itself. Language users work with the system they inherit; at the same time, linguistic meaning changes when terms are put to new use.[34] Any adequate definition of culture, then, has to keep both aspects—system and practice—in mind.

This book views culture as a work and world of meaning. Better, *culture is made up of "works" and "worlds" of meaning.* Culture is a *work* because it is the result of what humans do freely, not a result of what they do by nature. Culture is what we get when humans work the raw material of nature to produce something significant. Let us call the products of such work *cultural texts.* Why "texts"? Because a text is intentional human action, a work that communicates meaning and calls for interpretation. This is exactly what cultural works do.[35] Cultural texts include everything from the Sears Tower and Stravinsky's "Rite of Spring" to soccer moms, *The Simpsons,* and shaving cream. Each of these signs has meaning to the extent that it communicates something about our values, our concerns, and our self-understanding.

Culture is a *world* in the sense that cultural texts create a meaningful environment in which humans dwell both physically and imaginatively. Culture is the lens through which a vision of life and social order is expressed, experienced, and explored; it is a *lived* worldview. According to Paul Ricoeur, what we encounter in a text "is not another person, but a 'pro-ject,' that is, the outline of a new way of being in the world."[36] I have already distinguished the natural world from the culturally constructed world of human concerns. Increasingly, our children (and not children only!) are living in the worlds projected by television, movies, comic

Toward a Theory of Cultural Interpretation

books, video games, and the Internet—in the "media-world" of popular culture.[37] One child psychologist now speaks of "Nature Deficit Order" to designate our children's inability to "read" or attend to or understand the natural world, not least because they spend less and less time playing in or exploring it.

Cultural texts project worlds of meaning that invite us in and encourage us to make our home there. The world of a cultural text—say, for example, the world projected by *Friends*, *Survivor*, or *Desperate Housewives*—unfolds a possible way of living together, a possible way of being human. But we can go further. These culturally created worlds present themselves accompanied by the whisper of their creators: "And behold, it is very good." There's the rub. Should we accept the invitation? Should we appropriate the projected cultural world, enter in, and pitch our tent? It is a truism in Christian mission that we must go and address people where they *live*. Quite so. My point is that "they" (and we) frequently live in cleverly devised mythical worlds created by media and marketing moguls.

What Culture Does

To understand culture rightly, we need to grasp what it is and what it does. As to what it is, culture is the software that determines how things function and how people relate in a given society. Culture is both system and practice, a means through which visions of the meaning of life (cultural worlds) are expressed, experienced, and explored through diverse human products (cultural texts).[38]

Before we turn to examine the four functions of culture, we need to pause and consider another important moment in the history of the term. In the nineteenth and early twentieth centuries, "culture" stood for a standard of excellence. The purpose of this "high" culture was to improve humanity through a process of civilization. The English poet and literary critic Matthew Arnold wrote in 1869 that culture involves the "pursuit of our total perfection by means of getting to know, on all the matters which most concern us, the best which has been thought and said in the world."[39] On this view, culture is the preserve for a rather elite, educated group that Arnold called the "clerisy"—a secularized alternative to Christian clergy. Today, this distinction between high and low culture has been largely dismissed as an elitist construct.[40]

The study of popular culture—the everyday culture of everyday people—is alive and well, even thriving. There are entire sections now in bookstores devoted to "cultural studies." This new academic discipline got its start in the 1960s by questioning the restriction of the term "culture" to what the humanities—art, literature, and music—typically study. The humanities treat such masterpieces as texts existing "in isolation from the social and historical context of their production and consumption."[41] By contrast, exponents of the new cultural studies focused on *popular* culture in its broader *sociopolitical* context.

Let us therefore define popular culture as "the shared environment, practices, and resources of everyday life,"[42] that is, the texts and trends that fill and frame our days and nights.[43] Christians must read popular culture in order to understand the way in which it affects us, our neighbors, our children, and the church. In particular, culture does four things: culture communicates, culture orients, culture reproduces, and culture cultivates.

Culture communicates. Whether we are aware of it or not, culture is constantly communicating messages, both overt and covert, on a variety of levels and through a variety of means, including film, school assemblies, magazines, and especially advertisements. These messages express various human concerns, but if we were to generalize we could say that taken together these cultural messages communicate a vision of the meaning of life.

Cultural texts communicate their meaning as much by their form or packaging as by their actual content. Consider perfume, for example. Scent is a natural phenomenon; two scents differ from one another by virtue of their chemical composition. Yet what makes scent—the raw olfactory material—into perfume is a result of human work and cultural programming: in a word, marketing. The function of packaging—the name, the label, the shape of the bottle—is to "write" the scent into the larger semiotic system of perfumes. "It is the role of publicity to characterize perfumes, to differentiate them from each other in ideological (as opposed to merely physical) terms, to create distinct social signifieds for them, to give them meaning."[44] For instance, some perfumes are named after abstract, almost mystical notions like *Truth* or *Eternity*. Others have names that connote murkier moral ground: *Obsession, Decadence, Babylon.*

Connotations are not factual claims. By and large, cultural works and worlds of meaning do not make explicit thesis statements. There are exceptions: Forrest Gump, in the film of the same name, repeatedly asserts that "life is like a box of chocolates." Even this is not a straightforward indicative statement (if it were, it would be absurd) so much as it is a metaphor. The most effective metaphors become models, however, and

Toward a Theory of Cultural Interpretation

these models beget worldviews. Most cultural texts are like *Forrest Gump*: what they communicate in the first instance is not propositional information but something less tangible, though nonetheless powerful. Cultural statements are *vision* statements, and cultural texts have the ability to seize our imaginations. The power of cultural communication resides not in the information it conveys but in its role as an information *processor*. Culture tacitly communicates a program for making sense of life: a hermeneutic or interpretative framework through which we understand the world and read our own lives.

Culture orients. The second function of culture follows from the first. In providing us with framework for interpreting everyday life, culture draws mental maps that orient us in the world (e.g., "Life is like an episode of *Friends*"). Culture is "the logic by which I give order to the world."[45] And not logic only. While cultural works and worlds of meaning do have a cognitive dimension, affecting what we think, they also have affective and evaluative dimensions, influencing our likes and dislikes as well as our sense of right and wrong.

In the past, people received their basic orientation from the family, school, and church. In the present media culture, however, images and celebrities are "replacing families, schools, and churches as arbiters of taste, value, and thought."[46] Cultural texts—soap operas, the lives of celebrities, films—serve up ready-made "scripts" that provide templates for everything from the perfect relationship and the perfect kiss to the perfect crime. Whereas past cultural texts showed us how to live a life of faith, the texts of today's popular culture enact scripts of broken faith: of defiance or anger toward God; of fear of an indifferent or oppressive reality; of escape from sorrow over the absent God by finding joy in one's immediate mundane life.[47]

Cultural texts are maps and scripts that orient us in life and give us a sense of direction. Perhaps the most fundamental way that culture orients us, however, is by conveying a certain ethos (a sense of place, a feeling about the character of our environment). I spoke earlier about "moods" as our fundamental sense of being-in-the-world. It is particularly our stories (myths) about the nature of the world we live in that generate a particular mood. To state it in terms of a Greek formula, our world-picture—our *mythos* of the *cosmos*—gives rise to a certain *ethos*.[48] The stories we tell about where we have come from and why we are here will have an important bearing on how we think about everyday life.

Culture reproduces. "[C]ulture is the sphere of reproduction not of goods but of life."[49] Culture spreads beliefs, values, ideas, fashions, and practices from one social group to another. In some societies, culture is imposed upon people. British culture was imposed upon nineteenth-century India, for example, through the process of colonization.[50] Politics, then, is one means of reproduction. Schools are another. The chief noninstitutional means by which culture perpetuates itself, however, are mechanical and "memetic."

In former times, people had to travel long distances to see artistic masterpieces or to hear symphonies. Before machinery, the cultural texts available to be read by a given individual would be limited by a person's geographical and historical context: "One would imitate, absorb, and build one's world around the words, images, sounds, and gestures of one's family, neighbors, and local figures and institutions."[51] At present, however, thanks to new technologies anyone can see or hear just about any masterpiece.[52] Modern media give us access to cultural texts from virtually any place and any time, from ancient Greece to contemporary China: "The parade of alternative worlds that the privacy of the home once provided haven from now has around the clock privileges."[53]

Memetic reproduction is a less familiar, but no less important, notion. It relies on an analogy between genes and "memes." A meme is "an element of a culture that may be considered to be passed on by non-genetic means, esp. imitation."[54] Whereas genes are packages of biological information, a "meme" is a package of cultural information: "A meme might be a clothing fashion, a popular song, or a religious belief."[55]

The term "meme" comes from the Greek term *mimesis* ("imitation"). The general idea is that culture reproduces or replicates itself when people begin to copy certain cultural traits to which they have been exposed. The phenomenon of Beanie Babies is an example of "horizontal" (e.g., person-to-person) transmission. Some memes, however, are transmitted "vertically" from parents to children through the former setting examples and giving advice.[56] If culture is the programming software of our social world, memes are the bits of cultural information that are transmitted from one person to another.

According to the analogy, the information in both genes and memes—biological versus cultural traits, respectively—is "heritable."[57] Indeed, "Culture is a system of inheritance."[58] Of course, the way a meme is passed on to someone else or to the next generation is not via biology. Yet memes do resemble viruses. They are passed on from person to person as a result of proximity or contact, which would explain why some cultural trends (e.g., pet rocks) spread like epidemics: "Memes are spread from person to person by observation and social learning—either face to face or through media of communication like writing, television, or the Internet."[59]

Toward a Theory of Cultural Interpretation

Cultural traits thus resemble viruses, both the kind that affect our bodies and the kind that affect our computers. Is there such a thing as a cultural immune system? We shall speak more of cultural agency in due course. For the moment, let me simply say, yes. It's called the brain: "The brain should act as a sort of mental immune system, examining cultural ideas as they come in, considering their likely consequences, rejecting the ones that are liable to do harm and accepting those that are apt to help."[60]

Culture cultivates. Bacteria, we may recall, can be grown or "cultivated" in a petri dish. What exactly does culture cultivate? The short answer is the human spirit. We need to go further than Dilthey who saw culture as merely the expression of the human spirit. Given culture's ability to orient us and reproduce itself, we must acknowledge culture itself as a means of spiritual formation, a process that shapes our spirits, or "hearts."

Dallas Willard views the human heart as "that spiritual place within us from which outlook, choices, and actions come."[61] Spiritual formation is the process by which the human heart is shaped, oriented, and formed. The "form" of our spirit pertains to its character, that is, to our typical pattern of acting and reacting. A selfish spirit acts and reacts one way, a loving spirit another. In short, culture cultivates character traits—the habits of the heart—and in so doing forms our spirit so that we become this kind of a person rather than that kind. Just as culture projects ideal forms for our bodies, so it projects ideal forms for our spirits.

My point in describing culture as a process of spiritual formation is not to say that we are helpless and hapless victims but rather to call our attention to the fact that spiritual formation is happening to us and to our children all the time. Culture trains us in what philosophers call the transcendentals, honing our sense of what is true, good, and beautiful.

Take, for example, the spirit-forming cultural implement of television: "All television is educational television. The question is merely, 'What is it teaching?'"[62] I earlier acknowledged that cultural texts seldom make explicit statements. Television is a good case in point. Its teaching comes not in the form of explicit statements but rather through what it *does*, namely, through what philosophers of language call the *illocutionary* act (what is done with words).[63] Television performs the illocutionary act of *displaying* the world. It also performs perlocutionary acts (e.g., persuading) by and through these illocutions. In other words, "It is the cumulative effect of viewing the world portrayed in the popular arts that has the power to persuade—over time and with the influence of many, many films, TV shows, and CDs."[64]

Enough nurture of a particular kind produces in us a kind of second nature. Researchers at an Australian university looking into the neurophysiology of watching television discovered this telling fact: repeated and prolonged viewing destroys the capacity of the viewer to pay attention. Here is a kind of nurture, then, that corrupts nature.

Prolonged exposure to cultural texts—and we are always exposed—produces various types of effects for good or ill. Culture is always cultivating our spirits in one way or another, sensitizing or desensitizing us, and enlivening or dulling our capacity to attend to various aspects of reality. Many of us may be unaware of the effect that culture is having on our spirits. Yet disciples cannot afford to sleepwalk their way through everyday life. Those who confuse the real world with pathetic imitations can hardly be effective ambassadors for Jesus Christ.[65]

Here is an everyday example: How should we read the holiday season? How a culture "does" Christmas reveals much about its ultimate concern. On the one hand, Christmas is a theological event that marks the birth of Jesus Christ, the moment when the eternal Son of God became man. On the other hand, Christmas has become a cultural event that has evolved over time in an increasingly materialist direction. What is the meaning of Christmas according to twenty-first century North America? It is important to recall that culture does not often communicate directly: there are few explicit answers or thesis statements in the texts of popular culture. Yet there is copious *indirect* communication. Instead of addressing our belief-systems head-on, cultural works structure our daily practices and colonize our imaginations. Culture's power to shape our habits of thinking and acting is on conspicuous display during the Christmas season, the holiest of holy times for commercial retailers.

We need carefully and honestly to ask ourselves in what world of meaning do we dwell, at Christmastime or in ordinary time? Where do we spend most of our time, in our bodies and, just as importantly, in our imaginations? We need to guard what enters and inhabits our hearts. We should be dwelling in the real world displayed in Scripture, not the counterfeit worlds projected by other, non-canonical texts. Sleepwalkers of the world, awake!

Christianity and Culture

Christians have increasingly become aware of the need to engage culture as part of Christian mission and theology. Some commentators believe that popular culture affords new possibilities for evangelism and theology;

Toward a Theory of Cultural Interpretation

others believe that popular culture represents simply the latest variation on an idolatrous theme. It is better not to rush to judgment on this question. Everyday theologians must understand culture before they either exclude or embrace it. We must therefore do all that we can to resist two opposing temptations, each equally dangerous inasmuch as each compromises the integrity of the church's mission. The first is an uncritical acceptance of and fascination with the newfound religiosity and spirituality of popular culture. The second is to write off popular culture as one more symptom of sinful rebellion.

The spiritual dimension of culture. Culture is hardly a faith-free zone. On the contrary, in programming its members to live a certain way, culture also predisposes them toward a certain kind of faith. Nobody perceived this better than Tillich, who observed that "religion is the substance of culture, culture is the form of religion."[66]

One of the most surprising recent developments has been a newfound appreciation on the part of some evangelicals for what they perceive as an emergent spirituality in popular culture. To use Tillich's terms, they see popular culture as the form of something essentially religious. For these authors, culture is not merely "secular" in the sense of this-worldly, but an open window through which blows the fresh air of transcendence. One such book is William Romanowski's *Eyes Wide Open: Looking for God in Popular Culture*.[67] The authors of another book, subtitled *Finding God in Popular Culture*, declare: "We celebrate the rise of pop culture as among the most profound, provocative, exciting expressions of legitimate spiritual yearning in at least one hundred years."[68] These texts written by evangelicals are similar to those written by mainline theologians a generation earlier, such as John Wiley Nelson's *Your God Is Alive and Well and Appearing in Popular Culture*.[69] Andrew Greeley's *God in Popular Culture* expresses what these books have in common, namely, a conviction that popular culture "contains signals of the transcendent, the presence of grace, rumors of angels."[70]

Some authors go even further, proposing to use the texts and practices of popular culture as material for theological reflection—"a means of exploring issues including the nature of God, the possibility of meaning in life, the nature of sin and evil, and the nature of redemption."[71] For better or for worse, these authors contend that popular culture is an important "context within which theological reflection takes place."[72] Specifically, popular culture—more so than the academy or the church—has become the arena where most people work out their understanding of the true, the good, and the beautiful.[73] In sum: Christians must learn to read popular culture not least because it has become an important locus of everyday theology. Though our young people may not be learning their theology on the streets, they're not learning it in church either, but in the mall and in the all-encompassing media-world.

The cultural dimension of Christianity. It is impossible to construct a culture-free Christianity. The Christian faith is incarnational, after all, and even God became not a generic but a culturally located human being. Jesus' followers can do no less. Another reason to be able to read culture, then, is to ensure that the church at any particular place and time is serving the gospel rather than taking it hostage through acculturation.

We need to be aware of the way in which culture may be influencing or programming us, especially as this pertains to the way we "do" church. The church is never wholly isolated from its surrounding culture. Like cultures themselves, the church has "porous boundaries." Certain cultural "memes" have almost certainly entered the North American church. For example, pragmatism—a certain way of thinking about success—affects the way some churches conceive their very mission: "If our church grows, the rightness of our faith is somehow verified."[74] Those who ignore culture, like history, are doomed to repeat it.

Cultural competence and Christian performance. The most compelling reason I can give for learning to read culture is that the mission of the church demands it. Cultural illiteracy is harmful to our spiritual health. Christians need to know how to read culture because, first, it helps to know what is forming one's spirit. It helps to be able to name the powers and principalities that vie for the control of one's mind, soul, heart, and strength. Christians need to become culturally literate, second, so that they can be sure that the scripts they perform in everyday life are in accord with the Scriptures—the story of what God is doing in Jesus Christ through the Spirit to give meaning and life to the world—rather than some other story. Finally, Christians need to become culturally literate because we need to know where we are in the drama of redemption. The world is our stage, but culture is the setting for our next scene.[75]

Closely related to cultural literacy is the idea of cultural competence. The term "competence" was introduced into linguistics by Noam Chomsky, who used it to refer to the implicit knowledge that a native speaker has of a language.[76] Chomsky differentiated competence from "performance," which is the specific use we make of language in concrete situations. If culture is indeed like a language, then we can import Chomsky's distinction into our own project and speak of cultural competence (i.e., the tacit knowledge that a native actor has of his or her cultural world). Cultural

Toward a Theory of Cultural Interpretation

competence pertains to understanding the cultural system, while cultural performance pertains to our putting the system into motion and doing something with it.

The analogy is apt. Culture is as complex as a language and just as difficult to learn. On the other hand, we are all native speakers of at least one language and we all inhabit at least one culture. The challenge, therefore, is to make our implicit cultural know-how explicit.

The apostle Peter confidently assured his readers that the apostles "did not follow cleverly devised myths when we made known to you the power and coming of our Lord Jesus Christ" (2 Pet. 1:16 RSV). Quite so. The church's mission is to communicate, be oriented to, reproduce, and cultivate the reality of what God is doing in Christ through the Spirit for the sake of the world.[77] The mission remains, and it is as urgent as ever. For there are many contemporary hucksters employing more powerful media technology than ever hawking different gospels that lead in ways contrary to the way of Jesus Christ.

In order to be competent proclaimers and performers of the gospel, then, Christians must learn to read the Bible and culture alike. Christians cannot afford to continue sleepwalking their way through contemporary culture, letting their lives, and especially their imaginations, become conformed to culturally devised myths, each of which promises more than it can deliver: "Do not conform any longer to the pattern of this world, but be transformed by the renewing of your mind" (Rom. 12:2). The apostolic exhortation confronts us with a question: In which cultural world of meaning do *we* dwell? To what pattern have we conformed our imaginations? Will the real world please stand out?

How Should Christians Read Culture?

In addition to the Book of Nature there is now the Book of Culture. Faith's quest for understanding obliges us to "take up and read" this new book too. Many of us can no doubt identify with the Ethiopian eunuch in Acts 8. When asked by Philip "Do you understand what you are reading?" he replied: "How can I, unless someone guides me?" (Acts 8:30–31 RSV). Hence the purpose of the present section: to offer guidance to everyday theologians, to people of faith seeking cultural understanding.

Three preliminary remarks. To understand the Book of Culture is to engage in cultural hermeneutics. Hermeneutics is the art and science of interpretation, especially of Scripture or other written texts. The term comes from the Greek *hermeneuo* ("to interpret") and is probably derived from "Hermes," the name of the ancient mythological messenger god. As we have seen, the human sciences, insofar as they seek understanding rather than explanation, deal in interpretation and are thus hermeneutical in nature. The method set forth below therefore approaches cultural works and worlds as text-like.[78]

A second, and more subtle, point. Cultural hermeneutics treats cultural texts and trends as particular kinds of *discourse*: what someone says (or signs) to someone about something.[79] Yet cultural texts themselves, as we have seen in the previous section, exist not only to be read but to be used as interpretative frameworks. We don't simply read cultural texts but we read *through* them. In short: the cultural texts we love best come to serve as the lens through which we view everything else and as the compass that orients us toward the good life.

A final point. Interpretation is not an exact science. Understanding—be it of God, works of art, ourselves, or others—is both messier and more provisional than explanations that work with causal laws. Why should this be so? Three reasons: (1) because what we're trying to understand is often singular and unique, (2) because meaning is a matter of seeing the parts in relation to larger wholes of which finite human interpreters have only partial glimpses, and (3) because interpreters often have vested interests for seeing things in one way rather than another and lack the requisite virtues to see things as they really are *coram Deo* (before God).

The Method to be presented here is neither as objective as a geometric proof nor as arbitrary as a statement of one's personal preferences. It comes with no guarantee, either of infallible or of immediate results. No method for understanding does. What it does offer is concrete guidance for everyday theologians who want to make sense of everyday life and to read the Book of Culture, and the Good Book, with their eyes wide open.

The Conflict of Interpretations: Other Ways of Reading Culture

Disagreement is a prominent feature of everyday life. People hold varying opinions about every aspect of culture, from films and books to cars and clothing. Even reviewers and critics often disagree about the merits and the meaning of this or that cultural text. One reason for this conflict of interpretations is a deeper conflict between *theories* of interpretation. Anyone familiar with literary criticism or, for that matter, with biblical interpretation knows that there is a plethora of schools and approaches to interpretation.[80] Most if not all of the theories

Toward a Theory of Cultural Interpretation

used to interpret the Bible and other literary texts show up in cultural hermeneutics as well.

Every method of interpretation stems from some basic insight into textual meaning.[81] The danger of following one critical approach only, and hence of using only a single perspective or grid, is that it ultimately *limits* what one sees. I agree with the film critic Robert Stam: "Each grid has its blind spots and insights; each needs the 'excess seeing' of the other grids."[82] Stam rightly warns against investing in one approach only and calls instead for a plurality of methods. The critics themselves, however, are seldom as ecumenical. Be that as it may, I shall employ a plurality of methods and use theology to coordinate them.

In addition to disagreements over what cultural texts mean and how they should be read, there is an even more fundamental problem. What Ricoeur labels the "hermeneutics of suspicion" in the context of textual interpretation has its counterpart in cultural hermeneutics. Ricoeur points out that Freud, Marx, and Nietzsche alike—the so-called "masters of suspicion"—are skeptics concerning meaning. Each in his own way is guilty of a reductionism that explains what is apparently meaningful in terms of deeper causes. There are reductionists with regard to God, self, and world alike: with regard to God, Feuerbach says that atheism is the secret (i.e., the real explanation) of religion; with regard to self, the materialist says the mind is "nothing but" physical brain states; Freud "explains" morality by saying that it is nothing more than the attempt by society to repress natural human instincts, drives, and desires; finally, with regard to the cultural world, the suspicion is that all meaning is ultimately in the service of either power or profit. Such "nothing but" accounts may be true as far as they go, but they do not go far enough. They typically succeed not in explaining phenomena, but in explaining them away.

Reductionism in the natural sciences. The most radical form of cultural suspicion abandons hermeneutics altogether, jettisoning understanding in favor of scientific explanation. The competition between nature and nurture is no contest: it's nature—biology, to be exact—all the way down. Such is the claim of what we may call the sociobiological reading of culture.

Sociobiology bridges the natural and the human sciences by attempting to explain the latter in terms of the former. It is an outgrowth of evolutionary biology and attempts to account for human behavior, including the behavior of social groups, in terms of the now-familiar Darwinian metanarrative about the propagation of genes from one generation to the next.[83] The key conceptual move in sociobiology is to think of *society* as an organism that evolves by adapting to its environment and passing on those cultural traits that facilitate the group's survival. Perhaps the most radical exemplar of what I am calling the hermeneutics of cultural suspicion is David Sloan Wilson's *Darwin's Cathedral*, a book that attempts to explain religion itself in evolutionary terms: "I will attempt to study religious groups the way I and other evolutionary biologists routinely study guppies, trees, bacteria, and the rest of life on earth."[84]

In reducing sociology to biology—that is, in insisting that human behavior is "nothing but" the process of natural or adaptive selection—whatever legitimate insights sociobiology may have are dwarfed by its inability to do justice both to meaningfulness in general and to the work of the Holy Spirit in particular. For to the extent that the actions of the body politic are ultimately a matter of biological reflexes, they are bereft of meaning. Interpreted sociobiologically, human behavior is simply the epiphenomenon of what truly counts, namely, the drama of genetic propagation. Alas, there is little dignity, much less meaning, when art, romance, and philosophy shrivel up into a dry metanarrative about our DNA's struggle to survive to fight again another day.

Reductionism in cultural studies. While natural scientists may be expected to look for physical explanations for social phenomena, it is surprising to discover a certain kind of reductionism in the *human* sciences themselves. Yet this is precisely what we find in the kind of cultural studies associated with the Frankfurt School in the mid-twentieth century and the Birmingham School at century's end.

The Frankfurt School was the first group of academics to take popular culture seriously.[85] Developing Marx's suspicion that history is determined not by ideas but by economic factors, they viewed popular culture as "the culture produced by the culture industry to secure the stability and continuity of capitalism."[86] Popular culture, they argued, is "nothing but" a clever ruse by capitalists to ensure political conformity; it is ideology—"meaning in the service of power"—made flesh, or rather, made into a commodity. The "culture industries" maintain "the illusion that happiness can be found through the resources that are already available within everyday life, such as consumer commodities or mass-produced entertainments."[87] These post-Marxists say of popular culture what Marx said of religion: it is the opiate of the masses.[88] In response, the Frankfurt School advocated "critical theory," a kind of "liberation hermeneutic" of culture that offered economic and ideological explanations designed to expose the "real meaning" of culture ("It's about propagating capital, stupid!") and so free the masses from their commodified chains.[89]

The Centre for Contemporary Cultural Studies at the University of Birmingham represents another Marxist variation on the hermeneutics of cultural suspicion.[90] On this view, what culture is fundamentally about is not the meaning of life (the good) but socioeconomic power (the bad). British cultural studies set out "to understand how culture (the social production of sense and consciousness) should be specified in itself and in relation to economics (production) and politics (social relations)."[91]

The Birmingham Centre borrowed its most important concept—"hegemony"—from Antonio Gramsci, an Italian Marxist. Hegemony is the process whereby a society maintains its order by means other than police or military force. Hegemony works not by compelling people to do things against their will but rather by winning their consent. The concept of hegemony therefore reveals "how everyday meanings, representations and activities are organised and made sense of in such a way as to render the interests of a dominant 'bloc' into an apparently natural and unarguable general interest."[92] Hegemony is "the process by which dominant ideas accumulate the symbolic power to map the world for others."[93] As such, it pertains to what we have called cultural software. The dominant class achieves hegemony when its worldview or ideology wins the consent of the masses. Here too, then, popular culture is seen to exercise what is primarily an ideological function: using meaning to serve the interests of the powerful.

These attempts to explain "higher-level" or even spiritual phenomena (culture) in terms of more basic and material processes (economics) are prime examples of the reductionist temptation.[94] Such a hermeneutic of suspicion—that ideological concerns often lurk behind cultural texts—may nevertheless have more than a little truth. Christians can learn from these secular approaches, especially from their liberative concern and their prophetic voice: there *are* trends and tendencies, powers and principalities, in culture that *should* occasion our suspicion. Christians have nothing to gain from naive or superficial interpretations of popular culture that see only bright possibilities for new forms of spirituality and theological engagement and not the potential for new forms of idolatry as well. At the same time, to explain everything in culture in terms of hegemony and power goes too far inasmuch as it rules out the possibility that culture is meaningful—that at least some cultural texts speak to the question of life's meaning and, perhaps, in so doing point to that meaning's transcendent source.[95]

The challenge for Christian interpreters is to exercise a little suspicion for properly theological reasons (e.g., sin) without succumbing to a blinding reductionism in the process. The hermeneutics of cultural suspicion therefore has something to teach us about cultural texts, but by itself it takes us no further than "thin" description and thus falls short of true understanding.

Is Cultural Exegesis without Theological Presuppositions Possible?

There is a long-standing debate in biblical studies whether exegesis—the attempt to explicate textual meaning—is possible without the interpreter slipping something of his or her own interests into the exposition. Postmoderns and others have exploded the myth of neutrality: we interpreters never do approach texts as if we were generic human beings, as if our particular histories, identities, and traditions neither mattered nor existed.

Christians therefore need to be honest and acknowledge that we approach cultural texts as interpreters who hold certain convictions. After all, the banner under which a theological hermeneutic of culture marches is *faith* seeking understanding. Yet Christian interpretation of culture must not be content with claiming only "this is how my community sees things," for any interpreter from any community can say that. The challenge, therefore, is to seek to understand culture in ways that do not simply reflect community preferences, but disclose *truth*.

Two presuppositional desiderata. A first conviction: what is at stake both in cultural texts and in the process of their interpretation is the meaningful and the good, both of which are matters of universal human concern. All interpreters of culture work with some idea, however tacit, of what is or is not conducive to human flourishing. Christian interpreters will want to go even further and insist that what culture means is of *ultimate* concern because, in some way, it relates to God. While cultural texts have a fairly obvious "surface" meaning, they also have what Tillich called a "depth dimension" that pertains to the more perduring questions of human existence: What should I do? Why are we here? What may I hope?

A second presupposition is equally important. Notwithstanding our concern for God and the good, Christian interpreters acknowledge the importance of hearing culture "on its own terms," which is simply another way of saying that Christians recognize the importance of attending to what is really there. Understanding is not served by imposing Christian meanings where there are none. Christians must go the extra hermeneutical mile to make sure they do not simply project their own interests onto cultural texts. To do so would be to violate the Golden Rule of interpretation: do unto others' texts as you would have them do unto yours.[96] We do not want to give even more ammunition to postmodern reductionists who believe that interpretation is "nothing but" a function of one's race, gender, class, and religious affiliation.[97]

Three biblical dimensions. The Scriptures—what Calvin calls our "spectacles of faith"—serve as corrective lenses that enable us to see the world as it really is in the context of God's all-encompassing plan. Note that the redemptive-historical story line of the Bible—the narrative movement from creation through fall to salvation—is in no one single group's interest only. To view culture through the lens of biblical faith does not distort reality but offers a high-definition worldview.[98] Christian faith seeks true understanding of the real world.

The Bible narrates the story of God's presence and activity in the world. Elsewhere I refer to this story as a "theodrama" in which human beings have speaking and acting parts.[99] The cultural scenes in which the church finds itself may vary, but the play is always three-dimensional: creatures and structures originally created good have been corrupted by the fall; still groaning, they are presently being renewed in Christ through the Spirit. To understand a cultural text truly thus requires putting it into theodramatic context—reading it in light of the control-script; viewing it thrice over in terms of creation, fall, and redemption.

Four Christian doctrines. Christians must read culture theologically in an expository rather than impository manner in light of the biblical account of creation, fall, and redemption that sets culture in its real (viz., theodramatic) context. We turn now to the question of whether cultural texts themselves are properly theological. Can we find God in popular culture? There is indeed a present tendency to affirm God's work *outside* the church as well as in it. Tillich, for example, speaks of the "latent church" in secular culture and acknowledges its prophetic voice in challenging and even correcting distorted beliefs and practices in the church.[100]

Clearly, one's theology of culture—one's view as to how God relates to culture—will have a decisive bearing on the seriousness and openness with which the church approaches culture: is it a battleground on which to engage the enemy, a classroom in which to learn, a sanctuary in which to worship? If culture is our everyday environment, we must pose the question: Is it beneficial or harmful for our spiritual health?[101] Is the cultural atmosphere polluted and, if so, should we flee it or clean it?

A spate of recent books and articles suggests that "God shines through even the most debased pop cultural products."[102] For these authors, popular culture is itself an earthen vessel through which faith seeks to understand God. For example, David Dark reads a number of popular cultural texts as instances of "everyday apocalyptic" that open one's eyes to the cosmic stakes hidden just beneath the surface of everyday life.[103]

Four doctrines in particular have a special bearing on a theology of culture and, more specifically, on the issue of whether God reveals himself in and through popular culture: the incarnation, general revelation, common grace, and the *imago Dei*. Running through all four as a common theme is pneumatology: the doctrine of the Holy Spirit. Stanley Grenz raises this deeper theological issue when he says that reading culture theologically requires us to move beyond the assumption that the church is "the *only* location in which the Holy Spirit is operative."[104]

(1) The incarnation. Andrew Walls, a missiologist, argues on the basis of the incarnation—God's "translation" into humanity—that the gospel is "translatable" into any and every culture.[105] No one culture is allowed to claim for itself the sole rightful possession of what "Christian" means, for every "translation" of Christianity into another culture enhances our understanding of what the gospel means.[106] In Walls's words: "It is a delightful paradox that the more Christ is translated into the various thought forms and life systems which form our various national identities, the richer all of us will be in our common Christian identity."[107] Something similar may perhaps be said with regard to various *cultural* forms.[108] Yet the very fact of the incarnation reminds us that what God wants to make known of himself is *not* available in culture per se. The human cultural world provides the raw material, as it were, for the gospel; but the gospel cannot be reduced to the means of its cultural production.[109]

(2) General revelation. The doctrine of general revelation holds that some knowledge of God is universally available; it is a divine discourse delivered through the medium of creation, there to be "read" at all times and places. Could it be, then, that popular culture is not merely projecting vain imaginings onto the void but trying to grapple, even dialogue, "with *revelation* that precedes us, surrounds us, and saturates us"?[110] If so, then cultural texts have meaning not simply because they are cleverly constructed sign-systems but because they have ultimately "to do with this human-divine conversation, the play between revelational discourse and human cultural-counter discourse."[111] Cultural texts are, at least in part, our response to the *sensus divinitatis*—that general awareness of God or a higher power—that is part and parcel of the human condition.[112]

(3) Common grace. Though the presence of God in culture remains a disputed issue, there is no such controversy over the presence of good. Some everyday Reformed theologians wonder whether we should not account for everyday goodness in terms of common grace.[113] Richard

Toward a Theory of Cultural Interpretation

Mouw, for example, asserts that "God has a positive, albeit non-salvific, regard for those who are not elect."[114] Specifically, while Mouw contends that God has purposes for creation as such as well as a plan (e.g., salvation) for the elect only, he also believes that God appreciates goodness and beauty for their own sakes, quite apart from their role in the plan of salvation.[115] Revelation 21:24–26 depicts the kings of the earth bringing into the temple of the New Jerusalem their "splendor," which Mouw (along with Herman Bavinck and Abraham Kuyper) interprets as "the fruits of humankind's cultural labors."[116] It has been said that all truth is God's truth. Proponents of the doctrine of common grace want to say something similar about goodness and beauty.

(4) The *imago Dei*. Those who are uncomfortable speaking of "grace" outside the context of the forgiveness of sins or salvation in Christ have recourse to another doctrine in order to account for the residual goodness and beauty in culture: the image of God in men and women. According to this doctrine, we are able to produce works and worlds of meaning because we are created in the image of God. Some take the second half of the creation mandate—"fill the earth and subdue it" (Gen. 1:28)—along with the charge to work and care for the garden that was humanity's first home (Gen. 2:15) as a mandate for producing culture: "In these four tasks—ruling, filling, working, and keeping—we see culture in seed form."[117] To be in the image of God is, therefore, to be a culture-maker.

It is vital to keep in mind the creation-fall-redemption schema mentioned above as we consider the cultural significance of the *imago Dei*.[118] Because of the fall, we are no longer able to respond rightly to the cultural mandate: "The ideal of culture as thanksgiving was replaced by culture as a statement of autonomy."[119] Yet we have not lost the image entirely. Indeed, it is perhaps best to think of common grace as the Spirit's restraint and mitigation of the outward effects of our corruption such that even fallenness does not wholly erase the *imago Dei*.[120]

The Spirit also uses general revelation as a means to restrain sin and hence work common grace.[121] We may therefore conclude that the Spirit ministers God's *general* discourse embedded in creation and the human conscience as well as the special divine Christ-directed *canonical* discourse. The salient point is that the Spirit ministers divine discourse to sinners as well as saints. It follows that there may be vestiges of truth, goodness, and beauty outside the church—in culture. In Calvin's words: "If we regard the Spirit of God as the sole fountain of truth, we shall neither reject the truth itself, nor despise it wherever it shall appear, unless we wish to dishonor the Spirit of God."[122]

Thanks to the Spirit's ministry of general revelation to the fractured image of God that we are as fallen human beings, part of what culture says is true, good, and beautiful; other parts, however, are false, bad, and ugly. It follows that we must hearken to cultural texts as possible vehicles for appropriating new insights into justice and truth while at the same time maintaining Scripture as our normative framework of interpretation. The ultimate authority for theology is the triune God in communicative action. It is for this reason that the Spirit's canonical testimony to Christ ultimately trumps the non-canonical (e.g., cultural) testimony, helpful though the latter may be.

The Method: How to Read a Culture

How should Christians interpret culture? The following proposal advocates reading cultural texts on their own terms and in light of the biblical text. The goal of such reading is the understanding of faith: discerning the meaning of cultural texts and trends in light of the gospel of Jesus Christ.

Cultural discourse: The well-wrought world? Culture is a work and world of meaning. Both parts of this definition are essential if we are to avoid the kind of reductionism that yields abbreviated understanding only. A cultural text is a *work* of meaning because someone or some group has produced it. It is not enough, then, to read cultural texts as self-contained entities; we must be able to relate them to the contexts that produce and consume them.[123] A cultural text is a *world* of meaning because its work is precisely to provide form and shape for our world: cultural texts are meaningful works that shape meaningful worlds.

The meaning of cultural texts involves more than the communication of information, more too than merely decoding self-contained systems of signification. As we saw earlier, cultural texts convey not only messages but moods, not only explicit facts but an implicit ethos (i.e., a sense of the world). Cultural texts are communicative acts that achieve diverse aims through a variety of means. The best overall term for this phenomenon is *cultural discourse*.[124] "Discourse" is a matter of "what someone says to someone about something in some way." The concept of discourse enables us to go beyond a mere semiotics of culture, which treats cultural texts apart from the contexts of their use, to a *semantics* of culture that views cultural objects as texts that themselves have users—authors and readers—as well as extratextual contexts and references.[125]

Discourse happens when someone uses some medium to say or show something. Ricoeur analyzes discourse further in terms of "a hierarchy of subordinate acts distributed on three levels":[126] (1) "locution," or act *of* saying something, (2) "illocution," or act of doing something *in* saying something, and (3) "perlocution," or what we do *by* saying something. I believe that each of these aspects of spoken and written discourse has its counterpart in cultural discourse.

First, a cultural text, like written discourse, has a locutionary dimension and employs either language or some other signifying medium (e.g., art, television, film, music, products, social practices). Second, cultural discourse raises the same questions about its illocutionary act as does written or oral discourse, namely, what is a cultural text doing in saying/showing/signing such and such? Third, cultural discourse achieves certain effects (e.g., cultivation, spiritual formation) by saying/showing/signing.

Again, the meaning of cultural discourse transcends the immanent operations and elements that constitute its locutionary medium: "Popular culture is *about* something other than itself."[127] As we have seen, culture communicates, expresses, or objectifies human concerns, whether these be proximate or ultimate. What exactly are cultural texts doing? I have already suggested that cultural texts create worlds and shape our experience. Let us therefore refine our definition of cultural discourse: *something wrought by some one/group in some medium for world-building.* What culture is finally about is what it means to be human in this place and time; what culture ultimately does is "grow" humanity. Culture is the gesture a people makes toward the good life. It is the gesture—a shrug, a raised fist, folded arms, cupped hands—a people makes toward God.

Interpretation as theologically thick description. Hermeneutics, says Ricoeur, is "the art of discerning the discourse in the work."[128] Understanding is a matter of grasping what cultural texts are really doing and what they are really about. Everyday theology is faith seeking nonreductive understanding. Understanding is not served by simplistic theories that account for everything in culture in terms of one factor only, whether the factor be sin, technology, or economics. In order to make sense of culture as a complex whole, then, we must use a wide-angle lens. Accordingly, the approach set forth here is multiperspectival, multilevel, and multidimensional.

A *multiperspectival* cultural hermeneutic uses a variety of academic disciplines and approaches to illumine what is going on in cultural discourse.[129] To get light from various sources we must be light on our feet, prepared to move between history, economics, psychology, sociology, film studies, architectural engineering, marketing, and of course theology. We need to avoid looking at culture in one way only as much as we need to avoid explaining it in terms of one factor alone. Each method for studying culture proceeds from a certain insight. For example, the Frankfurt School's Marxist insight into the economic forces that drive the culture industry helps us to see part of what is happening beneath the surface of culture. Yet this approach, like any other, if taken to the extreme and isolated from others, ultimately distorts its subject matter. When this happens, insight dwindles into tunnel vision.

At this point the everyday theologian may be tempted to despair of ever achieving cultural understanding: "abandon hope all ye who enter in." Fortunately, a *multilevel* approach brings order into the plurality of possible methodological approaches by arranging hierarchically the various levels of complexity that characterize cultural reality. Just as we cannot explain everything about the biological in terms of physics and chemistry only, so we cannot understand everything about the cultural in terms of economics and politics alone.

It is possible to describe the same cultural phenomenon—say, one's high school prom—on a variety of levels: historical, psychological, social, educational, economic, musical, moral, political, etc.[130] Each level helps give a more complete picture of what is going on and may be accurate up to a certain point. Each level of description highlights a different aspect of the cultural reality we call *prom*. Some aspects of a cultural phenomenon only come to light, however, under a certain kind and level of description. The crucial point is that one cannot describe higher-level features of reality in lower-level terms without significant loss. For example, while the economic level is a relevant factor in understanding the practice of proms in North American culture, we cannot account for all aspects of proms in terms of economics alone without falling into the "nothing but" reductionist trap.

Understanding cultural discourse demands a thick description of what has been wrought, and this is best accomplished with the aid of those speech act categories (viz., locution, illocution, perlocution) that enable a thick description of the act of discourse. Ricoeur rightly observes that human action in general, precisely because it is meaningful, has the same traits as the speech act. An action is "locutionary" inasmuch as it works in some medium and has propositional content (e.g., breaking *the window*; opening *the window*). An action is "illocutionary" to the extent that it counts as a performance of one thing (e.g., *breaking* the window) rather than another (e.g., *closing* the window).[131] An action is "perlocutionary" when it brings about certain effects by being done (e.g., letting in fresh air).

Consider the following contrast between a thin and thick description of the same event. Here is the thin description: "He forcibly propelled

Toward a Theory of Cultural Interpretation

the round object with his left foot in an easterly direction." This is the kind of field note observation one might expect of a cultural anthropologist who does not really know what is going on. Such minimal descriptions have too narrow a view of the relevant context; they suffer from a poverty of meaning and do not yield much understanding. A thick description, by contrast, will attend to diverse levels of significance, to the broader context, and to the different dimensions (i.e., locutionary, illocutionary, perlocutionary) of the discourse. "He kicked the ball" clarifies the cultural locution (e.g., the medium of the discourse). "He scored a goal" clarifies the cultural illocution: it *counts as* a point in a soccer match. There is more: "He won the game"; "He led his team to victory in the final of the World Cup"; "He boosted Scotland's national pride." These latter descriptions concern the perlocutionary effects of his scoring the goal.

Whether one is reading the high-school prom or the World Cup, one clearly needs a multilevel understanding to fully appreciate cultural discourse, that is, to grasp what kind of world is being wrought in and through cultural texts. Arthur Peacocke argues that there is an ascending order to these levels: "Corresponding to the different levels in these hierarchies of the natural world there exist the appropriate sciences which study a particular level."[132] The lowest level is the physical world; one describes what happens on this level in terms of atoms and molecules. Peacocke sees a progression from the physical world to living organisms, another progression from living organisms to human persons, and yet another progression (i.e., another level of complexity) from human persons to culture.[133] Just as each level draws on lower levels and yet has an integrity of its own, so on the cultural level we discover materials from lower levels that are put to work for a more complex purpose—creating a meaningful world in which humans can dwell and perhaps flourish.

To interpret culture theologically is to have recourse to the highest level of description. On this level, we describe cultural discourse in terms of *biblical* discourse: we say how the world wrought by culture relates to God and to his purpose for the world that is summed up in Christ. Our understanding of what is happening in culture remains relatively thin to the extent that we fail to describe things at the theological level. To interpret cultural discourse as it relates to God and the gospel is, I submit, a *comprehensive* approach inasmuch as it enables us to give the thickest possible description of what is really going on in culture, and a *critical* approach inasmuch as it is concerned with true liberation ("It is for freedom that Christ has set us free" [Gal. 5:1]).

The Method strives for appropriately thick descriptions of cultural discourse, then, by making use of contributions from various disciplines and by ordering them according to increasing levels of complexity, culminating in the theological. In addition to the plurality of perspectives and levels, however, the Method is also *multidimensional*. To be precise, it situates cultural texts and trends in two distinct three-dimensional frameworks. The first three-dimensional framework applies to all kinds of texts and thus falls under what we may call a "general hermeneutic" of culture. It makes use of an author-text-reader schema. The second is the biblical-theological framework of creation-fall-redemption that we have already mentioned; this is a distinctly Christian contribution, a "special hermeneutic" of culture.

The world behind, of, and in front of the cultural text. Back to what I have called general hermeneutics. Just as various types of literary criticism focus on authors or texts or readers, respectively, so various schools of cultural criticism emphasize either the producers, the cultural products themselves, or the consumers of these products. I want to say the same thing about these three dimensions that I did about perspectives and levels: we need to attend to all three in order to gain an appropriately thick description—thick enough to understand what is going on.

Cultural texts and trends are meaningful works that convey either explicit messages or implicit pictures of the world. To interpret culture, we must describe what is going on in a cultural text at various levels and from a variety of perspectives. Readers of culture ought to be able to answer the following questions: Who made this cultural text and why? What does it mean and how does it work? What effect does it have on those who receive, use, or consume it? Perhaps the essential feature of a cultural text is the world it projects: its proposal about what it is to be human. Interpretations that focus exclusively on the "world of the text," however, ultimately prove too thin. It is better to take a multidimensional approach that attends to what is happening "behind," "in," and "in front of" the text.

Each of these three "worlds" represents an aspect of cultural discourse and may be described in terms of locutions, illocutions, and perlocutions. These three aspects of discourse also correspond to the three moments in the general hermeneutics of culture that attend to the author/producer, text/product, and reader/consumer, respectively.[134] "Faith seeking understanding" means doing justice to all three dimensions, grasping the worlds behind, of, and in front of cultural texts and, furthermore, doing so in relation to what Karl Barth calls "the strange new world of the Bible."[135]

Toward a Theory of Cultural Interpretation

The Method seeks to do for culture what Mortimer Adler's *How to Read a Book*[136] does for literature—promote literacy. Adler likens the reader to a catcher in baseball: not only is catching an activity, but catchers have to "read" various kinds of pitches (e.g., fastballs, curveballs, sliders, etc.). The question for readers is: How much can you catch? Adler's appeal to "levels" of reading also commends itself to the approach taken here. In what follows, then, I shall relate Adler's levels of reading to several triads: (1) author-text-reader, (2) locution-illocution-perlocution, and (3) the world behind, of, and in front of the text.

The "world behind the work" refers to the background context from which a cultural text emerges. Lynch identifies this with an author-focused approach that examines how a particular piece of popular culture "reflects the background, status, personality, and intentions of its particular author or authors."[137] Of course, many cultural texts do not have single authors. Who, for example, is the "author" of a film: the screenwriter, the director, the producer, the editor, some or all of the above?[138] If by "author" we mean "the person or persons responsible for the existence and nature of texts," then we may legitimately extend the notion and say that cultural texts and trends have either single authors or are the result of joint authorship.

The point is that all cultural texts originate somewhere and are produced by some person or group, and that this location may well have a bearing on what is going on in the text itself. Strictly speaking, this level is pre-text; consequently, some literary critics still believe that all we need to know is in the text itself. Though many literary critics explore the historical context of the author, Adler's account passes over this level in silence, which is a pity. For by exploring the world-behind-the-text, we come to know "that complex of the artist's beliefs and goals, convictions and concerns, which play a role in accounting for the existence and character of the work."[139]

As we have seen, culture is the objectification of the human spirit in concrete works. Cultural texts embody the worldviews of their makers. What we are ultimately trying to understand when we read cultural texts is how its producers view the meaning of life: "People's experiences of meaning are fundamentally structured by their inferences about the intentions of others."[140] We may therefore ask of any cultural text, as a proxy for its producers, not only "What are your intentions toward my daughter (or my son)?" but also "What are your intentions toward me? What do you want me to believe or do, and into what are you trying to fashion me?"

At the same time, we would be remiss if we simply equated the meaning of a cultural text with its authors' intentions. Here we may recall the lesson learned at the Frankfurt School: detailed textual analyses of cultural works are beside the point, for what matters is not the meaning of a cultural text but the power interest it serves. The (ultimately reductionist) assumption is that cultural texts always serve the interests (e.g., financial, political, ideological) of their producers. For this approach, then, the world-behind-the-text is everything. Christians have their own properly theological reasons (e.g., the doctrine of sin) for exercising a hermeneutic of suspicion with regard to the makers and producers of cultural texts; we cannot remain on this level indefinitely, however, without short-circuiting understanding.

The world "of" the cultural text refers to the particular way of being or "doing" life that the text embodies and displays and into which it invites us to enter and participate. Here it is a matter of looking not behind but *at* the text—at its rhetorical form and at its propositional content. The objective here is to discern how a particular cultural text—a television commercial, a brand name, a film—makes its point and projects its vision.

The first thing to do is to become familiar with the medium in question. Adler calls this "elementary reading." This reading pertains especially to what I have called the locutionary dimension of cultural discourse.[141] We will not understand Goethe's poetry unless we speak German. Similarly, we will not get much out of Orson Welles's "Citizen Kane" unless we "speak" film. Yes, film is like a language, complete with grammar and syntax.[142]

Adler's second level concerns "inspectional reading" and aims at providing an initial identification of the *kind* of text one is reading: its "genre." Having some provisional idea of the whole (a "preunderstanding") is most helpful when trying to make sense of the parts. Every cultural text has a genre. Films, for instance, may be classified, most broadly, as either "studio" or "indie." Under each of these two headings are more specific genres; comedy and drama are familiar from the world of the theater. Some genres, however, are distinctly cinematic: the Western or the screwball comedy.[143] In general, determining the genre of a cultural text represents a major step in understanding what it is all about.[144]

The third level that Adler discusses is "analytic reading." Here the aim is to give as thorough a reading as one needs in order to determine what the text is actually saying, and how the text is saying it. Whatever the medium, we must ask: What are the authors/producers of a cultural text *doing* with their locutions? Adler's third level thus corresponds to the illocutionary aspect of cultural discourse where the goal is to grasp what authors/producers are doing in, with, and through their cultural texts. For example, with regard to books, the goal is to grasp the author's proposition: a unit of thought or "an expression of the author's judgment about something."[145]

We can agree with Adler that understanding is a matter of "catching" what is being offered or proposed in a particular text. Yet, as we have seen, cultural texts seldom make explicit statements. Nevertheless, every cultural text contains some kind of proposition and carries some kind of illocutionary force.[146] Often the proposition is implicit; cultural statements are typically suggestive rather than blatant, but this does not stop them from performing the paradigm speech act: "Ads *make promises* to people all the time."[147]

Adler advises readers to "find the argument" of the book; he notes that "good expository authors try to reveal, not conceal, their thought."[148] Unfortunately, the same cannot always be said of producers of cultural texts. Many such texts, especially advertisements, bypass rationality altogether and appeal directly to the emotions. Indeed, I believe that most forms of cultural discourse speak primarily to imagination and not to reason.[149] Recall what we said earlier about culture's function in orienting us to the world through cultivating habits and moods. Cultural propositions are not units of thought so much as *units of life*. What a given cultural text ultimately proposes is a "world of meaning," a way of being human: "Texts speak of possible worlds and of possible ways of orientating oneself in these worlds."[150]

Let me summarize the argument up to this point in a thesis statement: *cultural texts convey their propositions—their proposals about what it means to be human—not by offering explicit arguments but rather by displaying them in concrete forms*. The world-of-the-text is often not demonstrated by logic but *displayed* in the products and practices that comprise our everyday life. For example, the world projected by many advertisements is a world in which one can be successful because of the clothes one wears or make friends by drinking the right beverage or be happy by taking the right medication.

Interestingly, *displaying a world* is also the illocutionary force associated with story and the narrative form.[151] Cultural texts offer us either narratives or bits of narrative that provide us with various "schemas"—storied frameworks—with which to make sense of everyday life. Taken together, these cultural schemas that make up the cultural world we inhabit form what Pierre Bourdieu calls the *habitus*: the "matrix of perceptions, appreciations, and actions" that script our social lives.[152]

Cultural texts thus offer what Stephen Pepper calls "world hypotheses": invitations to view the world, or human society, in a certain way and certain light (e.g., *as* a machine or *as* an organism).[153] Behind every world hypothesis is a "root metaphor" that encourages us to understand the whole world in terms of one part. Metaphors are powerful instruments for redescribing reality: "The essence of metaphor is understanding and experiencing one kind of thing in terms of another."[154] For example, one root metaphor might lead us to view life as a series of hard tests, while others might prompt us to view life as a race, a dangerous journey, a shopping spree, a sitcom, or a good party. When a metaphor takes hold, it changes the way we see things, and perhaps the way we live. Indeed, we relate to God differently when we view him as a loving Father rather than an aloof Monarch.

Cultural texts provide the flesh and bones, as it were, for what George Lakoff and Mark Johnson call the "metaphors we live by." These are the metaphors that shape our most basic understanding of the world as we experience it, metaphors that shape our perceptions and our practices without our even noticing them. As Lakoff and Johnson point out, the North American proverbial saying "time is money" is a root metaphor for a fundamental aspect of human experience and suggests that time is a valuable commodity.[155] This metaphor predisposes us to think about everyday life in terms of "spending," "saving," or "wasting" time. Once again, we see how culture exerts its hegemonic influence by taking captive our imagination.[156]

Taking the imagination captive is perhaps the ultimate perlocutionary effect. Adler's *How to Read a Book* lacks a distinct level that deals with the perlocutionary dimension of discourse (i.e., what we do *by* saying/showing something). He does, however, conclude his book with a section on the "ultimate goals" of reading, which, to summarize his own proposition, is "the growth of the mind"—cultivation! Good books, he says, "can teach you about the world and about yourself."[157] The problem, of course, is that not all cultural texts are good books. Part of what is involved in understanding cultural texts, therefore, is discerning what kinds of effects they produce: What kinds of persons do we become when we accept culture's invitation to indwell a certain world of meaning?

Each time I am confronted with the world in front of the cultural text, I have to make a decision about what to do and where to dwell. This is the moment of truth or, to use Ricoeur's term, of *appropriation*.[158] What we appropriate when we accept cultural texts is a certain way of looking at the world and a certain way of being-in-the-world: Do I accept the offer addressed to my imagination to view the world this way rather than another? Do I accept the offer addressed to my everyday existence to live this way rather than another? If we fall into step with a certain way of living in the world, we develop certain habits, habits that in turn shape our character.

What is ultimately at stake in reading culture is the reader's (my, our) response. Texts give us new capacities for knowing ourselves, new possibilities for being human. What Ricoeur says about written texts applies even more, I believe, to cultural texts: "It is the text, with its universal power of world disclosure, which gives a self to the ego."[159] In a real sense, in choosing how to respond to the texts of popular culture—to their propositions and to their projection of a proposed world—I also choose myself.

Culture is the environment and atmosphere in which we live and breathe with others. We are surrounded by cultural texts of all kinds, bombarded with messages, solicited by visions of the good life. To understand just what a cultural text is proposing one must take time and pay attention. The present chapter offers only some of the specific tools toward this end; more importantly, it has provided a broad interpretative framework and some general guidelines with which to read culture. The stakes are high. What the apostle Paul says about philosophy equally applies to culture: "See to it that no one takes you captive through hollow and deceptive philosophy" (Col. 2:8). When we appropriate the world hypothesis projected by a cultural text, we embody its proposal for our existence and make its vision visible.

Readers of culture must have some way of discerning whether and to what extent a given cultural text has the effect of imprisoning human imagination and existence rather than liberating it. What Jesus said about trees and prophets applies to cultural texts too: "By their fruit you shall know them" (Matt. 7:16). To be sure, Christians should not rush to judgment on the basis of superficial criteria. It is not enough simply to know that there are "bad words" in a film, for this takes us only as far as its locutions. Of much greater importance are the illocutions and perlocutions: what is the cultural text *doing* with these bad words and what effects does it bring about by using them in just this way?

Only the truth—that which corresponds to the strange new world of the Bible—can set us free. The truth is nothing less than what God is doing in Jesus Christ through the Spirit to bring about the transformation of this world. The gospel is the good news, authoritatively attested in the biblical text, that God is making all things new in Christ. The church is God's culture and God's building project—a new way of life, a new temple—that is being built up into Christ. In the meantime, we must heed the Johannine exhortations: Do not follow antichrists (1 John 2:18); "Test the spirits" (1 John 4:1); "Keep yourselves from idols" (1 John 5:21).

That last warning is especially relevant for all who read and engage culture. While there is nothing essentially idolatrous about popular culture, there is a persistent tendency in fallen human beings toward idol-mongering. With the exception of certain explicit cases (e.g., "American Idol"), idolatry remains under the surface of popular culture. But it is there. In Tillich's words, "Idolatry is the elevation of a preliminary concern to ultimacy."[160] Augustine was right to insist that only the triune God deserves to be the object of our ultimate concern.

Idols in today's world are no longer made of gold, at least not in North America. No, in our contemporary context the preferred materials for manufacturing idols are images and ideas: *ideologies*. Ideologies are "isms" like "materialism," "hedonism," "capitalism," "communism," "racism," etc.—systems of meaning in the service of power. Advertisements, for example, have been called "the most powerful art form on earth."[161] According to Marshall McLuhan, advertisements act as a mirror that reflects our values, hopes, dreams, and fears: ads are "the richest and most faithful daily reflections that any society ever made of its entire range of activities."[162] Ads clearly have an economic function, but they also exercise an ideological function, perpetuating the ideas and values that support and sustain the economic base of our society.[163]

Back to appropriation. Each of us is ultimately responsible for his or her way of life. After all, culture refers to all that we say and do *not by nature or instinct but freely*. We are not simply chips that have to obey their programming; we are not passive victims forced to swim with the cultural tide. To be sure, we are culturally conditioned, but this conditioning stops short of determinism. A vestige of the image of God remains in fallen human beings; there is raw material with which the Holy Spirit can work. At the same time, we have to acknowledge culture's tremendous nurturing force: what chance do individuals have against the multinational powers and principalities of popular culture? There, but for the grace (and the people) of God, go I.

Conclusion

Between Christ and Culture: The Church as a Community of Cultural Agents

To summarize: Why should Christians read culture? To get understanding; to grasp the meaning of the complex whole that is our everyday environment, an ecosystem of meaning that inevitably shapes our imaginations and nurtures concrete forms of life. How should Christians read culture? By offering theologically thick (e.g., multiperspectival, multilayered, multidimensional) descriptions of everyday texts and trends, products and practices. Well and good. But the understanding of the world of cultural texts for which faith seeks must not end here.

Faith's search for understanding of our everyday world is not merely theoretical. Everyday theologians must demonstrate their understanding in practice by becoming cultural agents. Indeed, if the church is a community of interpreters—of Scripture and of culture—it is for the sake of becoming an effective community of cultural agents. This involves, first, interpreting culture in light of a biblical-theological framework and, second, interpreting Scripture by embodying gospel values and truths in concrete cultural forms. The mission of the church is to witness to the truth of the gospel by participating in God's building project, realizing the well-wrought world redeemed in Christ.

A Community of Competent Interpreters

To be a cultural agent—a person able to make his or her own mark on culture rather than simply submit to cultural programming—one needs to be culturally literate and a critical thinker. Let me propose the following formula: Christian cultural agency = theological competence + cultural literacy + gospel performance. It is not enough simply to know doctrine; the competent disciple must also be able to read culture. With regard to popular culture, neither condemnation nor commendation alone suffices. Nothing is gained either by failing to recognize signs of common grace in culture or by reading the gospel into cultural texts where it is not present. Only when we truly understand what is happening around us can we engage our world intelligently and effectively (and evangelistically). "[Y]ou can *be* in the world more fully if you are a critical, thoughtful, insightful reader of the world around you."[164]

The church is to *be* a community of interpreters. The church interprets what is going on in culture by offering theologically thick descriptions that inscribe our everyday world into the created, fallen, and redeemed world narrated in Scripture. Hence the church also has to be a community of *biblical* interpreters whose task is to create forms of life that correspond to the biblical text in contemporary cultural contexts.[165] The church, as a community of cultural agents, must be able to make its distinctive mark—the cross of Christ—on culture.

Every culture proceeds from, embodies, and tries to reproduce a certain worldview. Similarly, everyday theologians must know not only how to preach but also how to practice Christian faith, for salvation is a matter not only of one's eternal destination but of one's present walk. The New Testament speaks to Christians as those who used to live in certain ways and now live in others. This is as it should be because behavior, as T. S. Eliot notes, is also belief. The vocation of the church is to perform the practices of Christ in ways that are both appropriate to and transformative of our particular place and time. Everyday theology is nothing less than the attempt to understand everyday life: to see it as God sees it and, with God's help, to be an agent of redemptive change.[166]

Everyday Politicians: Catalysts of the Kingdom

Culture is a testimony to what we think important (our values, our beliefs, our loves) and to what we think is more important than anything else (our ultimate concern, our first love). Christians belong to at least two cultures inasmuch as they hold dual citizenship in what Augustine termed the earthly city of man and the heavenly city of God, two cities characterized by love of self and love of God, respectively. Though it is tempting to equate the church with the city of God, such an identification is both peremptory and presumptuous. It is better to think of the two cities as two cultures, each with porous boundaries.

Christian cultural agency is the art of being "in between" Christ and everyday culture. It is the art of making Christian "space" in the dominant "places" that make up our cultural landscape. Everyday theologians are not helpless victims of popular culture. On the contrary, they can make their own cultural statements out of whatever the culture industries produce. De Certeau speaks of "adapting" or "poaching" elements from the dominant cultural system and using them for our own purposes.[167] Meaning is still a matter of discourse—as Wittgenstein put it, "meaning is use"—but consumers can use cultural texts in ways that subvert the uses and intentions of their producers (e.g., "mall walkers" who use shopping space as a place for indoor exercise).

John Fiske dubs this phenomenon "excorporation" (the opposite of "incorporation"): "the process by which the subordinate make their own culture out of the resources and commodities provided by the dominant system."[168] Cultural agents can use the locutions of popular culture (e.g., clothes, films) to perform new illocutionary and perlocutionary acts. We can speak *our* meaning with *their* language. We see this in Scripture itself.

The author of the Fourth Gospel "excorporates" the Stoic locution and notion of the "Logos" ("Word") and does something entirely unprecedented with it: he says that the Logos—the rational principle that runs the universe—"became flesh and made his dwelling among us" (John 1:14).

Christian cultural agents recognize cultural hegemony when they see it and take counter-hegemonic measures in response. Indeed, the church itself is a kind of counter-cultural industry, concerned not with making products for consumption (and worldly gain) but with cultivating certain practices: the practices of the kingdom of God. Gramsci, the cultural theorist who coined the term "hegemony," believed that "organic intellectuals"—intellectuals not sequestered in ivory towers but directly connected to a certain people group—are the ones who disseminate worldviews by calling into question customary ways of thinking and acting, thus challenging the people's consent to the prevailing order. These persons "are not just scholars and writers but anyone whose social function is to serve as a transmitter of ideas within civil society."[169] Gramsci's organic intellectual is not a traditional academic but a political organizer. This, I submit, is also a fitting description of everyday theologians, to the extent that they are concerned with how to live as citizens of the city (*polis*) of God and catalysts of a new eschatological order: the coming kingdom of God.

The kingdom of God is the "root metaphor" that fuels and fosters Christian world-building practices. For in Jesus Christ the kingdom of God came in concrete cultural form, specifically, in the form of certain focal practices that embodied for Jesus' time values that are of transcultural significance: "Focal practices are ways of being, living, and believing that express the vision of the good of a community."[170] It takes imagination for Christians to translate or transpose Jesus' kingdom practices—foot-washing, table fellowship with sinners—into the contemporary context. Others, such as prayer and preaching, need almost no adjustment at all.

My appropriation of Gramsci's notion of the "organic intellectual" is not only relevant to everyday theology but is an example of the kind of cultural agency I am advocating. I am taking a notion designed for use by the Italian Communist Party in the mid-twentieth century and putting it to twenty-first-century Christian use. As such, it is a case study in discerning how what is available in culture may be redeemed by taking it captive to the cause of Christ. This cause, I hasten to add, is not the project of Christendom, for it employs not the sword of the state (temporal, earthly power) but the sword of the Spirit (the imagination-captivating Scriptures). The hegemonic power of the mass media is indeed Goliath-like, but the church has the means to topple this giant, too: not five smooth stones but a single rock—the apostolic faith on which Christ builds his church (Matt. 16:18). The Word of God is as powerful a means of social change as the world has ever known. The only hegemonic power the church should wield is that of Word and Spirit, the very weapons the apostle Paul used to "take captive every thought to make it obedient to Christ" (2 Cor. 10:5).

A Sign of the End Time

The mission of the church is to cultivate the life of Christ in ourselves, our neighbors, and our neighborhoods. This means inculturating the way of Jesus Christ in concrete contexts. The church should be not only a "school of faith" but a "school of understanding" that trains the imaginations of its student-saints to see, judge, and act in the world as it really is "in Christ."

When the people of God fulfill their vocation, the church becomes not a sign of the times—this way lies cultural conformism—but rather a sign of the end time: a work and world of *evangelical* meaning. The church's life thus becomes an "apocalypse"—a revelation, an unveiling—that unmasks the powers that be and reminds us that they will not, contra appearances, be dominant forever. The church is to be a glimpse of the new world in the midst of the old, a reminder that the old order is passing away and a standing witness to the new. Accordingly, it is charged with the task of being a permanent revolution to prevailing plausibility structures. To "do church" is to engage in a different kind of politics, the "art of the *impossible*,"[171] an art that challenges our tired conceptions of what is possible. For "with God all things are possible" (Matt. 19:26).

The cultural understanding that faith seeks includes our response as cultural agents and is thus part and parcel of the Christian life. Whether we admit it or not, the worlds of meaning that we inhabit and create constitute our everyday lived theology. What Marx says of philosophy applies even more to theology: "The philosophers have only interpreted the world, in various ways; the point is to change it."[172] J. I. Packer agrees with the need to move beyond theoretical reflection, citing the Puritan John Perkins's definition of theology as "the science of living blessedly forever."[173]

When the people of God learn to read the signs of the times and to respond to culture so that they become a sign of end time, they will have achieved not only cultural literacy but counter-cultural wisdom. For the church is to be a contrast society, an ecclesial excorporation that demonstrates a way of living blessedly here and now by taking not only every thought but every cultural text and way of life captive to Jesus Christ.

Toward a Theory of Cultural Interpretation

What the world needs now are Christian cultural agents who demonstrate the understanding of faith by performing the gospel and giving concrete form to the kingdom of God wherever two or three are gathered: in the country garden, the city gate, the megachurch, the multiplex.

Suggested Readings

Cobb, Kelton. *The Blackwell Guide to Theology and Popular Culture*. Oxford: Blackwell, 2005.

Gorringe, T. J. *Furthering Humanity: A Theology of Culture*, Aldershot, UK: Ashgate, 2004.

Lynch, Gordon. *Understanding Theology and Popular Culture*. Oxford: Blackwell, 2005.

Tanner, Kathryn. *Theories of Culture: A New Agenda for Theology*. Minneapolis: Fortress, 1997.

Tillich, Paul. *Theology of Culture*. Oxford: Oxford University Press, 1959.

Methodological Coda: Guidelines for Everyday Theological Interpretation of Culture

1. Try to comprehend a cultural text on its own terms (grasp its communicative intent) before you "interpret" it (explore its broader social, political, sexual, or religious significance).
2. Attend to what a cultural text is *doing* as well as saying by clarifying its illocutionary act (e.g., stating a belief, displaying a world).
3. Consider the world *behind* (e.g., medieval, modern), *of* (i.e., the world displayed by the cultural text), and *in front of* (i.e., its proposal for your world) the cultural text.
4. Determine what "powers" are served by particular cultural texts or trends by discovering whose material interests are served (e.g., follow the money!).
5. Seek the "world hypothesis" and/or "root metaphor" implied by a cultural text.
6. Be comprehensive in your interpretation of a cultural text; find corroborative evidence that makes best sense of the whole as well as the parts.
7. Give "thick" descriptions of the cultural text that are nonreductive and sensitive to the various levels of communicative action.

8. Articulate the way of being human to which a cultural text directly or indirectly bears witness and gives commendation.

9. Discern what *faith* a cultural text directly or indirectly expresses. To what convictions about God, the world, and ourselves does a cultural text and/or trend commit us?

10. Locate the cultural text in the biblical creation-fall-redemption schema and make sure that biblical rather than cultural texts have the lead role in shaping your imagination and hence your interpretative framework for your experience.

Part 2
Reading Cultural Texts

Editorial Introduction

This first essay introduces us to how a theological hermeneutic of culture actually works. The authors take a rather lighthearted look at the grocery store checkout line—probably not the first place most of us would expect to find deep, underlying messages. Through an amusing catalog of the magazines, candy, and impulse items offered in the typical checkout line, the authors uncover a very consumerist message about what constitutes the good life, which they then analyze in light of biblical teaching. This essay points out that there are cultural texts all around us, each of them seeking to mold who we are and to make us into its own image. Discerning believers must first recognize such texts for what they are, then interpret them, and finally allow Christian wisdom to guide their response.

2

The Gospel according to Safeway
The Checkout Line and the Good Life

JEREMY D. LAWSON, MICHAEL J. SLEASMAN,
AND CHARLES A. ANDERSON

Navigating the Aisle

Scantily clad supermodels flash seductive stares and tabloids prophesy the next apocalypse as we are funneled through a modified version of Willy Wonka's Chocolate Factory. The magazine resting next to the super-sized peanut butter cups promises we can shed ten pounds in the next fifteen minutes. Have we entered the seventh heaven of hedonism? Or are we merely among the 90 percent of American adults who each month pass through the gauntlet of temptation known more commonly as the grocery store checkout line?[1]

The setup is virtually the same in every grocery store. Multiple rows of magazines guard the gates of the aisle: *People, US Weekly, Time,* and the like. The majority are geared toward women, who compose over 70 percent of the primary foot traffic.[2] The other side, if it does not also display magazines, often features a kiosk of individually wrapped snack foods and drinks to satisfy the urges worked up by this latest shopping expedition.

As we enter this hedonistic gauntlet, on the one side we find a narrow column of impulse items (razors, batteries, lip balm, toothbrushes, aspirin, pens, etc.), which hope to grab our attention in the approximately seven minutes we are likely to wait in line.[3] This is frequently the home of smaller seasonal items, such as Christmas bows and cheap toys, conveniently positioned within arm's reach for your toddler in the shopping cart. Farther in, a brightly colored assortment of breath mints, candy, and snack foods begs to be sampled.[4] On the other side rest such scholarly works as *National Enquirer* and *The Weekly World News* along with literary tomes by authors like Mary Higgins Clark, Nora Roberts, and Dean Koontz. Bellied up to these are columns of "micro mags" with the latest findings on alternative health remedies, recipe ideas, and astrological pontifications, along with the all-important *TV Guide* and *Soap Opera Digest*. Increasingly, we can also find the makings for a one-stop date as new-release videos and DVDs are offered in package deals with popcorn.

Other recent additions to the checkout line experience are gift and phone cards. Forgot to pick up that gift for the secretary, the in-laws, or tonight's housewarming party? Just purchase a gift card for use at the recipient's favorite AMC Theater, Old Navy, or Starbucks (now conveniently omnipresent). Not sure how many minutes are left on this month's mobile plan? Grab a five-hundred-minute phone card. In the checkout line we find a cornucopia of media and impulse items, but it is not simply a hodge-podge of consumer goods. The checkout line conveys a message, a message of what it means to live the "good life."

Marketing Strategy

The marketing strategy behind the checkout line is not unique to grocery stores; it has been appropriated in a variety of retail environments, including the payment stage of many online retailers. A few key components of that strategy shed light on the marketing forces in play. The location of a display is the most crucial factor in its success, which makes the checkout line twice as effective as some end-of-the-aisle displays in the back of the store. But why is the checkout line such a prime location? Because "the customer has downtime while waiting in line and his or her mind is free to consider possible impulse purchases"; as a result experts suggest that "the display should be as close to the customer's line of sight as possible."[5] Feel manipulated yet? Try this one from another marketing guide:

> People get fidgety waiting in line to have their purchases rung up. Capitalize on their desire to look at anything other than the line of people ahead of them by putting attention-getting impulse items on display near the checkout line. Remind lookers why they should buy now by hanging a sign above the display that reads, "Great Stocking Stuffers."[6]

We might learn as much about psychology as marketing from these resources. Indeed, one of the fastest growing areas of marketing research is how to tap the insights of psychology to sell more effectively to the consumer.[7]

Buying the "Good Life"

Psychology, indeed! Shopping today goes far beyond the purchase of life's necessities. In a study of consumers, John O'Shaughnessy probes behind the process of buying and selling: "Buying is a purposive activity, motivated and directed by the belief that the consequences of buying make life that much happier." He concludes that consumer buying "tracks certain goals that reflect a vision of the good life."[8] These goals are based on the ideas that people "are sensitive to contrasts in the human condition" and prefer to be, among other things, "Healthy *not* ill; . . . Loved and admired *not* hated and shunned; Insiders *not* outsiders looking in; Confident and *not* insecure; . . . Beautiful *not* ugly; Rich *not* poor; . . . Knowledgeable *not* ignorant; In control of life *not* at the mercy of events; Entertained *not* bored."[9] He acknowledges that advertising attempts to link these life goals with the product "by showing how the product enhances the 'good life.'"[10]

Here is the heart of the issue. Consumers want the American dream—the promise of the good life. We want the house with the white picket fence (preferably with at least four bedrooms and 2.5 baths), the SUV and the sleek sports car. We want our 401(k)'s well endowed and our children educated by the Ivy League, the latest iPod and the largest plasma TV, the highest gigs of RAM and the fastest processors for our broadband-connected media centers.

Businesses are more than happy to market their products as the road to El Dorado. The Holy Grail of the good life is reduced to a cost-efficient, high margin of return. Market research has analyzed our desire for the good life, then commodified, packaged, and mass-produced it. We are induced to believe that these products will provide us the good life, so that we will run right out to buy them.

There is, however, one more important step. Who decides what the "good life" means? What are its goals? Peter Berger's socialization theory offers some assistance: we influence society and society influences us.[11] Unless one lives in an isolated bunker somewhere, the media has the upper hand, if only by the sheer bombardment and saturation with messages. In the case of the individual versus corporations, usually the latter win. So we begin with a look at what the checkout line projects as the good life to its unsuspecting passers-by. Our discussion mimics the manner in which we encounter the checkout line itself. Starting with the experience of the cultural text, the grocery store checkout line, we become more critically aware of how the text promotes particular messages, versions of the good life. We can then begin to question what truly constitutes the "good life" from a Christian perspective. Finally, we initiate a preliminary response, a guide for being Christian cultural agents.

Browsing the Rack

Approaching the checkout line, there is the uneasy feeling that we, the customers, are in reality the ones being browsed. Dozens of digitally enhanced sirens call to us with hyper-real eyes (and breasts) as we strap ourselves to the masts of our shopping carts. Their songs are enticing: "Less Stress, True Bliss," "Make Him Ache for You," "Feel Happier in 24 Hours or Less," "11 Ways to Guarantee Financial Success." Many a person has crashed on these rocks, and quite happily too.

Judging from their headlines, these magazines cover about seven areas— a veritable "mini-summa" of our culture—that compose the good life, roughly similar to the goals mentioned by O'Shaughnessy. They include sex, beauty, health, information/knowledge, convenience, wealth, and celebrity. These categories have some overlap, but each one carries a distinct message.

Sex

The marketing cliché that "sex sells" is born out by the checkout line. *Cosmopolitan*, for example, has long positioned itself as a woman's guide to sex and always strategically places some story on how to have better sex as the top left-corner headline.[12] The September 2005 cover of *Cosmopolitan* plays along, offering: "Hot New Sex Tricks," "Guys Uncensored: What He's Really Thinking after Sex," and "50 Ways to Be a Better Girlfriend."[13] Though *Cosmopolitan* may have pioneered sexuality in women's magazines, it certainly does not stand alone. Scanning the headlines, we find "20 New Things You'll Be Happy You Tried in Bed" (*Glamour*), "Inside the Male Mind (Uh-Oh!)" (*Redbook*), and "7 Hottest Sex Tips of All Time" (*Marie Claire*), not to mention the sexually provocative poses by the models on the front covers.

All women should be sexually irresistible and fulfilled, according to these magazines. Never mind the fact that most women do not look like Victoria's Secret models and are not married to twenty-five-year-old, athletic, handsome, Italian venture capitalists. Sexuality is one package of the good life, and America is buying it in bulk. Of course, none of this is new, but still the quantity and explicitness of such messages are staggering. More distressingly, we are not discussing adult bookstores or late-night cable—this is the local grocery checkout line!

Beauty

How does one get that incredible sex life? By being beautiful, of course. From designer makeovers to models and actors, beauty seems to be divided into two main categories: body image and fashion. To be sexy one must be beautiful and dress beautifully. Many of the magazines with sex on the cover also emphasize beauty. Contrary to the proverb about beauty being in the eye of the beholder, magazines like *Glamour*, *Vogue*, and *Cosmo* set out to define, commodify, and mass-produce it. The majority of their pages are ads, not articles. In fact, you usually have to flip through twenty to thirty pages of ads just to find the table of contents. Remove all those ads and you would likely be left with a handful of articles tied in with the now-absent ads, a couple on dieting techniques, and a few on sex.

Body image is a primary topic. Evidently, thin is still in, judging from the headlines: "Fired for Getting Fat," "Stop Stress, Lose Weight, Love Your Life," "Burn Mega Fat in Less Than 4 Weeks." These messages, along with the presence of the pencil-thin cover models themselves, claim that the way to happiness is to weigh less. The estimated seven million women with eating disorders provide evidence for the effectiveness of such messages.[14]

With the right body comes the need for the right look. Headlines proclaim: "How to Find Jeans That Fit Your Butt," "Your Dream Haircut," "Fashion: 527 Best Buys" (Why stop at 527? You're on a roll!). Many purport to divulge some celebrity's fashion secrets, which often means a specific product or line of clothing. *Is it an ad or an article?* Can we tell the difference? Would it matter if we could?

These beauty magazines peddle unrealistic hopes to people desperate for some version of the good life. The rising popularity of designer makeovers, cosmetic surgery, and Botox are only a precursor of more significant cultural trends toward cybernetic augmentations and transhumanism, trends that a later essay in this book will examine.

Health

Health articles come in two main categories: physical, and emotional/mental. Some checkout line magazines, like *Shape*, *Self*, or *Muscle & Fitness*, devote themselves to the former topic. They specialize in physical fitness and images of people who seem to live at the gym. *Muscle & Fitness* and *Men's Fitness* typically show a picture of a tanned male body builder, sans chest hair, posing in gender-obvious shorts, with a female body builder clinging to his side. *Men's Fitness* often features articles on male sexuality, such as this classic from September 2005: "Orgasm Insurance." These are the masculine counterparts to women's magazines such as *Glamour*—while they claim to look at fitness, most of the articles are similar to the focus on beauty in *Glamour* or *Cosmo*. Health is a means to the end of looking good and being attractive. To be beautiful, one must be fit as well as pretty and fashionable. Some of the mini-mags, it should be noted, do devote themselves to more obviously health-related topics like breast cancer prevention, herbal remedies, and healthy dieting.

The goal of mental/emotional health, according to the magazines, is to be happy and stress-free. *Cosmo* boasted in a headline, "The Article That Can Make You Feel Happier Almost Instantly," while *Woman's Day* once told us about "The Healing Power of Friendships." These magazines presuppose that most people are stressed-out and unhappy. Of course, people might be so unhappy because they have come to the realization that they are missing out on the good life because they are not body builders, supermodels, or tycoons. Or perhaps they have realized they are so busy living the good life they cannot enjoy it.

Information/Knowledge

In the information age, Americans constantly want to be in the know, and the checkout line is another dispensary. Tabloids provide valuable information about the last, brave days of some aged celebrity or the shocking breakup of last week's couple of the century. More reputable magazines like *Time* or *Newsweek* keep us up to date with politics and cultural trends, while *People* and *Us Weekly* provide the inside celebrity scoop. No need to go to the library when we can learn right here how to create the perfect garden, or become a gourmet chef or an interior decorator—all in ten minutes or less. But who are these experts? And what is their information based on? It doesn't matter as long as we are in the know. Because of their location in the checkout line, it is the tabloids that have the last word.[15]

Convenience

To want things quick and easy is a hallmark of contemporary America, a characteristic on which these magazines capitalize. O'Shaughnessy states that "anything that reduces effort will contribute to sales."[16] This mania for efficiency permeates nearly all of society. (A later essay explores the trend of busyness amid our caffeine-saturated culture.)

Most magazines trumpet their commitment to your convenience. Headlines offer to help you "Jump Start Your Weight Loss: Easy Fixes for Your Toughest Obstacles" and "Speed through Your To-Do List." One magazine, *First for Women*, positions itself for "Women on the Go," according to its masthead. Its headlines regularly promise "The 15 Best New Cuts for 2005" or "173 Holiday Shortcuts." Its publisher specifically promises advertisers that "every article is written in a positive and optimistic tone, benefit-oriented with a 'you-can-do-it' attitude to make her *already good life even better*."[17] Most of the magazines themselves are convenient in that they are easily accessible, offer quick tips, and give instant access to "life-changing" information. They therefore embody the quality of being "good." Wherever the road to El Dorado leads, it better be a quick and easy ride.

Convenience in the checkout line, however, can cut both ways. Grocery stores have begun to allow customers to scan and bag their own items, in the name of convenience (and corporate cost-cutting). This process allows less time for browsing, and the space for magazine racks and all other items is reduced significantly. The obvious result would seem to be fewer magazine sales.[18] Related to this is the emergence of online grocers like Peapod, which allow you to skip the checkout line altogether.[19] Such convenience-inspired trends may eventually prove the decline of much of the traditional checkout line.

As for the snack foods, soft drinks, and candy in the checkout line, they represent convenience in edible form. Their presence, though, does contradict some aspects of the "good life" message, especially the idea that one should weigh less than a Mr. Goodbar. On the other hand, there is instant pleasure to be had in the sugar rush. Also, the sheer ubiquity of breath mints in these displays demands comment (one line offered some 30 brands of mints). Either bad breath has become a "code red" epidemic, or kissing has become our favorite national pastime.

Wealth

Who wants to be a millionaire? Who doesn't? A few magazines deal directly with finance including *Fortune* and *Money*, but they typically do not make the checkout line racks. They cover mostly investments and retirement, the ultimate destination of the good life. Other magazines, more directly geared to the primary foot-traffic of the checkout line, likewise offer financial advice: *Woman's World* featured a 2002 article on how to "save $3,275 on groceries."

To live the good life means, at the least, financial security, but more often it equates to having a bottomless pit of money. One magazine pictured a twenty-something man hanging out of a limousine sun roof, with stacks of cash flying through his ring-covered fingers into the street behind him. Money means pleasure and power—it is the means by which the good life is accessible. Sex, beauty, knowledge, convenience, health, even celebrity, are all available if you have the cash (or credit limit). Even for those who would explicitly reject this message, the ubiquity of such images still has an impact. If we are honest, it is not just the naïve who are influenced.

Celebrity

This last area of the good life is one the checkout line particularly loves. The majority of magazines devote much attention to celebrities. They are the physical manifestation of the good life. This pantheon of cultural gods is portrayed as sexually fulfilled, beautiful, healthy, educated, and wealthy; as a result, they are worshiped. Thus, they are used to promote both the magazines and the products advertised therein. To live the good life ultimately means to be like a celebrity. They represent the pinnacle and culmination of the checkout-line vision.

Sometimes the intersection of celebrity and the checkout line comes into special focus. A television talk show celebrity like Oprah Winfrey has ascended to the status of expert to whom we turn for information on any number of topics. Oprah's magazine, appropriately titled *O*, features articles on relationships, spirituality, health, celebrities' lives, and helpful tips on just about everything. Recently, *O* offered advice on "mistake-proof money smart shopping" and the "Yes, I Can! Diet." Oprah has established an entire media empire that includes the magazine, her own top-rated talk show, a production company that produces "Dr. Phil," and her own cable network, Oxygen. Her cultural influence particularly came into focus with her book club, as it propelled previously obscure authors atop the best-seller lists.[20] Oprah, the celebrity and cultural guru, aptly pictures and invites us to participate in the good life.

Conclusion

The good life according to the checkout line projects a vision of happiness that comes from having the best physically (sex, beauty, and health), intellectually (information/knowledge), and financially (wealth). We want all of it quickly and effortlessly (convenience), and we find the epitome of this good life in the celebrity media star. This is the message, sometimes subtle and other times blatant, that comes to us as we simply wait in line at our neighborhood grocery store.

The Good Life according to the Gospel

What does the checkout line have to do with Jerusalem? In one sense, they overlap and compete, for there is a Christian vision of the good life, what we may call the good life according to the gospel. If the point of the good life presented in the checkout line is to become like a celebrity (or at least to dream about it), then the goal of the good life according to the gospel is to become like Jesus. In redemption, God is at work to perfect us in his image and make us like his Son.[21] He speaks a word of new creation to make light shine in our lives, and thus we are transformed into the likeness of Christ, who himself is the image of God (2 Cor. 3:17–4:6).[22] In this process, we become like God in true righteousness and holiness (Eph. 4:22–24). This is the purpose for which God has predestined his people—to be conformed to the image of his Son (Rom. 8:29). So the good life of the gospel is wrapped up in our growing likeness to Jesus. We will look, therefore, at each of these seven components from the checkout line to see what a gospel-centered vision of the good life has to say about them, concluding with Christ, the anticelebrity.

Sex

Sex, often perceived as the dirty little secret of Christianity, is actually accorded a special place in the good life envisioned by the gospel. In the biblical worldview, sex is a mutually enriching relationship that is grounded in love and commitment. In fact, marriage, the sexual relationship ordained by God, takes on even greater significance when we realize that it points beyond itself to image the relationship between Christ and the church (Eph. 5:31–32). The purposes of sex are procreative, as God uses it to create life and fulfill the first commandment (Gen. 1:28), and unitive, as its enjoyment and intimacy culminate in the union of a husband and wife (Gen. 2:23–24). Furthermore, because a married person's body does not belong to himself or herself alone, sex is a gift given to another (1 Cor. 7:4). Its primary concern, therefore, is not outward attraction or selfish satisfaction, but internal connectedness. So both the checkout line and the gospel think very highly of sex, but for different reasons and in divergent ways. Yet, as important as sex is, it is not all important. Jesus proclaimed marriage to be part of God's good design for creation, and yet said some are called to renounce it for the sake of the kingdom of heaven (Matt. 19:1–12).[23] In the good life of the gospel, sex is an incredible gift from God, but faithfulness to the Giver remains primary.

Beauty

The commodification of beauty is evident in its omnipresent mass-production. From the checkout-line magazines to Barbie dolls and Victoria's Secret, all of us are immersed in a culture obsessed with the surface of our skin. Christians are by no means immune to this concern.[24] Initially, though, some might think there is little scriptural concern for beauty. After all, didn't Paul say that the outward is wasting away, while the inward is being renewed (2 Cor. 4:16)? On this view, Christians should repudiate any interest in physical beauty.

The biblical vision, however, is more balanced than this misinterpretation might initially lead us to believe. Outward beauty is understood to be a gift from God, something that applies to all of creation in its time (Eccles. 3:11). Such beauty can even be celebrated, as when the lover sings of his beloved's lips resembling a scarlet ribbon and her breasts the twin fawns of a gazelle (Song 4:1–7). Moreover, beauty will have its place in the new heaven and new earth: the New Jerusalem is described as "a bride beautifully dressed for her husband" (Rev. 21:2). Yet there is another side of beauty where, paradoxically, it actually manifests an inner ugliness. The prophet Ezekiel describes the king of Tyre—a reference many interpret to be also about Satan—as perfect in beauty, yet because of it, his heart became proud (Ezek. 28:12, 17). Similarly, God promised to judge the proud and fashionably adorned women of Judah: he would replace their nose rings and tiaras with sackcloth and desolation (Isa. 3:16–26). Outward beauty is fleeting (Prov. 31:30), while the real fashion adornments are the fruits of a godly wisdom (Prov. 1:9). The truth is that there is a world of difference between looking beautiful and being beautiful.[25]

The life of Esther captures a biblical conception of beauty. Esther is a looker. Of all the eligible women in the kingdom, she catches the king's eye. To Xerxes, much like contemporary America, looks are what matter. The biblical narrative, though, is not concerned with the radiance of her complexion, but with the radiance of her character. It is her courage to stand for her people and oppose Haman's genocidal plans that draws biblical praise. This is a profoundly different way of looking at beauty from what we are marketed. A culture infatuated with surface-level beauty and blown about by the winds of fashion trends is miles away from the inward "beauty of a gentle and quiet spirit" (1 Pet. 3:4). The truly beautiful are those who embody the good life of the gospel by fearing God and telling others about that life. Indeed, how beautiful are the feet of those who bring good news (Isa. 52:7).

Health

Unlike Count Rugen in *The Princess Bride* ("If you haven't got your health, you haven't got anything"), the vision of the good life in the gospel sees health as a blessing but by no means a necessity. Healing was central to Christ's ministry as a sign of God's in-breaking kingdom. Indeed, Matthew understands healings and exorcisms as integral to Jesus' redemptive ministry (Matt. 8:16–17, quoting Isa. 53:4). The heart of Jesus' ministry was reconciling people to God, chiefly through forgiveness of sins. He points out that while on the surface it may seem harder to heal someone who cannot walk, the greater miracle is to forgive that person's sins

(Mark 2:8–12). Healing was indeed central for the Great Physician, but the primary focus of health was not physical, mental, or emotional, but spiritual. The good life of the checkout line has confused the incidental for the essential. The good life of the gospel places the emphasis on a healthy relationship with God. Likewise, the contemporary obsession with physical exercise has its place within a broader conception of stewardship and responsibility, but the greatest exercise should be the practice of godliness (1 Tim. 4:8).

Information/Knowledge

To be in-the-know looks very different in the good life envisioned by the gospel than that of the checkout line. It starts with our point of view, the vantage point from which we try to navigate the contemporary information overload. As Paul describes it, believers should "regard no one from a worldly point of view. Though we once regarded Christ in this way, we do so no longer" (2 Cor. 5:16). Paul is explaining that it is possible to regard the same reference point from very different perspectives. We can know people (and things) from a worldly perspective, but to be in-the-know for a Christian is to know and be known by Christ, and for this to transform how we see everything else. Faith should so decisively shape our vantage point that we take all thoughts captive to Christ (2 Cor. 10:5).[26] Such a point of view radically changes the motivation, source, and outcome of our knowledge.

Given this Christ-shaped point of view, our ultimate source for information and education is Scripture (though without eliminating the need for other sources). Both Christ and Scripture are called the Word of God (Rev. 19:13; John 10:35); as Luther put it, Scripture is the manger in which the Christ child is laid. As the ideals of the checkout-line good life form the person who pursues them, how much more should the word of God form the Christian? We do not read Scripture merely to be in-the-know, but rather to be transformed by the renewing of our minds. Proverbs appropriately begins with the declaration that "The fear of the LORD is the beginning of knowledge, but fools despise wisdom and discipline" (1:7). Christians should be interested not just in mere information, but in wisdom that finds its significance in obedience to God. Information and knowledge, then, are to be conceived within the framework of equipping believers as cultural agents who, just as the men of Issachar, can discern the times and know what the church should do (1 Chron. 12:32). This is at the heart of what it means to influence culture.

Reading Cultural Texts

Convenience

The pursuit of twelve easy steps to success takes on a new light in the gospel vision of the good life. Though it offers many benefits, convenience is often antithetical to Christian formation and discipleship, where the emphasis is on the quality of the end product and not the speed with which it is achieved. There are no quick and easy steps to the Christian life; in many respects, it is one of patience and waiting. We must wait upon the Lord in prayer, for Christ's return, for God's judgment against wickedness, for the redemption of our bodies, and for a new heaven and new earth. Peter warns us that we will endure suffering even as we participate in Christ's sufferings (1 Pet. 4:12–19). Patience is a fruit of the Spirit (Gal. 5:22). The only thing we are ever told is easy about the Christian life is Christ's yoke (Matt. 11:30). Our salvation was not wrought by an act of convenience and cheap grace; it was a costly endeavor requiring the shed blood of the Son of God. The good life of the gospel offers a lifestyle of stewardship and a vision of peace and rest as we—in blood, sweat, and tears—anticipate the second coming of our Lord.

Wealth

Wealth is seen in Scripture in both worldly and godly terms. In the Old Testament, wealth was often a manifestation of God's blessing, but one that frequently led to complacency and forgetfulness. God brought the Israelites into a bountiful land that provided them with valley springs, olive oil, fine houses, and much more, but their temptation would be to forget God and credit themselves for these things (Deut. 8:6–18). Sadly, although God delivered them and blessed them so abundantly, the people did indeed turn away to idolatry, and thus God promised to tear down their ivory mansions (Amos 3:15). We too, like the Israelites of Amos' day, are prone to forget the provision of God when we reach the checkout-line good life of the fat 401(k).

In the New Testament, the blessing of earthly wealth remains, at least in the opportunity it offers to do good for others (e.g., Luke 7:4–5; Acts 4:36–37). Generous giving is commended, yet wealth itself is not condemned (1 Tim. 6:17–19). Still, the dangers of wealth become all the more apparent. Jesus starkly presents our choice ultimately as either to serve God or to serve money (Matt. 6:24). In fact, money is one of his most frequent teaching topics. In the divine economy, financial wealth pales beside what is truly valuable. Jesus points to the kingdom of heaven as the ultimate treasure worth more than all our worldly possessions (Matt. 13:44–46). The famous hymn "Be Thou My Vision" captures this truth when it states, "Riches I heed not, nor man's empty praise. Thou mine inheritance now and always." Our true, spiritual wealth has come from Jesus, who willingly became poor so that we might become rich—this is the gospel (2 Cor. 8:9). The Christian retirement plan is not necessarily received in this life, but it is enjoyed eternally.

Celebrity

The Bible has its share of celebrities but never holds them up as models for Christians to imitate. Perhaps the prime example of biblical celebrity is Solomon. He had an active sex life (to say the least) with 700 wives and 300 concubines. His wealth and wisdom were world-renowned for his time, drawing even the Queen of Sheba for a state visit. He built the temple of the LORD, and an even more extravagant palace for himself (a likely candidate for MTV's *Cribs*). Under his leadership, Israel enjoyed some of its greatest days. Yet, in the end, the evaluation of Solomon's life is tragic. All these gifts did not lead him to the Giver but to pleasure and idolatry—Scripture concludes that Solomon, unlike his father David, did evil in the eyes of the LORD (1 Kings 11:6). Later generations did not laud Solomon as a celebrity; they lamented his faithlessness (Neh. 13:26). Solomon demonstrates the temptation of a creeping syncretism that suggests we can have everything, that we can pursue both the checkout-line and the gospel visions of the good life. No sacrifices, just supersize it all.

The incarnation of Christ is the antithesis of celebrity culture. Just as the celebrity *du jour* represents the checkout-line good life, so Jesus is the model and author of the good life according to the gospel. He had more glory than the checkout line could ever imagine but set it aside to take on the form of a slave (Phil. 2:6–8). Though he had close relationships with women—even some scandalous ones—he remained celibate. Scripture comments little on his appearance, but our best clue comes from Isaiah 53—a chapter frequently applied to Jesus—which says the servant had no physical beauty to catch our eye (Isa. 53:2). We know even less about how healthy he was, though crucifixion at such a young age is never doctor recommended. He knew Scripture intimately, able to quote it in the midst of temptation (Matt. 4:1–11) and even to derive doctrine from its details (Mark 12:26–27). Very little about his life was convenient, from leaving the perfections of heaven for a fallen world where he had no per-

I Want That! How We All Became Shoppers

The supermarket checkout line may represent the state-of-the-art in commercial salesmanship and consumer psychology, but where did the idea of shopping really come from? In a society where toddlers are encouraged to pay for their own candy, most of us cannot remember a time when we didn't shop. Exchanging money for goods is as natural as breathing in and out.

Thomas Hine's *I Want That! How We All Became Shoppers* (New York: HarperCollins, 2002) reminds us that in order to understand the present we have to understand the past. His book is an excellent case study in cultural history that examines how people throughout time have acquired objects, a survey that includes everything from medieval fairs to Priceline.com.

Hine offers a thick description of a long-time cultural trend aimed at helping us understand ourselves better. He is at his best discussing why people shop: "Shopping is the contemporary expression of our complex relationship to things" (x). He argues that we spend much of our lives in what he calls the "buyosphere," a place of possibilities where we can imagine our lives differently and choose who we will be: what we will wear, what objects will furnish our homes, what class we identify with and belong to.

Shopping is literally an "objectification" of what it means to be human. Each of Hine's chapters focuses on a force that drives us to shop: power, responsibility, self-expression, belonging, celebration, convenience, etc. We learn that the concept of taste "is based on the idea that objects have meanings, and that people who share the taste can agree on the meaning" (144). So, be careful what you pick up in the checkout line—"By the choices you make . . . you tell the world who you are" (66).

Kevin J. Vanhoozer

manent home, to traveling constantly for the sake of his mission (Luke 9:57–58; Mark 1:38–39). In terms of wealth, he took on poverty as part of his rescue mission (2 Cor. 8:9) and was supported financially by others, particularly women whom he had healed (Luke 8:1–3). His work seemingly came to an abrupt end, not in the halls of political influence in the nation's capital or amid the success of a Fortune 500 boardroom—not even in a Florida retirement home—but on a cross, which was the death of a criminal among criminals. Only on the other side, having poured out his life, do resurrection and vindication come, to which the rehabilitation of a Martha Stewart—or the latest "celebrity redemption" story—pales in comparison.

Conclusion

What emerges from a biblical consideration of these seven areas is that most of them (with the exception of celebrity and perhaps convenience) have their place, but only *a* place. Sex, beauty, health, information, and wealth can all be good things in the good life of the gospel, but not if they are elevated too highly. The checkout line puts our loves out of order, an indication itself of how culture can have a subtle impact on our idea of the good life. In contrast, the good life envisioned by the gospel relativizes what the checkout line sets forth as essential. Most important are relationships, primarily to God and then to others whom he has made and the creation in which he has placed us. We must keep the main thing the main thing, that God in Christ was reconciling the world to himself, not counting peoples' sins against them (2 Cor. 5:19). Reorienting ourselves toward the good life of the gospel acknowledges with Augustine the importance of rightly ordered loves. Only with such a focus on the gospel can the truly good life come to fruition. Here we may declare with the psalmist, "Taste and see that the Lord is good" (Ps. 34:8).

"In" the Checkout Line But Not "of" It

So where does this vision of the good life take us? Many Christians and non-Christians alike have expressed concern over the explicit images and headlines of checkout-line magazines. Consumer groups like the American Decency Association and Morality in Media have accused stores of indecent exposure.[27] In response, Kroger, the largest grocery chain in the U.S. with more than 3,000 stores, placed covers over the more racy magazines. Such a step, though significant, can easily blind us to the deeper and wider troubles. The explicit sexuality of the magazines is only one part of the checkout-line good life. The subtle temptation of the easy road to financial independence, the instant gratification of a gluttonous sugar rush, and the juicy dish of Hollywood gossip are all dangerous, and no less so than the damning rocks of unrestrained sexuality embodied in the digitally enhanced, scantily clad supermodels calling our names. These other sirens call us just as seductively—though perhaps not as visibly—and require just as much diligence on our part. Christians need to realize the impact that the media has on us, even in the grocery store. Just like the Matrix, it has us; it is all around us. Being wise as serpents means that we understand what the checkout-line good life proposes and commit ourselves to seeking the good life that Christ himself makes possible and embodies. Though we find ourselves "in" the checkout line, we must not be "of" the checkout line.

Editorial Introduction

Popular music opens up a window into the soul. Cultural studies have increasingly reflected upon the lyrics and musical styling of various artists to discern key themes and messages that resonate with the audiences that flock to these musicians. This next essay looks at one of the most provocative and controversial musical artists of our time, the rapper Eminem. By thoughtfully examining the lyrics and music of Eminem, so taboo to many Christians, the author taps a valuable resource that offers insights into the desires and fears of a generation that embraces him.

Despair and Redemption

A Theological Account of Eminem

D A R R E N S A R I S K Y

Coming to Grips with Eminem

Since its inception in the 1970s, rap has undergone a transformation in terms of audience and popularity. Rapper André of the group OutKast describes this change from his own insider's point of view:

> Rap . . . *is* the mainstream now. People are saying, "We're keeping it underground. We're keeping it underground." But really, that's b*******. Because . . . once they start putting rap songs in commercials and rap is outselling country music . . . it's not the same any more. It's a different type of white kid that listens to it now. It used to be kids listened to it for the same reason they liked punk—it was a rebellious thing your parents didn't like. To those kids, it was cool to listen to N.W.A. say, "F*** the police." That was like your music while you're skipping school and partying and drinking. . . . Rap was something those white kids discovered, it wasn't just there in front of them. Now, it's everywhere.[1]

I would like to thank Colleen Sarisky for her many valuable contributions to this essay.

No one better represents rap's move from the margins to the mainstream than Eminem. He began competing in small-venue rap battles in inner-city Detroit in an effort to make ends meet, and a decade later consistently appears on *Rolling Stone*'s list of top money earners alongside artists he has mentored and from whose success he profits. Eminem is by no means "keeping it underground" at this stage of his career. One writer went so far as to taunt him by saying that, on his current trajectory, he is bound to start hearing his music on elevators.[2]

Even as Eminem has become a figure in mainstream culture, Christian leaders have, by and large, advised people to steer clear of him because of his unabashedly vulgar and violent lyrics. Certainly, a theological account of Eminem's music must counsel a degree of separation: his material is just that raw. But Christians who make avoidance the first and final word on the subject of Eminem deprive themselves of an opportunity to understand the powerful trends in contemporary culture that make him so wildly popular, especially with younger audiences. As Eminem's record sales demonstrate, his music resonates with millions of people. Why? If the Christian church aspires to address the gospel message to people where they are, it will be of great value to inquire how Eminem fits within popular culture.

Eminem as a Cultural Phenomenon

The World of Eminem: Music and Film

As this book goes to print, Eminem has released five solo albums, along with a number of collaborative ventures, and a recently released greatest hits collection. Obviously, then, space constraints do not allow for a comprehensive survey of his music; selectivity becomes a necessity. Focus will fall on two songs from the *Marshall Mathers LP*, an album that nearly won the Grammy for best album in 2001 despite protests against it from both ends of the political spectrum. This album is important not simply because of its notoriety or because it sold well but primarily because it illustrates what makes Eminem distinctive as a rapper. Whereas rap traditionally has provided a vehicle for social commentary and critique, especially from the perspective of people who felt they had no other way to voice their concerns, the *Marshall Mathers LP* consists, in large part, of forthright discussions of Eminem's own personal story—hence the inclusion of Eminem's real name in the album's title. (His previous two albums, the *Slim Shady EP*

[1998] and the *Slim Shady LP* [1999], while autobiographical in part, often involve the extreme and sadistic antics of Eminem's alter ego, Slim Shady.) In addition to reflection on two tracks from the *Marshall Mathers LP*, the autobiographical movie *8 Mile* will also enter this discussion. The film deserves analysis for reasons similar to those that pertain to the *Marshall Mathers LP*. First, the movie drew a large audience: Eminem's feature film debut grossed $54.5 million at the box office the weekend of its U.S. release, which at that time represented the second highest opening tally ever for an R-rated film. Second, *8 Mile* provides a window into the life of the rapper, even while it makes a concerted effort to downplay his offensive side. Third, "Lose Yourself," a song from the *8 Mile* soundtrack, won Eminem a Grammy for best original song.

The rap "The Way I Am" from the *Marshall Mathers LP* is as good a place as any to begin to understand Eminem and his music. Unlike some of his songs, this track is not just an effort to get a laugh out of his audience. According to Eminem himself, "The Way I Am" is "where I really dump out my true feelings."[3] By the time Eminem recorded this song (1999), he had already racked up a number of MTV and Grammy awards, and he owned his own record label.[4] This professional success delivered Eminem from the poverty that had dogged him growing up, but he nonetheless found his new fame a profoundly mixed blessing. In fact, what provoked Eminem to write "The Way I Am" was the pressure to deliver a popular hit that would make as much of a splash as his previous hit, "My Name Is" (*Slim Shady LP*).[5] For this track (as for most of Eminem's work until *The Eminem Show* and the *8 Mile* soundtrack), the music creates a background for the rhymes, which are the point of focus. Over a simple three-note loop with ominous bells tolling in the background, Eminem admits, "I'm not gonna be able to top on 'My Name Is.'" Nor does he want to get caught up in a game of maintaining his popularity. His aim is not to be "pigeon-holed into some pop-py sensation / to cop me rotation at rock 'n' roll stations." Eminem says his piece regarding these matters,

Studying music for the sake of cultural engagement requires attention to several aspects. The primary focus belongs to the lyrics of particular songs, which most directly convey the message. The advanced exegete may want to consider further the relation of songs on a particular album. Do these together convey a unified message? Likewise, it is important to remember that we are talking about *music* and not just poetry. How does the form of the music either advance or stand in tension with its content?

yet there is much more. The song turns into a full-blown rant against every-body, even his fans. To them, he says pointedly, "at least have the decency in you / to leave me alone, when you freaks see me out in the streets when I'm eatin' or feedin' my daughter / to not come and speak to me." (On "Stan," a previous track from the same album, Eminem is gracious with a fan who is enamored with him; here he is harsher.) Even more than his fans, the media receive rough treatment: "All this controversy circles me / and it seems like the media immediately / points a finger at me / So I point one back at 'em, but not the index or pinkie / or the ring or the thumb." Eminem voices his frustration that when violence occurs in a middle-class school (an allusion to Columbine), the public blames artists like him and Marilyn Manson, while no one draws attention to the violence occurring in the inner city every day. Pressure to perform, fans who will not give him space, negative attention from media outlets—all of these things infuriate Eminem. The very act of rapping about what vexes him is, for Eminem, the answer: "Since birth I've been cursed with this curse to just curse / . . . And it sells and it helps in itself to relieve / all this tension dispensing these sentences." An exchange during an interview between radio show host Howard Stern and Eminem captures the essence of this song, "'Let me tell you something pal: you got a lot of pain inside you, you need therapy,' Stern told [Eminem]. 'My music is my therapy,' Em replied."[6]

A second song from the *Marshall Mathers LP* that warrants a closer look is "Kim," a track Eminem's critics often refer to as an example of the rapper's misogyny and violent tendencies.[7] Understanding this song requires some stage setting. For Eminem, 1999 brought professional achievement (which itself was fraught with ambiguities, as demonstrated in "The Way I Am") as well as numerous sources of personal turmoil. First, his mother filed a $10 million defamation of character lawsuit against him because he referred to her as smoking dope in "My Name Is." Second, Eminem's grandmother threatened to sue him if he sampled a track recorded by his uncle. Third, Eminem entered what would become a troubled marriage to Kim Scott. Kim married Eminem despite being depicted as dead in the trunk of his car on the front of the *Slim Shady LP*. The two divorced not long after marrying. Difficult relationships with many of the women in his life serve to explain, yet—let it be said—certainly not to excuse, the hateful rage that explodes in "Kim."[8] According to Eminem, when he sat down to write "Kim," at a time when the two were estranged, he intended to compose a love song; but, not wanting to resort to trite sentimentality, he instead gave free rein to quite the opposite emotion.[9] (Factoring into all of this is the fact that Eminem penned the song while on the mood-amplifying drug Ecstasy.)

Reading Cultural Texts

"Kim" is a "murder ballad" fictionally narrating how Eminem kills Kim and her son after first killing her lover, with whom she supposedly had an affair. Given its basic subject matter, it is odd that the song begins with Eminem talking softly and sweetly to Hailie ("daddy's baby girl"). The mood darkens quickly, however, as a heavy backbeat formulated by the Bass Brothers begins and Eminem turns on his wife. Eminem's voice portrays two characters in the song: himself and Kim. In threatening tones, he says to her, "Don't make me wake this baby / She doesn't need to see what I'm about to do." In a terrified, high-pitched voice representing Kim, Eminem protests, "Let go of my hair, please don't do this baby." This shrieking and pleading are all the more harrowing because when Eminem impersonates females he usually does so in a contrived voice intended to mock them. As the song progresses and the tension mounts—will he follow through on his declared intention?—the chorus periodically gives what relief there is to be found in the song.[10] Reflecting on the situation, Eminem reveals himself to be both tormentor (via obvious physical violence) and tormented (by the thought that his wife is disloyal): "So long, b**** you did me so wrong / I don't wanna go on / Living in this world without you." Eminem swings back and forth through a whole range of emotions in the song, often spewing forth rage ("I hate you! I hate you!") but at times reversing himself ("Oh my God I love you"). In the closing lines of the song, Eminem does the awful deed, taunting his wife even as he kills her, "Now bleed!" In concert, Eminem would often perform this song dressed in a hockey mask intended to evoke Jason of the *Friday the 13th* movie series. As he kicked around and stabbed a blow-up Kim doll, his audience would chant "Kill Kim!"[11] Eminem has said that in real life he would never do the things he portrays in his music; what

BEHIND THE TEXT

The author reflected on his own struggle in listening to "Kim." He noted: "'Kim' poses a challenge to those Christians who listen to Eminem in order to understand contemporary culture. As I listened closely to the song a number of times, my wife was in the next room. I felt disturbed. Husbands are supposed to love their wives as Christ loved the church and gave himself up for her (Eph. 5:25). A man should be willing to die for his wife; nothing could be more opposed to that than murdering one's wife. People who are especially sensitive should be cautious about listening to music like this. Youth are inevitably more impressionable than adults and therefore should also tend toward avoidance." This is a caution that must be addressed particularly as those involved in Christian agency seek to carefully navigate being in the world but not of it.

he is doing, by his account, is spontaneously expressing how he feels at a certain moment.[12] In this case, sadly, life and art came to resemble one another in a way. After seeing video footage of a concert performance, Kim tried unsuccessfully to kill herself.[13]

In light of the depravity that characterizes some of Eminem's songs, such as "Kim," how was a film about him supposed to attract a large audience? The writer hired by Universal Studios to create the screenplay for *8 Mile* initially offered up something that "reflected [the] outrageous humor and cartoonish violence of his records."[14] Universal was not pleased: "They were like, 'Uh, no,'" the writer reported to *Entertainment Weekly*.[15] The studio wanted to create a drama that would reach an audience with reservations about Eminem. So, instead of violence against homosexuals ("My words are like a dagger with a jagged edge / that'll stab you in the head whether you're a fag or a lez / Hate fags? The answer's yes"), *8 Mile* has Eminem's character, Jimmy "Rabbit" Smith Jr., defending a gay man in the workplace.[16] Instead of misogyny, *8 Mile* features Rabbit sticking up for his mom when her boyfriend badmouths and shoves her. Instead of flippant violence, *8 Mile* portrays Rabbit and his buddies undertaking juvenile pranks such as shooting paintballs at pedestrians and a police car.

The film depicts a single week in the life of Rabbit and his friends as they try to make it on the streets of inner-city Detroit in 1995. The action is framed by two incidents that take place at a rap club called the Shelter. In the opening scene, Rabbit nervously rehearses gestures and lines in a bathroom mirror before taking the stage for a rap battle. When he eventually participates in the verbal joust, he freezes up and slips offstage as the crowd chants, "Choke!" Rabbit spends most of the movie trying to live down that failure. Rap is his only way out, yet if he is to pursue it he must face up to his fears and conquer them. As the movie draws to a close, Rabbit squares off against a member of a rival Detroit posse, members of which have recently beaten him up and stolen his girl. A coin toss determines that Rabbit will go first, ensuring that he will have no chance to respond to his rival, who can trot out a long list of ways in which he and his friends have recently gotten the better of Rabbit. In true Eminem style, Rabbit decides to preempt his opponent by exposing all of his own weaknesses. When he finishes, he hands the microphone to his opponent and challenges him to tell the crowd something they do not already know about him. His opponent cannot say a word, and Rabbit wins the battle. Rabbit's friends are exultant, thinking that they will now be able to garner all the trappings of success because of Rabbit's victory. If viewers make the leap and associate Eminem's character with the man himself, it would seem that after this victory he may well be on his way to a successful rap career. The film, however, does not end with the guarantee of glory. Just before the credits roll, Rabbit heads back to work his shift at a pressing plant. This ending prompts Roger Ebert to ask wistfully, "What has happened to our hopes, that young audiences now embrace such cheerless material, avoiding melody like the plague?"[17] An assessment of this generation will have to wait. What is already clear, at this point, is that the mood of *8 Mile*, where even victory is tinged with melancholy, is not fundamentally different from the feel of Eminem songs like "The Way I Am." The closing rap battle in *8 Mile* also resembles "The Way I Am" in that Eminem lays himself bare in both cases: just as Rabbit exposes his own weaknesses before his opponent can capitalize on them, Eminem confesses in the autobiographical song that he fears he may never surpass the popularity of his previous material.

Eminem's Place in the Genre of Rap

The list of successful white rappers prior to Eminem is exceedingly short, consisting of, for example, Marky Mark, 3rd Base, and Vanilla Ice, none of whom enjoyed the sustained popularity of Eminem. Rap is a genre deeply intertwined with African-American culture. There are historical reasons for this association. First, rap music harkens back to similar cultural idioms from African culture. In tribal African cultures, "griots" were storytellers who performed against the background of drums and other instruments. Griots would extemporize on current events, thereby demonstrating their verbal dexterity, and would provide quick comebacks to those who disputed with them.[18] There are clear similarities between this phenomenon and the rap battles of *8 Mile*. Second, rap also bears similarities to the slave work songs of antebellum American history. Such music often carried a double meaning, the hidden side subverting the authority of the slave masters.[19] For its part, rap music abounds with messages that criticize authority, although contemporary rap artists usually do not bother to camouflage critique with double meanings. A classic example of this challenge to authority is N.W.A.'s song "F*** the Police." Set up as a courtroom scene in which Ice Cube takes the stand against the police, the song proclaims a desire to avenge years of police prejudice and brutality against young African-American males. "Why don't you tell everybody what . . . you gotta say?" asks Dr. Dre, the presiding judge. "F*** the police," says Ice Cube. Another rap group, 2 Live Crew, was acquitted of obscenity charges after a scholar testified that rap is part of an African oral tradition that criticizes elements of society.[20] Rap

Finding out about the artist, and therefore accessing the world-behind-the-text, can include learning the biography of the band members as well as checking out their inspirations and musical influences. Often this information is available on a website maintained by their record label, or on fan websites, which frequently have invaluable links to one another and mainstream press coverage.

had been tied to these elements of African-American culture, at least before its recent emergence as music for the mainstream.

Then came Eminem. Usually black rappers dismissed white rappers as phony since they did not share the black inner-city experiences on which the music was built.[21] Vanilla Ice, for example, had little opportunity to sell albums on a wide scale after it was revealed that he grew up in a middle-class neighborhood. On the other hand, the African-American community has, for the most part, accepted Eminem as a rapper. Rapper and producer Dr. Dre took on Eminem as his protégé. In "The Way I Am," the charge that Eminem is "some wigger"—a white guy who tries, unconvincingly, to act black—comes from "cocky Caucasians," not from people of color. The lawyer representing Eminem's mother was never able to substantiate his assertion that it would soon come to light that Eminem was really a white middle-class boy.[22] Howard Stern, who himself grew up in a predominantly black neighborhood, said to Eminem: "You know what man: you can talk like a black guy, you've earned it."[23] Along the way there were certainly people who tried to gain an advantage on Eminem because of his race. But their voices have not predominated. The secret of Eminem's success in this regard has been that he did grow up in a rough part of Detroit, and he is honest about all of his experiences. He does less critiquing of oppressive social structures than many rappers do; rather, he raps about his personal experiences and feelings as much as anything else. One commentator says with regard to Eminem, "There is vulnerability. There's self-examination, and boy, that has a lot more power than the tough-guy thing. He has the bravery of the real artist to put himself out there. That's the secret that's distinguished him from the others."[24]

Perceptions of His Work

If there is any common denominator among the vast array of reactions to Eminem's work, it would be that in some way or other they are all strong. His fans flock to his concerts in droves, buy his albums by the millions, and, in the most personal of terms, defend him against his critics. For example, after a critical review of *The Eminem Show* in *Slate* magazine, one reader had this to say to the reviewer:

> If you were a real music lover then you would listen to some of his songs and break down and cry. Country music is all about *love*. Lost love, true love, and broken hearts. Well in a way so is this. Just listen to the man. He may not sugar coat it. But what he is saying is insightful. Sometimes I listen to him and think he is singing about me.[25]

On the other hand, Eminem's opponents on both the right and the left denounce him in the most severe terms and go to great lengths to convince others of their viewpoint. Even those who take a more nuanced position on Eminem, saying that he is a symptom of an underlying, real problem, find themselves speaking passionately about that issue.

Conservative Christian groups have spoken few words of praise on behalf of Eminem. For example, Focus on the Family's review of *8 Mile* curtly characterizes it as "an obscenity-strewn *Rocky* for the gangsta rap generation."[26] The reference to *Rocky* misses the point of Rabbit's return to work as the film closes: this is not a rags-to-riches story. The review continues by noting that while Eminem displays the ability to project the full range of human emotions as an actor, the movie's viewers should recall the type of lyrics he sings as a rapper. The review ends with a litany of bad behaviors in the film, including more than 300 instances of profanity. The conclusion: eight miles "becomes the distance teens should put between themselves and this movie."[27] In *Campus Life*, a publication of *Christianity Today*, a questioner named Sam asks how he should handle his friends' interest in Eminem.[28] This time the response is more thoughtful. The writer identifies a number of reasons why teens might be drawn to Eminem (e.g., he is talented), provides a few scriptural passages that speak to issues like vulgarity and hate (Eph. 4:22–32; Phil. 4:8; Col. 3:8–10), and suggests that when Sam has the opportunity to play some music for his friends he could choose from rap artists whose lyrics have a redemptive message. These examples from Focus on the Family and *Campus Life*, while different in tone and style, work toward a similar bottom line: Eminem is bad and to be avoided.

Although on many issues they would find themselves at loggerheads, in their opposition to Eminem these Christian groups share common ground with some of a more liberal bent. In 2001, when the *Marshall Mathers LP* was nominated for album of the year, the Gay and Lesbian Alliance Against Defamation organized a protest called Rally Against Hate.[29] The Alliance enlisted the support of a dozen other activist organizations in a large-scale demonstration outside of the Grammy Award ceremonies. In addition, the group pressured the National Academy of Recording Arts and Sciences, which produces the Grammys, not to grant the award to Eminem. Finally, the Alliance condemned the duet Elton John performed with Eminem during the awards show, even though only a year previously it had awarded Elton John one of its highest honors for combating homophobia.

There are other instances of opposition to Eminem originating from camps typically considered liberal. In an article from *Village Voice*, an alternative New York newspaper, a writer criticizes the claim that Eminem's music is simply an encapsulated experience, an artistic form that is not tied to real life: "There *is* a relationship between Eminem and his time. His bigotry isn't incidental or stupid, as his progressive champions claim. It's central and knowing—and unless it's examined, it will be free to operate."[30] The writer asks: Do anti-Semitic messages become acceptable simply because they are expressed in art? No, he answers, and Eminem's misogyny should be no different. Kim's suicide attempt certainly backs up the suggestion that art and life connect. In addition, controlled studies indicate that young people who expose themselves to rap videos are more likely to accept dating violence and materialism.[31]

There are, in addition to the foes and champions of Eminem, those who take a middle position on what he represents. These voices, often speaking from within academia, want to push the point that Eminem is not the root issue; something much deeper and more pervasive has gone awry. First, some members of the African-American church want to look behind rap music and shine light on problems lurking in the background. In a piece of provocation that would do even Eminem proud, one African-American leader says this: "Gangster rap's greatest sin, in the eyes of many of its critics, is that it tells the truth about practices and beliefs that rappers hold in common with the black elite."[32] The charge is that the church has failed to get its own house in order (for instance, it has not treated women with due respect) and is therefore guilty of some of the same sins that generate criticism of rap. Second, though he sees Eminem's violence and vulgarity as deserving critique, Shelby Steele suggests that the "cartoonish bravado" of rappers is not as bad as "what it compensates for."[33] From what does all of rap's bluster stem? Steele points to a sense of alienation and helplessness. These feelings, which have haunted many African-Americans since the time of slavery, now have a much wider resonance. The injury to family life over the past 30 years—high divorce and illegitimacy rates, a sweeping sexual revolution, dual-career households, etc.—may well "have given us the most interpersonally alienated generation in our history. Here the suburban white kid, gawky and materially privileged, is oddly simpatico with the black American experience."[34] The solution: "Everything about rap—the misogynistic lyrics, the heavy swagger, the violent sexuality, the cynical hipness—screams 'I'm bad because I don't feel.' Nonfeeling is freedom."[35] Roger Ebert's question about *8 Mile*—"What has happened to our hopes, that young audiences now embrace such cheerless material?"—receives an answer in Steele's reflections. Rap embodies a resolute refusal to feel in the face of unbearable pain. Its broad appeal derives, in large part, from the sad fact that so many people today are searching for anything that acknowledges and validates their experience of hurt, alienation, and disaffection.

Eminem as a Spiritual Phenomenon

Spiritual themes surface frequently in rap music, including Eminem's. Especially in the eyes of the working poor and those in the underclass, rap itself can represent a vehicle of salvation, one's last hope for transcendence.[36] Consider the plot of the movie *Get Rich or Die Tryin'*, a film that stars Eminem's protégé Curtis "50 Cent" Jackson: an orphaned street kid leaves behind drug dealing in order to make a go of a rap career. Yet, rap seldom fulfills the hope people invest in it. In response, rap music often parodies the idea of transcendence itself.[37] Eminem's own "Lose Yourself," a commentary on the life of Rabbit/Eminem, illustrates the point. An intense rhythm pounds through most of the song, summoning a level of energy in listeners that will match the song's own. "Lose Yourself" shows why experts call rhythm "the universal life force."[38] Over this stirring beat, the chorus proclaims, "You only got one shot, do not miss your chance to blow / This opportunity comes once in a lifetime." Within the context of the movie, the idea is that Rabbit has already choked during an earlier rap battle, and he has exactly one chance to redeem himself. If he does not, he is doomed to live out his days in a trailer park or, even worse, jail. By the second verse, he has achieved superstar status. Yet this does not offer relief: "It only grows harder, only grows hotter / He's grown farther from home, he's no father / He goes home and barely knows his own daughter." Just as the movie ends on an uncertain note, the song portrays even a successful rap career as one that is difficult and fraught with disappointment. Rap, then, speaks of and can even stand for transcendence, but it fails to deliver.

TAKING IT *FURTHER*

The author of this essay has identified several spiritual themes that surface in Eminem's lyrics. This is a similar phenomenon with most artists. The theological themes listed in this section are not exhaustive, but rather are an entrance into the discussion. More could be found for Eminem, or any other artist for that matter. Other spiritual themes commonly found in lyrics include love, forgiveness, purpose/meaning, and hope.

Christianity offers a "better hope" (Heb. 7:19). The balance of this essay will consider Eminem from an explicitly theological vantage point, discussing ways in which biblical-theological themes come to bear on rap and what it represents.

Salvation

The Gospel of Luke's special concern for the downtrodden and marginalized makes it a highly relevant text to reflect on in this connection. Here, Jesus' primary mission is to "preach good news to the poor" (Luke 4:18). What does this mean? The term "poor" in contemporary English is an index of economic status, indicating a low position on a scale of annual household income or in relation to an established poverty line. This, however, is not exactly the sense it carries in Luke.[39] Some background on the concept of status will help to make this clear. Leviticus 21:16–24 indicates that one's membership in the community of priests depended on factors outside one's control. First, being a priest meant being born into a priestly family. Second, numerous genetic "defects" would disqualify one from membership in the priestly community (examples include being blind or lame, having a hunchback or a broken foot, etc.). Religious communities from Luke's time used similar membership criteria, which were recorded in similar lists. In Luke's Gospel, things operate very differently. Again, there are lists of people considered "impure" or of low status, but Luke presents these as the very people who are to be included, not excluded. Most of the occurrences of the word "poor" in Luke are to be found in these lists (4:18; 6:20; 7:22; 14:13, 21; 16:20, 22 RSV). Jesus' ministry of "preaching good news to the poor," then, entails overturning previous measures of status. Anyone may freely receive the grace of God. The good news that Jesus preaches to these people is holistic. As one commentator puts it:

> Luke holds together what the contemporary church has often partitioned into discordant elements: empowering the disadvantaged, seeking the lost, reconciling persons across social lines, calling people to repentance, healing the sick, forgiving sins, initiating people into the community of God's people. All these and more are constitutive of salvation in the Third Gospel.[40]

Luke's narrative teaches contemporary Christians two lessons. First, if Jesus focused his own ministry efforts on the alienated, the church today can do no less. Many of those attracted to Eminem can relate firsthand to the tough, impoverished streets of inner-city Detroit where Eminem grew up. Many others who listen to Eminem are well heeled but have been stung deeply by life's hardships. The church should welcome all people, particularly the disenfranchised. Second, churches should approach ministry holistically. Conservative churches tend to think first of all about meeting an individual's spiritual needs, while liberal congregations often major on structural solutions to tangible, physical problems. Luke envisions salvation as an encompassing reality that does not respect these false disjunctions. By God's grace all of creation can be made new. No hurt is beyond the reach of God's gracious, healing hand.

In this connection, consider the case of *8 Mile*. Christians are rightly appalled by many of the things that happen in the movie, even though it is cleaner than many of Eminem's songs and his actual life. Some Christian groups, however, focus so narrowly on what offends them that they fail to comprehend the mentality of the marginalized—the very people they are especially obligated to reach. Focus on the Family's review is an unfortunate case in point. The review totals up the instances of vulgarity in an effort to underscore the crassness of *8 Mile*. Obviously the movie is crass, and those completely unfamiliar with Eminem deserve a warning regarding the film's content. However, fervor to enumerate swearwords should not displace an intent to understand the film's genre and mood. Rabbit does not go from rags to riches as Rocky does, but from "rags to slightly better rags."[41] And, crucially, as Roger Ebert notes, there is something about this generation that gravitates toward *8 Mile*'s cynicism. Eminem's fans testify that they identify with the difficult aspects of his life as depicted in the film: he does not get along with his mom, he has financial problems, he grew up in a single-parent home, he has broken up with his girlfriend, etc. Christians can begin to reach those on the margins of society by acknowledging and entering into their pain. Perhaps Eminem can remind the church how important that is. The church of Jesus Christ should follow its Lord's example by reaching out with a sympathetic ear and a helping hand.

Holiness

To the extent that the church has been reluctant to engage in the task of understanding Eminem, or to engage those on the margins of society, it has usually been out of a well-intended concern to establish and guard the church's holiness. The idea is that separating from evil leads to holiness. There is certainly a need for the strategy of separation, but Christians should see that motif in a fuller theological context. Reflecting further on the biblical notion of holiness, and most importantly on its reference to God, is critical at this point.

In 2 Corinthians 6, holiness is a cleansing that involves both a radical separation from what is unclean as well as fellowship with the Father.[42] God is the ground of holiness. It is first and foremost an attribute of God, and only derivatively a quality of the church or of a Christian. Holiness cannot be transposed onto the level of purely human action and thus made into a function of conformity with a moral law (as important as such a law is). Just as the origin of the church's holiness lies outside of itself, so does its goal. With reference to the church, 1 Peter 2:9 says, "You are . . . a holy nation . . . that you may declare the praises of him who called you out of darkness into his wonderful light." Separation is imperative not simply to keep the church from being defiled but also so that those outside the church "may see your good deeds and glorify God" (1 Pet. 2:12). Except for the sake of understanding the culture, Christians probably ought not listen to Eminem. But Christians' choice of music in and of itself does not confer holiness upon them. Only God can do that. When Christians lose sight of this, "rightful moral outrage," at Eminem for instance, "has mutated into self-deceiving moral smugness."[43] Such smugness, in turn, undercuts the very witness that is the goal of holiness.

Mission

The opening lines of John's Gospel illustrate a couple of countervailing tendencies that have always characterized Christian mission. When John says, "In the beginning was the Word" (1:1), the key term "word" (*logos* in the original Greek) would have been immediately familiar to his readers. They were used to thinking of a "word" as a rational paradigm according to which something was fashioned. Communicating the Christian message to people unfamiliar with it inevitably involves taking up forms of language and, in turn, whole ways of thinking and living with which a community is already at home. This tendency is an entailment of the gospel. God accepts us as we are, on the ground of Christ's work alone, not on the ground of what we are struggling to become. If that is so, God does not accept us as autonomous individuals but as people conditioned by culture. Call this first inclination of mission the indigenizing principle.[44] On the other hand, there is the pilgrim principle, which stands in tension with the indigenizing principle.[45] Not only does God take people as they are; he does so in order to transform them into what he wants them to become. This second principle puts a degree of friction between Christians and their cultural surrounding. Readers of John's Gospel would have been scandalized to learn that "the Word became flesh and made his dwelling among us" (1:14). The concept that John's audience knew was too abstract to be enmeshed in the physical world. So, in Christian mission and proclamation there is a moment of unconditional acceptance as well as a moment of challenge.

Just as John draws a concept from his context, Christians should feel the freedom to take up and transform art forms like rap that have currency in the culture and that can become bearers of the message of redemption. Christians have a long history of doing this with music: in the nineteenth century, for instance, William Booth's Salvation Army co-opted popular drinking songs and made them into Christian hymns. As important as it is to ask the question "Can Christians listen to Eminem?" fixating on that query can limit Christians to a mode of retreat. Maybe Eminem is indeed "the most dangerous threat to American children since polio," as George W. Bush allegedly stated (the authenticity of which some doubt due to the small number of media outlets that reported it and its hyperbolic ring).[46] Even if Eminem represents such a grave threat, an aspect of the Christian response should be to create an alternative attractive enough to draw listeners—both Christians and non-Christians—away from Eminem. In the Christian community, there is a deep vein of artistic talent that ought to be tapped, and indeed is already being tapped. *Campus Life* reports on a rapper who goes by the moniker KJ-52 and whose nickname is the Christian Slim Shady.[47] The task of all such musicians is to match the artistry of their non-Christian counterparts. Fulfilling that task gives the music its best chance of being heard by people not yet persuaded by its message.

Christianizing an artistic form that has traditionally involved violence, anger, and all the rest, has come across to some commentators as an exceedingly odd development in the genre.[48] Considering only the roots of rap, this change is indeed strange. But in light of the dynamics of how Christian witness articulates the gospel, it comes as no surprise. The real challenge is to engage in the process of appropriation and adaptation well, which is to say, by utilizing as much skill as one can summon and by keeping the indigenizing principle in productive tension with the pilgrim principle. In regard to the latter requirement, wisdom becomes the watchword. An example from a slightly different context will help. A former missionary to Africa relates what he discovered about adopting native instruments in worship services: "I learned that the first generation or two of Christians after initial evangelization had no wish to use drums or dance because they evoked features of the tribal culture that they had explicitly renounced. Later generations began showing an interest in recapturing in some sense the ancient heritage."[49] Likewise, rap music, regardless of its lyrical content, may remain something that certain individuals associate with former patterns of sin. For them, Christianizing rap is not the best path. Handling situations like this requires good judgment. The only reliable principles are "eternal vigilance" and a burning desire to see the Lord glorified.[50]

Retrospect and Prospect

Christians should continuously try to understand rap's place in contemporary culture, for such music provides a window into popular spirituality. Understanding how the rap community reaches for transcendence, for instance, will suggest angles from which Christians can bring the gospel of Jesus Christ to that audience, though of course no audience analysis will change the essential content of the message. The gospel consists of a compassionate and holistic message of salvation, a call to be holy as God is holy, and a charge to bear witness in relevant, intelligible, and challenging ways. The church's mandate will endure long after Eminem relinquishes his hold on popular imagination. The value of understanding Eminem consists not only in lessons that emerge from a study of his career (e.g., the importance of giving candid acknowledgement of deep personal hurt) but also in the lessons that apply to a whole array of figures in rap. Even when Eminem passes from the scene, popular culture will doubtless continue to generate rappers who, like Eminem, channel into music the hurt, anger, and brokenness that so many people feel. At the very least, the prominence of Eminem's protégés and those who have signed onto his label guarantee that his legacy will be felt for years to come. By giving due consideration to themes of salvation, holiness, and mission, the church can rise to the challenge that these artists present.

Suggested Readings

Bozza, Anthony. *Whatever You Say I Am: The Life and Times of Eminem.* New York: Bantam, 2003.

Dyson, Michael Eric. "Rap Culture, the Church, and American Society." *Black Sacred Musicology: A Journal of Theomusicology* 6 (1992): 268–73.

Reading Cultural Texts

BOOK LINK

Popular Music Genres: An Introduction

One of the best-known forms of popular culture is popular music. For almost two generations now, it has become the *lingua franca* of our multicultural, postindustrial age, perhaps the only language "spoken" everywhere on earth. Like shopping, popular music has a cultural history too.

While this chapter focuses on both the author of a text and the world-behind-the-text, the present book link tries to help readers think about popular music as a cultural text. In interpreting written texts, one of the most important things to determine is *what kind of a text am I reading?* The first step toward understanding, then, is to discern a text's literary genre. That's why readers may find Stuart Borthwick and Ron Moy's *Popular Music Genres: An Introduction* (New York: Routledge, 2004) so helpful.

The book devotes a chapter to each of the eleven popular music genres: soul, funk, psychedelia, progressive rock, punk rock, reggae, synthpop, heavy metal, rap, indie, and jungle. We find Eminem, for example, under "rap," a chapter that discusses the historical roots and antecedents of that genre (in which we learn that rap, together with turntablism, graffiti art, and breakdancing form the "four central pillars of hip-hop culture" [157]), some musical texts that exemplify the genre, as well as rap's social and political contexts.

Popular Music Genres does not purport to offer religious interpretation, nor are its authors even remotely interested in theology. Even so, the book has much in common with the methodology set out in *Everyday Theology*. The authors take an interdisciplinary approach and are concerned to do justice both to the musical texts and to their social, cultural, political, and economic contexts: "We firmly believe that an examination of the relationship between musical texts and their various contexts tells us far more about music and its importance to the societies in which it is situated than a purely musicological approach" (1–2). The authors helpfully remind us that textual genres are often "tied to an era, a mode of production, a *Zeitgeist*" (3). In short, they are interested in what popular music means and in what it does.

Kevin J. Vanhoozer

Haskins, James. *The Story of Hip-Hop*. London: Penguin, 2002.

Steele, Shelby. "Notes from the Hip-Hop Underground." *Wall Street Journal*, March 30, 2001, A14.

Stubbs, David. *Cleaning Out My Closet: The Stories Behind Every Song*. New York: Thunder's Mouth, 2003.

Westfield, N. Lynne, and Harold Dean Trulear. "Theomusicology and Christian Education: Spirituality and the Ethics of Control in the Rap of Hammer." *Black Sacred Music: A Journal of Theomusicology* 8 (1994): 218–38.

Editorial Introduction

With this essay we come to what at first appears to be a very different kind of cultural text than the music of Eminem. The UN's Universal Declaration of Human Rights represents a seminal moment in the political and intellectual history of the twentieth century. Certainly, the type of text under consideration shapes what tools one might use. Yet, in many ways, the approach remains the same, whether the text is from popular or intellectual culture. This essay surveys the historical and intellectual context in which the UDHR took shape. It then pays close attention to the claims of the text itself and widens the inquiry to see how it has influenced and shaped the world. Finally, it engages theologically with the UDHR and points Christians forward as proponents for human rights.

4

The High Price of Unity

The Universal Declaration of Human Rights

DAVID G. THOMPSON

All human beings are born free and equal in dignity and rights. They are endowed with reason and conscience and should act towards one another in a spirit of brotherhood.

Everyone is entitled to all the rights and freedoms set forth in this Declaration, without distinction of any kind, such as race, colour, sex, language, religion, political or other opinion, national or social origin, property, birth or other status. Furthermore, no distinction shall be made on the basis of the political, jurisdictional or international status of the country or territory to which a person belongs, whether it be independent, trust, non-self-governing or under any other limitation of sovereignty.

Everyone has the right to life, liberty and security of person.

Everyone has the right to recognition everywhere as a person before the law.

All are equal before the law and are entitled without any discrimination to equal protection of the law. All are entitled to equal protection against any discrimination in violation of this Declaration and against any incitement to such discrimination.

—*Universal Declaration of Human Rights,* Articles 1, 2, 3, 6, 7

U2 and the UN

In May 2005, I attended a U2 concert in Chicago and stood in wonder as 30,000 screaming fans hushed to listen to a small child on the Jumbotron screen read from the Universal Declaration of Human Rights. Bono, the lead singer of U2, has become one of the leading human rights activists of our day. He has led the fight for debt relief for developing countries and helped create the ONE campaign, which is bringing together NGOs, governments, and citizens from around the globe in order to combat poverty. Bono has become the spokesperson for this message, repeatedly bringing it to the attention of presidents, prime ministers, and even the pope. For these efforts, he has been nominated for a Nobel Peace Prize and named one of *Time*'s "Persons of the Year" for 2005. So as the articles scrolled across the screen, I realized Bono was trying to make a point: the ONE campaign as such will eventually end, but its long-term goal—real respect and opportunity for every individual, no matter his or her background—must not. As he sings on U2's 2004 album, *How to Dismantle an Atomic Bomb*, "Where you live should not decide, whether you live or whether you die." So why the Universal Declaration of Human Rights? Simply put, there can be no end to poverty without a profound valuing of human rights. For millions of U2 fans, many of whom had probably never heard of the Declaration, Bono directed them to this profound text in the hope of undergirding the fight against oppression and injustice.[1]

Prior to the Universal Declaration of Human Rights (hereafter the UDHR) the first truly global affirmation of fundamental human rights was the 1945 preamble of The Charter of the United Nations. That was, however, only a broad vision statement. In order to preserve its fragile ideals, namely, "the value of human rights and freedoms," UN leaders saw the necessity of enshrining defensible and specific directives.[2] The time for spelling out the details was upon them. The UN Commission for Human Rights (UNCHR) was formed, with Eleanor Roosevelt as chair; she exercised tremendous moral authority as the standard-bearer of her late husband Franklin D. Roosevelt's vision for peace.[3] From 1946 to 1948, leaders from 56 nations composed the UNCHR and together hammered out a collection of articles from the raw materials of legal, political, and philosophical thought. Since that time, these 30 articles of the UDHR have served as a source for treaties and a soapbox for pronouncements against human rights violators.

We will examine the UDHR as a cultural text, discerning its impact on developments in international law while also examining the way in which it grounds human rights. Focusing in order on the three "worlds" of the text, we investigate first the precursors that led to the UDHR's inception. Next, we turn to the actual claims of the document, noting the inherent tension of a universal declaration of human rights that squarely ties its validity to the shifting winds of cultural consensus.[4] Thirdly, we analyze the repercussions of the cultural text both intended and unforeseen. We conclude with a Christian response to the UDHR that relocates authority from a nebulous human consensus about human rights to their grounding in divine creation and Christology.

The Long Road to Never Again

The UDHR was the genesis of the modern human rights dialogue, its creation an effort to salvage hope out of the burning ashes of WWII.[5] As one commentator remarks, "Rights did not begin with 1948 and the UN Declaration of Human Rights, but that moment gave a formal shape and quasi-universality to human rights."[6] In the harrowing aftermath of the war, the international community came to a critical juncture where abuse of citizens by governments was so reprehensible that all nations agreed, at least in word, on the necessity of international prohibitions against atrocities.[7]

The horrors of WWII thus served as the historical catalyst for the UDHR: "The very origin of the Declaration was to say, 'Never Again' to the genocidal abomination of the Nazi period."[8] Réne Cassin, France's representative on the UNCHR who himself lost dozens of relatives to the Nazis and would later win a Nobel Peace Prize, pointed out that Hitler would justify his denial of rights to certain citizens by first "asserting the inequality of men before attacking their liberties."[9] But what grounds did the international community have for protest? The principle of national

BEHIND THE
TEXT

A difficulty with which the author of this essay struggled was identifying and limiting the world-behind-the-text to the most relevant data such that it did not overwhelm his interpretation of the UDHR. Any examination of human rights could take on board thousands of years of philosophical and legal reflections on these questions. We are likely to face this initial difficulty whenever we step into new areas of cultural studies, especially ones so broad and significant. The guiding concept to keep in mind is what we need to do to establish competency as a Christian cultural agent. Many of us will never be experts in a particular field, but if we are going to enter into a discussion we must make sure that we understand the key ideas and players before we start making judgments.

sovereignty, whereby a nation's government holds absolutist rule over its territory, was enshrined in Europe by the Treaty of Westphalia, exactly 300 years prior to the advent of the UDHR. Nations, therefore, held scant legal precedent to protest neighboring governments' actions against their respective citizens. National sovereignty for centuries precipitated only international silence, even in the face of crimes against humanity. Theologian Jürgen Moltmann contends that, "Right down to the end of the Second World War, it was internationally accepted that the way a country treats its own people is a matter solely for its own sovereign decisions."[10] World War II brought this issue to the forefront of international relations. As one commentator states, "Hitler had shown that a country which violates human rights at home may eventually violate human rights overseas."[11] The rules of the international relations game had in hindsight proved untenable.

Since their inception as such, nation-states bore all rights in society. All duties were to be rendered to the king, whose will was, in essence, law; later, each discrete national government ruled its own people in a similar monarch-like fashion. The UDHR was a turn from the traditional locating of rights solely in the hands of the state. Disputing the idea that governments ought to be left unaccountable in the global public square, the UDHR authors claimed that each state owes rights to its citizens indiscriminately. Moreover, they held that the international community of nation-states, through the mechanism of the UN, was the witness to these rights. The UDHR's inversion of the classic superiority of the state over its citizens brought to realization the previously contentious moral claim that every citizen was like a king or queen; moreover, this "right" was now on the international books.

"Ideas do not make their way in history except they be carried by persons and institutions."[12] Ironically, one of the main contemporary challenges to the Declaration's validity was that its creators were overwhelmingly of European origin—either in nationality or education—and thus its "universality" was in serious question. But this is only half the story. In fact, many of the chief contributors came from non-Western countries, including Charles Malik (Lebanon), P. C. Chang (China), General Carlos Romulo (Philippines), and Hernan Santa Cruz (Chile). The voices of many smaller states participated in the creation of and voting on each of the UDHR's articles. Thus, the argument that the origins of the UDHR are "European" not only falls prey to the genetic fallacy but also is empirically incorrect.[13] Malik made no idle claim when he said the UDHR did not fall from the pens of isolated Western philosophers. Rather, it underwent

Reading Cultural Texts

extensive review by hundreds of representatives from various religious and political traditions. It was affirmed, then, not by fiat but through critique, compromise, and argument.[14]

As the drafters reviewed relevant precedents for human rights in theology, philosophy, and legal theory, they sought to move beyond the concept of "rights" in order to flesh out a significant and safe space for the individual within society. Throughout the debates of the three primary gatherings of the UNCHR, Malik and others sought to flip the sovereignty of the state on its head and give it to individuals, placing the sanctity of the individual freedom of conscience off-limits to the state. This was an outgrowth of the so-called "first generation" of political and civil rights, which underpins the constitutions of most Western democracies. Various modifications, however, overlaid the original focus on liberty with the "second generation" of rights that champion work, education, and basic subsistence, rights that Communist and non-Western states consider essential. These nations refused to grant such spacious and near-absolute control to individuals. In contrast, their hierarchy of rights distinctly prioritized economic and social prerogatives, thereby sustaining the rule of society by the government over against its body of individual citizens. This conspicuous tension helped set the background for deliberations over the UDHR.

The Terms of the Debate

The UDHR synthesized divergent visions of human nature and its relation to the divine realm into one international moral claim on all humankind. Malik, who later served as UN president, defined the drafters' goal as "inquiring how much . . . we could define and protect what belonged to the essence of man."[15] Accordingly, the UDHR, while utilizing contractual language similar to the most famous of revolutionary declarations, grounds human freedoms and obligations no longer in America's "Creator" or France's "Supreme Being" but exclusively in humanity itself.[16] The accession of global universal human rights occurred, then, under the specter of a complete separation of humanity and God. The horizontal relationship between human beings became sufficient: heaven was eclipsed.[17]

While much was lost by such a move, a great deal remained. Never before on a worldwide scope had nations agreed that proper governance required a basic inviolability of every human being: male, female, black, white, yellow, etc.—no matter gender, race, religion, or any other such marker; what counted was being human. This categorical endorsement of

Often, when Christians talk about cultural engagement, they are referring to interpretation of movies or other popular cultural texts. Rarely do they examine intellectual texts, like the UDHR. A balance between both is needed, under the recognition that while Eminem's music, for example, is more immediately accessible and its influence obvious, texts like the UDHR often have deeper and farther-reaching effects.

all human beings as equal before the law is a common thread through the thirty articles, contributing to the process whereby the starting point for rights shifted from the state to the individual.[18] Yet, this shift was not mere radical Western individualism in the guise of universality. It was, in fact, the Western powers, whose colonial interests and national sovereignty—seemingly one and the same—were served least by this transformation. In contrast, Third World nations were significant champions of the rights of all individuals. Syria's representative to the UNCHR, Abdul Dalmsa Kayla, describes the broad support of the UDHR: "The Declaration was not the work of a few representatives in the Assembly or in the Economic and Social Council; it was the achievement of generations of human beings towards that end."[19] This end of which Kayla speaks underlines the UDHR's Preamble, that "the peoples of the United Nations have in the Charter reaffirmed their faith in fundamental human rights, in the dignity and worth of the human person and in the equal rights of men and women."[20]

What specifically was affirmed through this complex diplomatic process? Article 1 acts as a fountainhead, declaring, "All human beings are born free and equal in dignity and rights. They are endowed with reason and conscience and should act towards one another in a spirit of brotherhood." Article 2 affirms the corollary that these rights belong to all individuals, without any possible distinctions of race, gender, creed, etc. The following articles begin to unpack the content of these rights that all possess by virtue of their humanity. For example, Article 3 mandates a right to life; 4–5 prohibit slavery and torture; 6–11 deal with individuals' full standing before the law and its courts; 13 affirms freedom of movement; 16 declares the right for men and women to marry and have families, since "the family is the natural and fundamental unit group of society"; 17 declares the right to own property individually and with others. Article 18 holds a key concept for Christians, "the right to freedom of thought, conscience and religion"; similarly, 19 delineates the right to freedom of opinion and expression. The first 21 articles center on the first generation of rights closely tied to liberty and equality.

The second generation of rights begins in earnest at Article 22 with man's "right to social security [and] . . . the economic, social and cultural rights indispensable for his dignity." This article hearkens back to the language of Article 1, which speaks of rights belonging to people by virtue of intrinsic human dignity. Articles 23–27 unfold these economic, social, and cultural rights: 23, to work; 24, to leisure; 25, to an adequate standard of living; 26, to education; and 27, to participate in a community's cultural life. Articles 28–30 draw together the Declaration's argument, specifying the need for a social order in which all these rights can be realized (28), reminding individuals of the duties they owe to their communities (29), and finally, providing a blanket clause that protects these rights from encroachment by any party (30).

Returning to the Preamble, we see that it begins with the inherent dignity and inalienable rights of all *members* of the human family and follows through with a pledge from member states to protect and promote these rights. Indeed, both the individual and the state continue as the chief actors in society and not, for instance, families (despite Article 16), or religious or community associations. The final "Whereas" clause in the Preamble emphasizes the need for common understanding of these rights if they are to be realized fully, so again the universality of the Declaration is in view.

The interdependent nature of humanity's existence also helps to unify the document. The UDHR places value on the state insofar as it protects and promotes individual rights. This signals that the chief end of governments is not self-referential but must have in view all individuals, because their humanness and unique personhood entitles them to obligations from the state. Individuals, however, must be joined together—a person has, as Article 29 points out, not just rights but also duties "to the community in which alone the free and full development of his personality is possible." Interestingly, it is not until the next to last article that the UDHR speaks of the duties of individuals to the state. Thus, the classical importance of duties of individuals to society is not abandoned in the UDHR, but it is diminished and set in a new light; first, the development of individuals as their own *raison d'être*, then the community.

The UDHR went through seven revisions, starting from the legal precedents amassed by the Canadian John Humphrey.[21] After Humphrey's work, Réne Cassin acted as scribe for the committee and provided an internal logic to the document, philosophically and linguistically weaving the articles together to build what he would later call a "portico" for the UDHR: its foundation being dignity, liberty, equality, and brotherhood. After subsequent

T FOR THE TOOLKIT

This essay treats a particular text, but one that is symptomatic of an important trend, namely, the human rights movement. In the interpretive task, we will sometimes have to decide whether to look at a cultural text or trend, when they are closely linked, and both approaches have merit. One advantage to focusing on a text, as this essay does, is that it can prove more manageable and yet, at the same time, provide a window into understanding the trend as well.

UNCHR general committees and a worldwide "peer review" by political leaders such as Gandhi, the final draft passed 48–0 with 8 abstentions.

In issuing the UDHR, its framers worked to bring to life a reference point for common principles of right governance. The UDHR's "lofty principles" are the result of compromise and common goals.[22] Early in the deliberation process, Eleanor Roosevelt and her allies dreamt of ratifying an International Bill of Rights, compulsory in force, through international convention.[23] They wisely abandoned that unattainable goal, however, and settled for a consensus declaration that included no negative votes. The UNCHR, amid contentious cultural, political, and philosophical disputes, walked a fine diplomatic line between ambitions and passage. According to the Preamble, the UN General Assembly proclaims the Declaration to be a common standard and aims to promote it through teaching and education rather than the enactment of legally binding norms. As a result, the final passage of the UDHR, although not without dissent (though not explicitly in the final vote), allowed its creators to make a credible claim for the text's universality.

We owe the ubiquity of the human rights dialogue in large part to the momentous decision by the UDHR's authors to speak universally on the subject.[24] Their reworking of international law was not mere window-dressing; it was a paradigmatic revolution that fostered later human rights advances. They managed to create a common global vernacular for dialogue about conflicting values.

Admittedly, the UDHR does try, in a way, to be all things to all people, and does so with the inherent tension of attempting to reach "universal" consensus by agreeing to global rules while not possessing a common warrant. The vision of humanity and its rights enumerated in the UDHR was to have persuasive, exemplary power. The UNCHR built the Declaration on a foundation of social consensus, the best raw materials available to them. This inevitable situation led to a weak assertive statement that left the "inherent dignity" of humanity and our being "endowed with reason and conscience" as an ambiguously grounded notion. No reason is given

Reading Cultural Texts

for why human beings have rights, other than the fact that they have reason and conscience (though, that too is not argued for); it is simply asserted.

Hints, Allegations, and Things Left Unsaid

The UDHR is undoubtedly fundamental for international deliberation about rights. As one scholar puts it, "There is no question that 'Human Rightsism' has become the dominant political ideology of the international new class, and the common currency of the UN treaties, academic conferences, and charitable foundations mission statements."[25] The UDHR developed into the North Star for emerging anti-colonial leaders, serving as a reference point for causes such as colonial "self-determination . . . of struggles for national independence" for the later solidarity movements of the Czech and Polish labor unions.[26] From a legal standpoint, the UDHR has, in essence, been universally accepted. As John Humphrey noted in 1978, "whatever its drafters may have intended in 1948, it is now part of customary law of nations, therefore binding on all states."[27]

The very success of the UDHR, though, has carried with it some nettlesome entailments, as nations consider whether they can place even more weight on it. At the Vienna Conference on Human Rights in 1992, the UN struggled in revising many of the articles of the UDHR.[28] Some detractors even charge that the UN confuses the discussion of rights through the proliferation of new entitlements like "the right to third world debt relief."[29] What constitutes human rights is the center of the disagreements. The balkanization of human rights has redoubled the danger that the document's purchase on the international community will lose what power it has gained over the past fifty years.

Critics continue to attack the UDHR, arguing that it fails to ground its claims properly. Many have concluded that its failure to provide a foundational basis for human rights greater than a *prima facie* argument from humanity itself renders the "Universal" aspect of the UDHR null and void.[30] The universal claim of the document has alternately been likened to the "eternal Scriptures" of the human rights movement and ridiculed by postcolonial leaders like Robert Mugabe of Zimbabwe or Lee Kwan Yu of Singapore for its alleged preference of Western values such as freedom of expression and private property.[31]

Michael Ignatieff enumerates the three main contemporary challenges to the universality of human rights: the Islamic rejection of "western" values, postmodernism's suspicion of their "universal" nature, and the East Asian assertion of greater focus on community norms.[32] The common denominator for the critiques is their rejection of universality as a Western ploy. Conservative Islam questioned the UDHR from its inception, calling many of its articles "alien to the jurisprudence and political thought of the Islamic tradition."[33] They dispute the very idea of humans holding autonomous rights as contrary to Allah's absolute authority. Thus, on religious grounds, the universality of the UDHR is rejected. The postmodernist critique describes the Declaration's principles as no more than a prime example of "Western intellectual hegemony."[34] This view rejects universal human rights as the latest manifestation of the West's attempts to impose its values on other nations.[35] Finally, the East Asian critiques turn upon a proposal of "communitarian values." Singapore, Indonesia, and China lead the cadre that defend their tailored version of human rights as a proper corrective to the radical individualism decried as the headwaters of the UDHR.[36] Asian nations assert their freedom to embrace the global economy upon the terms of their national interest,[37] reaping the economic benefits of globalization, while rejecting the "Western tradition" of individual rights.[38]

The grand goal of universality for the UDHR, together with the absence of sufficient warrant supporting this claim, has triggered sharp critiques and stymied its acceptance globally. As one commentator has made clear, "Weakness about the foundation of human rights has led to a serious weakness in their moral heft."[39] Despite the UDHR greatly furthering its laudable goals of protecting the oppressed and unmasking their oppressors, the document fails to substantiate what it claims; we are not told *why* humans have the rights the document ascribes to them.

Yet the UDHR's greatest liability—its universal claim—also empowers it to function as a conscience for the international community, employable in response both to al-Qaeda's attacks or controversies over the scope of democracy.[40] If the Universal Declaration of Human Rights were instead known as "A Declaration of Human Rights" or "Forty-eight Nations' Declaration of Human Rights," one doubts it would still be under debate fifty years later.

If the protection of the powerless and rule of law among the nations is worth the fight, then that leads to the question: Does shifting the grounds for human rights from the Creator to creatures amount to anything more than circular reasoning—making the grounds, claims, and warrant of human rights logically vacuous? Merely to hope that every generation will take up the goals of UDHR afresh, without compelling reasons, is at best wishful thinking.

At this critical juncture we must ask whether, under the pressure of an increasingly skeptical international community, the UDHR has splintered beyond repair. Yes, some argue that the UDHR is in its last throes, decrying it as abstract idealism that no longer aligns with specific traditions. Yet the underlying themes of the UDHR, particularly the granting of rights to all human beings universally and indiscriminately, are themes that Christians cannot passively allow to be thrown into the dustbin of geopolitical history.

Christ, the True Human, as Foundation for Human Rights

Whereas the UDHR was an amalgamation of beliefs that coalesced into a progressive common standard, a Christian theological position insists that we can maintain human rights only in right relation to God. The primary avenue for understanding universal human rights flows out of the doctrine of the image of God, *particularly Christ as true human and the perfect image of God*. A christocentric starting point for human rights might at first appear paradoxical, but as Peter Berger has noted, some of the "deepest and sturdiest" roots of human rights sprout from the soil of the Judeo-Christian ethic.[41]

At the same time, the UDHR is by no means a "Christian" document. We will do well to remember Jürgen Moltmann's insight: "There are no copyright claims to human rights. They are neither exclusively Jewish-Christian, nor do they derive solely from Enlightenment humanism."[42] Alongside many others who hold diverse beliefs and come from different backgrounds, we can affirm the inherent dignity that every human being *qua* human being possesses. At the same time, the foundations for that affirmation (*why* we affirm this is true) will be distinctly Christian. Moreover, what we understand as our duty to other people also differs somewhat by virtue of the gospel. Our love for God and our love for others cannot be separated. Jesus intentionally connects the two love commands—to love God radically and others sacrificially (Mark 12:28–34).[43] Love for neighbor means loving anyone in need (Luke 10:25–37). When Paul exhorts Christians to do good to all, especially other believers (Gal. 6:10), that minimally includes the defense and promotion of the rights inherent to them as persons; the fact that we follow a crucified Savior, though, means it may include much more.

How can one offer this christocentric foundation and not be dismissed as appealing to inadmissible evidence in a culturally relative world? If we bear in mind the problem—the failure to ground the universality of this "universal" declaration—we realize that anyone who wishes to propose a solution faces the same dilemma. In fact, one theorist admits "a (strong) foundation can compel assent, not just ask for or induce agreement. In this sense, human rights have no foundation."[44] This statement, from an ardent supporter of the UDHR, acknowledges that the emperor has no clothes—this seminal document lacks a compelling foundation. It makes its claims on the basis of what it means to be human but cannot buttress that any further. Thus, *any* suggestion as to a good foundation for human rights faces this problem, not just a Christian one. Moreover, foundational claims are always vulnerable to skeptical questions; this situation is not "specific to human rights."[45]

Christians can rightly shore up the weaknesses in the UDHR by supplying a theological justification.[46] Human dignity from a Christian perspective stems from the belief that we have been created in the image of God. The incarnation of his Son, Jesus Christ, confirms the inherent dignity of humanity even in a sin-tarnished world. To look at Christ is to see the image of God (Col. 1:15; Heb. 1:3) in which we are all created (Gen. 1:26–27), though now damaged and marred through the fall. Christ shows us what humankind was meant to be, and by his death and resurrection he restores us in that image (Col. 3:9–10). The "inherent dignity" of the UDHR's Preamble receives a striking endorsement in the fact that Christ came, not as a spirit or vision, but as a human. By being made like us in every way, Jesus Christ—fully God and fully man—confirms the inherent worth of every human being. This truth serves as the bedrock for the basic values beneath them all. Max L. Stackhouse put it well:

> For Christians specifically, to deny that any absolute universal can be connected to the realities of concrete historical experience in ways that lead to a redeemed future, is in fact a denial of the deepest insight of our faith: that Christ was both fully God and fully human, and that his life both fulfilled the commands of God, was concretely lived in the midst of a specific ethos, and nevertheless pointed to an ultimate future that we could not otherwise obtain.[47]

Christians Active for Human Rights

One implication of the idea of the image of God for cultural agency is its questioning of the principle of unrestrained national sovereignty. The

BOOK LINK

Rights Talk: The Impoverishment of Political Discourse

Human rights, as this chapter reminds us, need to be grounded in something greater than humanity. The concept of universal human rights is not the brainchild of Enlightenment philosophy but an implication of the doctrine of creation. Human *discourse* about rights, however, is an entirely different matter; "rights talk," along with political correctness in general, shows all the signs of cultural conditionedness.

Mary Ann Glendon, a Harvard Law School professor, provides an insightful interpretation of the way people in the United States typically speak about human rights in her *Rights Talk: The Impoverishment of Political Discourse* (New York: Free Press, 1991). Our contemporary discourse on rights is yet another mirror in which, if we look and listen hard, we can discover much about ourselves ("our current rights talk is a verbal caricature of our culture" [xii]). Of special note is Glendon's belief that our common values are borne not by shared history or religion so much as by the law (cf. her comments on the "legalization" of popular culture [3]).

Glendon views contemporary American discourse on rights as a dialect, a particular way of speaking that is peculiar to our place and time. American rights talk is distinct both from the way Europeans talk about rights and from the tradition of our own founding fathers in its starkness and simplicity, its hyperindividualism, and its exaggerated absoluteness (x). Combine these themes with today's rhetorical weapon of choice—the sound bite—and you can see why, in the home of free speech, "genuine exchange of ideas about matters of high public importance has come to a virtual standstill" (x). Welcome to the era of dumbed-down political discourse.

Glendon argues compellingly that more and more political issues are framed not morally but legalistically in terms of individual rights; the notion of individual rights has captured our political imagination, making it difficult to think of pressing social issues in any other terms. The problem, however, is that rights talk has displaced responsibility talk, so much so that Glendon calls for the rehabilitation of the "missing language of responsibility." Our single-minded concern with the rights of individuals has similarly led to "the missing dimension of sociality." An obsession with individual rights can be hazardous to your community's health.

Kevin J. Vanhoozer

growth of the gospel is not limited by nor does it recognize modern political boundaries; on the contrary, the gospel asserts the dignity that belongs to all members of the human family, without distinction. Ultimately for the Christian it is human beings whose value comes prior to that of the state, since human rights properly follow from Christ's incarnation. Granted, in a contemporary climate rightly concerned about terrorism, there is a place for attention to the sovereignty of nation-states, but it should not, from a Christian perspective, override human rights. When we pass by actions taken by states, including democracies, that overturn the legal rights of citizens and abuse their people as a means of gathering information or for other purposes, we risk ignoring the admonishment of Scripture to respect the dignity and value of every individual.[48] Put bluntly, the human dignity of the inmate at Guantanamo Bay should matter as much to us as the dignity that you or I or his incarcerators have, or even the dignity that the president has.

Furthermore, in taking seriously our responsibility to champion the inviolability of every human being as God's image bearer, we need to seek out organizations that defend the value God places on every individual. While we must carefully examine the overall message of groups like Amnesty International, a positive step toward understanding and working alongside the human rights movement might include joining their email lists and participating in letter-writing campaigns and the like. The dissemination of information empowers prayerful consideration of petitions that "speak truth to power," helps free human rights activists, and challenges governments that place their own interests above the law. There is no longer such a thing as an innocent bystander in an increasingly interconnected global society, particularly now that there are indeed effective methods of challenging the international community to honor its commitments to human rights treaties.

Of particular note in this regard is the International Justice Mission (www.ijm.org). Based in Washington, D.C. and led by internationally recognized human rights lawyers and activists, IJM is a distinctly Christian agency that works to free the oppressed and challenge human rights violations both on the ground and at the highest levels of state power. Supporting their work financially, in prayer, and by raising their profile in our churches is a poignant way for all of us to participate in the defense of the powerless. Each of these steps takes the abstract words of the UDHR and applies them in the world in a practical way. Together we can support human rights to protect human dignity to the glory of God our Maker and the advance of the gospel among the oppressed.

In conclusion, Christians can find much to support in the UDHR: emphasis on the dignity of every single member of the human family; rights not only of liberty, as in freedom of religion and expression, but rights to a basic standard of living; and the call for nation-states to adhere to and promote these rights. Nonetheless, we must question its support beams. These will prove unstable if left on the shaky foundation of a humanity that thinks itself to be self-sufficient. On that anthropocentric reading of human rights, we find the unraveling of international agreement on the UDHR and the rise of regionalization. Rather, Christians should winsomely argue for and act from a theological foundation of humanity's creation in the image of God. Rooted in the drama of the gift of salvation through Christ, who as the one true human taught us what we owe to God and to each other, these human rights become an expression of how God has created us in his image and part of our responsibility to love our neighbor.

Suggested Readings

Bucar, Elizabeth M., and Barbra Barnett, eds. *Does Human Rights Need God?* Grand Rapids: Eerdmans, 2005.

Glendon, Mary Ann. *A World Made New: Eleanor Roosevelt and the Universal Declaration of Human Rights*. Repr. New York: Random House, 2002.

Hauerwas, Stanley, and William H. Willimon. *Resident Aliens: Life in the Christian Colony*. Nashville: Abingdon, 1989.

O'Donovan, Oliver. *Resurrection and Moral Order: An Outline for Evangelical Ethics*. 2nd ed. Grand Rapids: Eerdmans, 1994.

O'Donovan, Oliver. *The Ways of Judgment: The Bampton Lectures, 2003*. Grand Rapids: Eerdmans, 2005.

Editorial Introduction

Beginning with the premise that buildings themselves are expressions of culture, the author of this essay explores how contemporary evangelical megachurches interact with and are influenced by culture. What does the way a church building is constructed say about what that congregation values? The reader is challenged to become more aware of the intentionality of the structural design of the world around him or her, realizing that even bricks and mortar convey messages.

5

Between City and Steeple

Looking at Megachurch Architecture

PREMKUMAR D. WILLIAMS

Open Doors

A local church recently remodeled its sanctuary, moving the pipe organ tubes from alongside the platform to behind newly angled walls that increased visibility and better accommodated the choir. The church elevated the platform, expanding it to include the mini-orchestra that formerly had rested on the floor below; rearranged the pews so that they were directed toward the pulpit; and raised the chandeliers. Aside from the increased visibility and better coordination between organ, choir, and orchestra, these adjustments were made, more importantly, because they promoted the biblical value of community (at worship), uniting more closely preacher and worshipers, musicians and members.

This essay is a modification and application of materials from my doctoral dissertation, "Shaping Sacred Space: Toward an Evangelical Theology of Church Architecture" (PhD diss., Trinity Evangelical Divinity School, 2005).

The contemporary megachurch takes the desire for community to a higher level. Megachurches are typically defined as churches with a weekly attendance of at least 2,000 people and a strong commitment to reaching their communities for Christ.[1] Making no apologies for their size, their leaders "saturate" themselves with growth strategies and proportion their growth to match the potential that the wide stretches of suburban sprawl offers.[2]

Nestled among such suburbs, the megachurch draws people from miles around, inviting them to hear God's word and experience true community. Most megachurches offer seven-day-a-week programs catering to the person and his or her relations in community: "It is a place where we can go if we want to learn a foreign language, or if we're interested in how best to handle home finances, or if we need marriage counseling."[3] Making room for such a large variety of social activities obviously involves some changes to more traditional spaces. For instance, one newspaper article reports that the architect for one church, "left out a few key items: crosses, stained-glass windows, flying buttresses, altars and wooden pews. Instead, he replaced them with food kiosks, water fountains, cappuccino carts, convenient parking lots and a shopping mall feel."[4]

Providing for such large numbers of people requires a lot of space and civic amenities. Taking advantage of freeway access, cheaper land, and amenable zoning restrictions, many megachurches think big, building entire complexes of buildings.[5] Entrances, parking, and exits to the area are controlled so that in a significant way the experience "is similar to attending a professional sporting event or rock concert."[6] Intentionally interested in drawing unchurched crowds, these churches keep religious symbolism to a minimum. Willow Creek Community Church is a good example because of its firm commitment to being a seeker-sensitive church. Its architectural setting is an immaculate, deliberate prelude to its programs. The curves in the entry road gently flow past a lake and toward a complex more corporate than religious in appearance. No steeples or church bells, but rather a place that invites visitors by expressed values such as "neutrality, comfort, contemporary, clean."[7]

With respect to the central evangelical ritual of worship—preaching—megachurches have efficiently structured their sanctuaries to produce some of the finest auditoriums around. Following a theater style, they have semicircular seating along with huge media screens to neutralize the distance between the preacher and the last row. The platform often thrusts out into the audience, bringing the speaker as close to the people as possible. This promotes a sense of intimacy, making the individual listener feel directly addressed and personally challenged to follow Christ.

The megachurch shares a family resemblance with many Evangelical churches. Here, the steeple (as a vestige of the bell tower that once stood over the entrance to call people to gather in God's name) is a signboard for the stage inside. The sanctuary with its stage prepares people for the spoken word to reach out and stir their imaginations, and challenge their wills. It is no accident that these places are styled like the theater, maximized for sight lines and clear speech, shutting off the outside world and its interruptions. By its very form, the space generates a sense of anticipation similar to that of the theater, as people eagerly await the main events like the music and the popular (in many cases, celebrity) preacher.

Common Places

With the shift from place (temple) to person (Christ) in the New Testament, the early church expressed an appropriate ambivalence toward sacred space. They understood that it was the Spirit who helped constitute such spaces by gathering true worshipers, and thus worship could take place anywhere. Catalyzed by the mission to communicate the gospel to the ends of the earth, this diffusion of the sacred into what was once profane space increased exponentially as the gospel entered new cultures. From houses and basilicas to market halls and theaters,[8] Christians have willingly drawn on cultural forms that could be adapted for worship and witness, and the megachurch is a contemporary example of this process.

Evidence from a third-century house church in Dura-Europos (Syria) suggests that the theological restructuring of cultural forms began quite early in church history. For example, two of the house's rooms were merged to create an assembly hall, while another was converted to a baptismal chamber covered with biblical frescoes.[9] Soon Christians would adapt the Roman basilica (used for government buildings in the empire) to represent Christ's body and eventually bring aesthetic expression to full flourishing in the medieval cathedral, a monumental icon of worship space.

While Protestant churches are often quite aesthetic, there are many whose theological expression is restricted. A large number of Protestants understand this restriction to be warranted by the apparent trajectory that Scripture sets for God's people from physical space (Old Testament temple) to spiritual space (Eph. 2:20–22). When combined with Scripture's emphasis on proclaiming the word and its silence on liturgical expressiveness, this means that even though many buildings are quite aesthetic in their own right they are not interpreted and appropriated theologically.

One architectural historian observes, "The temple of stone or wood is no more than an insignificant shell surrounding the living congregation of the faithful which assembles within its walls."[10] Thus, with Protestant churches typically characterized by spaces for congregations to hear God's word, it seems natural that the theater (being "non-sacred") would be a useful form to adopt. Even mall-like spaces are useful because the megachurch wants numerous places that both invite people to hear the gospel and encourage them to practice it.

Theater

Though pulpits and pews have been common features of churches through history,[11] it was in the early nineteenth century that the evangelist preacher Charles Finney took over the Chatham Theater in New York City and made it a platform for his revival meetings.[12] This architectural transition impacted preaching for it challenged the preacher to work harder on such a large stage to catch and keep people's attention. Architectural historian Jeanne Kilde notes the social dynamic:

> For revivalists, as for actors, authority on stage derived not from erudition nor from connections to elite society or respected institutions but from charisma—from their popularity as speakers, from their ability to personally connect with the audiences, from their authenticity and sincerity, and from the skill of their performances. Finney was a master of performance.[13]

There has been a tradition of theater-like auditorium churches (including the famous Moody Church in Chicago), and most churches today to some degree exhibit similar features.

Mall

Church leaders readily admit that the megachurch has adopted mall-style architecture from the culture. Along with the earlier example of a church designed with pools of falling water, and numerous kiosks offering everything from cappuccino to popcorn, another church (Community Church of Joy, Glendale, AZ) has, along with a large child-care center, a multipurpose conference/banquet complex that looks like a multiplex and is preparing for a full-fledged "intergenerational community" that will include a retirement resort, performing arts facility, chapel, hotel, and an aquatics and recreational center.[14] The pastor of this seeker-sensitive church

BOOK LINK

Theology in Stone:
Church Architecture from Byzantium to Berkeley

Especially in Europe, but to some extent even in parts of North America, we inhabit spaces—churches, schools, homes—that have been shaped by those from another time. Buildings, more than any other cultural artifact, are visible expressions of the silent majority that has gone on before us. Perhaps this is why Kenneth Clark once suggested that architecture is the most informative index of the character of a civilization. Similarly, church buildings are standing witnesses to both the culture and the theology of a certain age. As such, they afford an interesting case study of how to read cultural texts.

Richard Kieckhefer's *Theology in Stone: Church Architecture from Byzantium to Berkeley* (Oxford and New York: Oxford University Press, 2004) is more academic than the other book links we discuss, but it is nonetheless helpful. The book suggests how one might go about *reading* a church (4). Specifically, how does the shaping of space also shape our experience of the sacred, our experience of God?

To his credit, Kieckhefer wrestles with the question of the locus of meaning. Do buildings speak? If so, how is it that the same church says different things to different visitors? Do architects speak through their churches? Is there a meaning in this nave? Other scholars focus on the people who planned and built churches and thus on their form and purpose, but Kieckhefer chooses to focus on the observers and participants, and hence on the use to which churches are put by worshiping communities. Of course, the shape of the church affects its use.

Kieckhefer spends four chapters considering the basic elements of church architecture: the overall arrangement of space; the central focus of attention; the immediate aesthetic impact; the gradual accumulation of impressions. He then examines three architectural types: the classic sacramental church, which focuses on the altar; the classic evangelical church which focuses on the pulpit and the preaching of the gospel; the modern communal church that focuses on the gathering of the people as itself something for celebration. He argues that what makes for sacred space is ultimately not a matter of separation from the world but of association with the Word, that is, with the images and narratives and symbols that have Jesus Christ as their ultimate focus.

Kevin J. Vanhoozer

---

has used what he calls "entertainment evangelism," which, like the mall, provides a sense of community and is designed to "attract people of all ages and walks of life with programs that provide a positive influence in their lives."[15]

The mall is rooted in twentieth-century American culture, particularly the post–World War II interstate highway program and the consequent rise of the American suburb.[16] Corporations, developers, and landowners have moved to the periphery of the city, setting up new centers and establishing vast suburban alternatives to the city, connecting them "by a network of more than thirty-two thousand shopping centers and malls."[17] In such places, plants, water fountains, kiosks, and specialty shops are all enclosed within a large complex rather featureless on the outside because marketers want you to go inside rather than loiter outside.

The genius of the mall is its appeal to the human spirit. James Rouse, a pioneer of profitable urban land reform in America, exhibited a kind of Christian humanism when he privileged the public's comfort over the architect's creativity:

> The family wants to feel at home in [the marketplace]; to be comfortable, important, uplifted by the spirit of it. They want not to be overwhelmed—set apart—but to feel a sense of ownership and pride in it. It should gratify the sense and the spirit.[18]

If these places are meant to nurture a religious kind of wholeness and identity, then they are quite unlike traditional religious buildings that mark the distinction between sacred and profane more strongly. Rouse's malls invite rather than command.

Dramatic Stages

There is much to commend in the popular megachurches, for they rightly attempt to integrate the evangelistic commission (Matt. 28:19–20) with the cultural commission (Gen. 1:28). This does not imply the long-term investment in the transformation of cultural institutions as much as it does the short-term process of meeting people's needs.[19] As such, the megachurch is both branch and tributary to the mainstream of evangelicalism. It reveals its common Christian source by the ease with which it adapts culture to communicate, with its emphasis on proclaiming the gospel, and its desire to sacralize the profane. It also contributes to the liturgical tradition by the distinct cultural forms it assimilates and applies to Christian life, forms that include a combination of theater and mall.

Control, quality, and efficiency are architectural values associated with theater and mall forms, and equally so with the megachurch. The hard work that preachers and their teams put into their art (much like the practice that goes into perfecting a concert recital) pleases God, stirs people's souls, and witnesses to the world. The use of common places to help restore the human spirit makes the megachurch a less threatening place and fosters amicability toward the gospel and the life of the church. Expressing a biblical view that all Christian living is worship, these common places recollect the mall, which provides a comfortable environment so that people might stay, where staying might lead to spending (and any spending is good spending). Similarly, megachurches also encourage staying, which might lead to Christian living, *and any Christian living is good Christian living.* The stage connotes the dramatics of a performance and creates a sense of relaxed anticipation. One usually sits before it with the feeling that all is well with one's soul. It adapts the prophetic voice to contemporary culture in making Christian "comedy" comedy that cuts. By recalling the artist's profession, by becoming the canvas on which to paint with dramatic colors and a prop to manipulate for thrilling effect in order to point to the possibilities in Christ, the stage largely symbolizes the appeal and potential of that theological category we call common grace—those faculties for aesthetics and conscience that God has granted to everybody.

Maybe there is room at this point, however, for the critic (or even the prophet). With this in mind, one can raise thoughtful questions with respect to such values like control and choice when considering megachurches that have adopted theater- and mall-like architecture.

Control

William Kowinski found himself one night at a mall restaurant long after the other stores had closed. In looking around, he spotted large courts, tiles "of the kind you associate with . . . a sunny path around a garden," and a stairway that might belong more inside a house. These different elements were put together to create a new world, "pulled out of time and space, not only by windowless walls and roofs" but by a variety of elements like interior landscaping, controlled lighting, and temperature, all of which work together to create a closed, protected, and controlled space. He says,

> The mall banishes outside threats of disruption and distraction: no cars are allowed in the mall, no traffic, noise or fumes. The natural world can't even intrude; there's no rain or snow, heat or cold, no seasonal change—not even gathering clouds to cause concern.[20]

It does not come as a surprise, then, when Kowinski associates the mall's "unreal perfection" and strong sense of nature with *theatrical* space: "For a space to be theater, the outside rules of time and space must be banished."[21] The temptation for this kind of control is real to many churches; it is part of our culture. Now, we know that control is not bad in itself, and it can be a virtue expressed in innumerable worthy activities. But we also know the lure of image.

In contemporary culture, image is everything. Models pore over their portfolios, singers over their music videos, and preachers over their sermons. Yes, we can do these for Christ's sake, but when this involves advertising, programming, management, and leadership of a large number of people responsible for a variety of activities all geared toward creating the best impression on the visitor, there is a tendency to control the process so as to guarantee the product. This can tempt one to squeeze the Spirit out of the scene and lean on the dynamics of performance.[22] The larger the church "corporation" and its image, the greater the pressure to maintain and promote its image. For architecture, this might raise a tension between cultural image and Christian identity. One could ask, for example, whether Willow Creek's corporate image of "neutrality, comfort, contemporary, clean" precludes the possibility of any architectural manifestation of Christian identity, or whether its banishment of time and space is always good.

The heavens tell of God's glory, and creation makes known his invisible attributes (Ps. 19:1; Rom. 1:20). What are we losing when, in a theatrical world of our own making, we ignore architectural opportunities to know God not only as Creator but also as provider?[23] Certainly, we cannot go back to a farmer-like dependence on the changing seasons, but can we not thank God for these simple but clear signs of his provision for the earth and thus for us as well? How can we remember that it is not we but God who makes the gardens grow and the seasons change? It might be that inward-looking spaces, closed to the outside and artificially giving a sense of nature, are detrimental to our spiritual well-being if they are the places where we cannot worship God as *Creator*. Spaces open to creation tell of God's glory and of our dependence on him for the preservation of our lives and the provision of our needs: "*Look* at the birds of the air . . ." (Matt. 6:26; emphasis added).

Choice

Control can often confine choice, and it is amazing how malls disguise their motives with the environments they create. Mark Gottdiener interprets the mall as a pattern of signs that point to deeper ideological processes.[24] He argues that the intersection of the seller's ideology of profit-taking and the buyer's ideology of consumption determines a mall's spatial arrangement. These spatial arrangements express a single motif calculated to captivate visitors while at the same time disguising the mall's primary purpose, which is to get consumers to buy. Gottdiener mentions four techniques used to motivate crowds to buy: First, with their blank exteriors, malls not only promise a protected, secure environment for shopping, but also hope "to prevent loitering outside . . . and to quicken the pace with which shoppers leave their cars." Second, much like the spontaneous festivity and social fellowship of traditional city centers, malls include large spaces with attractions (fountains, performers, etc.) *unrelated to shopping*. Third, directions and signs are made simple in order to ease the movement and flow of large numbers of people. Fourth, paths are made irregular (by things like plants, benches, and store displays) in order to slightly disorient people and thus facilitate browsing and impulse buying.[25]

While a comparison is not completely analogous, the megachurch does include numerous activities not directly related to *formal* worship, and in so doing gives them worship value. One must ask, though, whether some of these activities distract us from fully worshiping, much like one might buy things at the mall one really did not need. In desiring to create an atmosphere where the visitor is amicable toward what is being offered, do megachurches also create the opportunity for distraction or self-indulgence as much as—or more than—self-examination?

Scripture speaks of places that orient one to a true relationship with God. In Psalm 73:17, it was the Lord's temple: "till I entered the sanctuary of God, *then* I understood their final destiny" (emphasis added). And in 1 Corinthians 11:22, it was a place defined by the fellowship of Holy Communion: "Don't you have homes to eat and drink in?"[26] Surely there is a time and place for eating, and a time for communion. Should we think it appropriate that the food court now replaces the Lord's Table and the architecture of crowds that of communion? One difference between the two is that while the food court spotlights the present disassociated from the past and the future (by encouraging food for the stomach more than food for thought), the Lord's Table infuses the present with both past and future, drawing us to our place in the drama of redemption. The food court provides a relaxed atmosphere compared to the reflective one encouraged by communion space. Its many restaurant options seem to divide us rather than draw us into sharing one loaf and one cup. Further, the option of choosing one's companions that the food court allows is quite different from the exhortation to overcome personal differences that the communion table requires, for in so doing, the latter strongly proclaims the gospel and is theologically more expressive.[27] Given its mission to culture, one might think that the megachurch could include both kinds of spaces.[28]

Church Buildings and Culture

These architectural values of control and choice, useful when wisely employed, can also damage the church's image and identity when they become indiscriminate imitations of culture. Expressed in architecture, they can communicate that the process of meeting people's needs today often acquires the professionalism and efficiency of an economic transaction. We would not want our architecture to elicit an evaluation like this:

> The Super Savers of evangelicalism discovered that the key to spreading the Good News and increasing the size of their congregations was to blend the evangelistic and cultural mandates into the imperatives of Christian capitalism: Find a need and fill it; find a hurt and heal it.[29]

Church spaces must do more than remind people of their culture, they need to recall them to Christ. Maybe a communion place as the spatial focus of Christian community at worship is such an option.

Communion Tables

Church, More Than Cells

A singular objective of Willow Creek Community Church is not so much size as it is "to create the kind of intimate spiritual community in Acts 2, which describes early Christians caring for each other as if they were family."[30] Accordingly, Willow Creek has spent thirty years creating the appropriate environment (including architecture) for such community. Still, one is prompted to ask, "How much does the specialized nature of service-oriented churches encourage Christian community?" Since the appeal is to Acts 2, consider the situation then: The local church was actually comprised of many house churches. Households typically included far more than the parents and children of whom we think today—they encompassed slaves and others who worked for that house as well.[31] Consistent with that, architecturally, these houses featured residential quarters along with shops, workrooms, and accommodations for workers and guests.[32] These were the basic social units of society, and their members were interdependent. It is this imagery that helps describe Christian community as "a living and growing family whose life together requires mutuality of service and care, recognition of responsibilities, and a sense of identity, belonging and protection."[33] It is important to note that the household church reflected Christian fellowship among people of varied age, status, and gender. This is different from the megachurch, which reduces community experience by often defining cell groups on the grounds of their sameness rather than diversity. In the megachurch (as in many churches), groups defined by common interests, age, gender, or life circumstances could likely be found. Like a clubhouse, spaces are so independent of each other that they accommodate their activities without interfering (that is, manifesting the value of interacting) with each other.

The cell group is not organized to be a church in itself, while the house church is. The lack of direct interaction between the diverse cell groups individually connected to the megachurch invokes a mechanical image, like that of identical spokes on a wheel. But the constant—and often necessary—interaction of a house church's diverse subgroups invokes a more organic image, a web of relations that might be more illustrative of community. There is theological potential here, where the boundaries of private space expand to include the outsider. There is something profound about crossing the threshold of a stranger's home to share in a common unity, and often this sense of profundity comes from sensing the symbolic nature of what is being given up by an individual family (merely human space) for what is gained by the whole community (spiritual, holy space). One questions whether the megachurch's exponential increase in spatial size is able to sustain the intimacy of a home. The architecture of a house communicates a strong cohesive unity, and to the eye each distinct part expresses its function and appears necessary to the whole. This necessary cohesion is not a feature of mall-like church architecture. Apart from the basic elements (food court, stage, atrium), classrooms for cell groups can be cloned without limit, making them compatible but not distinct. For cell space is neutral space, where one is unable to discern its function apart from the people who are using it.

Symbols, More Than Stages

Symbols can be very potent in the way they bring order to our seemingly chaotic experiences and give them appropriate meaning. At a ball game, the singing of the national anthem might mean more to a veteran than to the person next to him. His training and time spent away from home, views on life and sacrifice, scars and skirmishes, all are brought to attention when he stands with his hand over his heart. By itself, the anthem is but a piece of music, but for him (and many others) it is a potent symbol. Shared memories and experiences are embodied in the symbols that accompany a healthy community. Recalling a common past is a significant way to re-member (put the body back together)[34] who we are. We mark our calendars with special "sacred" (set apart) days to remember who we are, and we organize community events like festivals and parades to celebrate this identity. Not doing so can have pernicious effects: "The numbing of memory, or the failure to discipline memory in ways that most traditional cultures do . . . can lead to a loss of resonance, often a loss of meaning"[35] or, one might say, a loss of identity. The contemporary church gets its identity in part from a history stretching back two thousand years and, for megachurches in particular, in large measure from sixteenth-century Reformation commitments and their later American expressions through common meetinghouses and steepled churches. One way to recall this past is for contemporary churches to allude to past forms (mere imitation might make them seem irrelevant). Another might be to continue the practice of ancient (but relevant) traditions that would require the appropriate theologically expressive space, such as a quiet, private room for confession and reconciliation, or a place for meditative reflection, like a personally tended garden or a symbol-rich chapel.[36] Confession, prayer, discipline, celebration, faith, hope, love . . . these are distinctly theological activities—ancient yet relevant because they embody God's work in our lives.[37] And their spaces invite us to truth that is deep, dramatic, and dangerous, truth that is able to forge a community of spiritual power and beauty.

Communion, More Than Crowds

The Old Testament prescribed an elaborate system of rituals and sacrifices that helped people transition from profane space of everyday life into God's most holy presence. In the New Testament, Jesus transforms this system by offering himself as a sacrifice for people's sins and ushering them into God's presence. He is the new temple in whom God meets us, and in giving us the Spirit, God constitutes his people as a "holy temple" and "a dwelling" of God (Eph. 2:13–22). In remembrance of his priestly work on the cross and in anticipation of his royal return, Jesus institutes

Reading Cultural Texts

the communion meal—the broken bread and the poured-out wine. With no servant to wash the disciples' grimy feet when they gathered in that upper room, Jesus takes up the task of menial servitude and sets an example of Christian love (John 13). Paul confirms that this meal was to be celebrated in the church's gathering together, not out of selfish motives, but out of deep unity and concern for others (1 Cor. 11:17–30), and takes up Christ's sacrifice for sins as the prime example of this servant love. If having communion in Christ is one of the church's central, identity-shaping activities, then both the "old rugged cross" and the "old rugged communion table" (other cultures might have old rugged communion mats) are theological symbols that invite people to contemplate Christ and his work on their behalf. Architecturally, then, a space useful for preaching might be equally useful for participation, that is, communion space. This is not a case of either/or, but of both/and. The pulpit or stage can and should be a platform for drawing people into God's drama of redemption as played out in the pages of Scripture and history. But because of its participatory nature, communion (and thus communion space) has equal potential for the formation of Christian community.

Signboards

How should we pay attention to church architecture? Buildings introduce themselves by their sheer physical presence. Their size and scale, materials used, and sense of proportion and unity can draw our attention, bore us, or even repel us. Once past the initial "introduction," interesting buildings invite us to engage in a meaningful "conversation," holding out the promise of richer experiences embedded in their symbols and spaces. In order to better understand the signs, we might ask three initial questions: (1) What is it about the building that engages our sense of the aesthetic? Maybe it is the materials used, or the way intricate, complex parts integrate into a harmonious whole, or a certain architectural style. These aspects not only "feel" good but they also engage the mind, inviting us to understand them through associated images, metaphors, and values. (2) Is there a sense of *fittingness* about the way the worship is related to the building? Do the two complement each other in productive ways? Maybe the sanctuary is sealed off from the outside world and draws us to a place of quietness in the presence of God's assembly; or maybe (as in many countries of the two-thirds world) the sanctuary is open to the sounds from the street and this encourages us to sing our new songs amid the world's cacophony.

(3) Is there something about the worship itself that needs to change in light of God's word and our witness? Maybe the genre and content of our music is irrelevant; or maybe we leave no room to confess our sins to one another. If there needs to be a change in worship then maybe a call for a complementary architectural renovation is also needed.

Further, we could focus on specific theological values that might be especially appealing. I have already hinted at creation and community. Church buildings open to God's creation can show evidence of our stewardship over the earth (Ps. 8) while more strongly proclaiming God's providence and care for all that is his (Ps. 104; Matt. 6:26–27). A pond might be better than an aquarium; patches of woodland might balance manicured lawns; doors and windows can open (once in a while) to the sun and sky to counter the artificiality of a controlled environment. More earthy materials can be used and technological ostentation avoided. Thus, one might ask: How does this building encourage a sense of divine providence and Christian stewardship with respect to nature? How does the building incorporate nature into the praise of God (Pss. 98, 148)?

With respect to community, Hebrews 12:18–24 notes that through Jesus we have access to God and are in the presence of his assembly, not so much the fearful and spectacular theophanies of the past. Let us beware of spectacular buildings where we do not find God's spiritual people. Let us also beware of places where we find worship focused on the merely social, for as Hebrews 12 reminds us, the joyful assembly gathers with full access to God's presence. And the signs of that access today are in the theological, communal practices of word, water, and wine. How do our buildings reflect and complement these practices?

Another theological value to consider is cultural location. Church buildings are places for memory and promise, identity and witness. Vernacular forms of architecture, rising as they do from the particular contexts of peoples and places, have potential to recall a theological heritage and express the identity of a people called to witness in a given culture.[38] Earthy building materials such as wood, stone, brick, and clay mark their duration with the symbols and signs of generations gone by, thus calling us to remember. Artwork can be a subtle yet impressive way of show and tell, of imagination and experience, making vivid our sense of history and hope. Here, one might ask: How does this building help us remember our cultural place (our "tribe and tongue" Rev. 7:9) in the expansion of God's kingdom? How does it speak in the language of the people, telling the culture our ancient story and indicating our citizenship in a worldwide realm?

BOOK LINK

Heaven in Stone and Glass;
Angels in the Architecture

Kieckhefer believes that most modern churches are easy to understand: "They have the plainness and the familiarity of prose" (*Theology in Stone*, 17). The classic sacramental models, by contrast, are filled with symbolism and require sustained interpretation. Such churches are hard to interpret, he says, in much the way a dense and highly allusive poem is difficult. Thank goodness, then, for books like Robert Barron's *Heaven in Stone and Glass: Experiencing the Spirituality of the Great Cathedrals* (New York: Crossroad, 2000).

Barron opens his book with a chapter entitled "A Cathedral Must Be Read." To read the great cathedrals of Europe, we "must move into the medieval mind" and become comfortable with its "symbolic imagination." For the medieval person, the ordinary things of our world were symbolic manifestations—signs—that point to spiritual realities. Indeed, everything on earth, especially a cathedral, is a sign that ultimately directs our attention to God. In Barron's words: "The cathedrals, as embodiments and expressions of Christ, constitute a way of seeing, an avenue to another world" (13). The rest of the book consists of a walking tour through the medieval cathedral that interprets its textual features, everything from stained glass to gargoyles.

Angels in the Architecture: A Protestant Vision for Middle Earth, by Douglas Jones and Douglas Wilson (Moscow, ID: Canon Press, 1998), contains little about architecture, apart from its title. But there is much about medieval culture of which the cathedral is exhibit number one. The book is a plea for what its authors call "Medieval Protestantism"—a culture that, like its medieval forebear, would be shaped throughout by Christian concerns. In the midst of the barren wilderness of modernity, Jones and Wilson remind us that, once upon a time, the Christian concern for truth, goodness, and beauty was actually embraced and embodied in culture. It can be done because it has been done.

Christian culture is "the Gospel in bodily form" (213), and the medieval period is the closest humanity has come to realizing its promise. What we have in modernity and postmodernity, in contrast, is a secular culture on the way to ruin. Medieval Protestantism is the vision of what a culture-wide desire for the truth, goodness, and beauty of the gospel would look like if it were embodied today, and includes a love of beauty, a covenantal wholeness of family and society, a discipline in developing technologies, a community shaped by rural rhythms, and the predominance of poetic over rationalistic knowledge. And, to come back to the theme of the present chapter, it would include the centrality of the catholic church as something greater than ourselves and demanding our discipleship not only when we worship but in all areas of life.

Kevin J. Vanhoozer

Steeples and Cities

So where do these megachurches stand among the basilicas and meetinghouses of church history and the skyscrapers, malls, and theaters of today? How might they continue to use bricks and mortar for the glory of God? Our mall-like churches ought to be in transition to something more theological, a transition from city to steeple (so to speak) and beyond. For the steeple itself is in transition to a greater theological reality, a *holy* city (Rev. 21). By too closely copying the human city (or the suburb) it might be that the mall-like church is less along Scripture's trajectory for theological community than it hopes to be. Symbolically speaking, God calls us, as we are living in time between human city and holy city, not to the suburb or even the steeple but to the communion table—the holy space of identity in Christ, the locus between the past and the future, the locus of the now but not-yet. In coming to the megachurch, we have entered through its open, inviting doors and have enjoyed its common places for rest and refreshment. Its stage has stirred our spirits through presentation and proclamation. But the stage need not be the end of the architectural tour.[39] Could we not move from common places to communion places, seeing that both are necessary for Christian community? In throwing open its doors, the megachurch has challenged us to be more culturally relevant. In turning to the world to call people out of it, all churches can affirm the potential for theologically expressive architecture to help us take our place in God's plan for the ages. For the fulfillment of days envisions not a monstrous steeple staring down its long shadow at people on the periphery but a gigantic cube city of natural and symbolic beauty in which each place is theologically equidistant from its center, for God is its center (Rev. 21:15–22:2). Each place is a place of Christian community, and people praise more than perform or prophesy. There is potential, then, for the megachurch to stand not only between the human city and steeple, but also between steeple and the holy city, with the compelling bond for community being the stage-stirred imagination *as well as* the table-worn memory.

Suggested Readings

Bruggink, Donald J., and Carl H. Droppers. *When Faith Takes Form: Contemporary Churches of Architectural Integrity in America.* Grand Rapids: Eerdmans, 1971.

Fleming, Daniel. *Heritage of Beauty: Pictorial Study of Modern Christian Architecture in Asia and Africa Illustrating the Influence of Indigenous Cultures.* New York: Friendship Press, 1937.

Gorringe, Timothy J. *A Theology of the Built Environment: Justice, Empowerment, Redemption.* Cambridge: Cambridge University Press, 2002.

Kieckhefer, Richard. *Theology in Stone: Church Architecture from Byzantium to Berkeley.* New York: Oxford, 2004.

Turner, Harold W. *From Temples to Meetinghouses: The Phenomenology and Theology of Places of Worship.* The Hague: Mouton, 1979.

As the grocery checkout line essay highlighted, one key idea in Western culture, specifically contemporary American culture, is the pursuit of happiness or the "good life." The "good life," that for which we hope, is one among a number of key cultural ideas or competing visions of culture. This next essay turns to address a concrete cultural text, the film *Gladiator*, and seeks to demonstrate that this movie struggles to express a vision of hope. As the only movie included in this volume, this essay serves as a guide for how one would approach this important medium that is so popular in our contemporary culture.

6

Swords, Sandals, and Saviors

Visions of Hope in Ridley Scott's Gladiator

MICHAEL J. SLEASMAN

Introduction

Want to interpret culture? Engaging films might come to mind, for cinema is all the rage these days in cultural studies. Any number of Christian websites have jumped on this bandwagon.[1] Indeed, film has become the new text by which many around the globe now pose the crucial questions about life. The water cooler phenomenon may gather people to discuss last night's primetime offerings, but it is film that captures the sustained interest of the masses. If cultural texts express ideas deeply rooted within the fabric of a culture, what sorts of ideas would a blockbuster film express?

It is these sentiments that invite us to engage the film *Gladiator* (2000). Some may question whether this particular film is still relevant. Has not our attention moved on? There is a sense in which the interpretation of certain cultural texts, especially movies, has a *kairos*—a moment in which the text's relevance achieves its place on the cutting edge. Typically these texts disappear into the memories of the culture; only a select few survive as classics that have affected the culture itself. *Gladiator*, however, has demonstrated a staying power that places it among the classics of contemporary film.[2] After a thirty-plus-year hiatus, historic epics of the sword and sandal genre have been revived by *Gladiator*'s success, which opened the box-office door for more recent offerings such as *Troy* and *Alexander*.

This film was chosen because it affords an intriguing prospect for developing the notion of deep structures of culture. Though it may initially surprise the casual viewer, this essay proposes that the theme of visions of hope is a hermeneutical key to the best interpretation of *Gladiator*. Grappling with hope gives this film deep relevance in a culture where so many are disillusioned by hopes that disappoint; there is a ripeness in the air for a hope that lasts, a hope that is eternal, a hope that does not fail, and *Gladiator* gropes blindly after such a hope.

After a brief explanation of deep structures, we examine *Gladiator* by means of the three worlds of a cultural text, and then turn to survey a number of possible interpretations, ultimately suggesting that this film is best understood as an expression of hope. Finally, we open a discussion that understands hope from a proper biblical-theological development that finds ethical expression in Christian agency as a *habitus* of hope.

From Texts to Film: Understanding Deep Structures

The sounds, images, and ideas of our world are manipulated into expressions or embodiments of culture that convey the ideals, moral guidelines, and histories that serve as frameworks for our thinking or familiar points of reference for our social existence. Creators (authors) of these intentional "expressions" are themselves situated within a culture and, whether they embrace this situatedness or not, inevitably express aspects of that culture through their works. Sometimes these embodiments manifest realities that deeply undergird the very fabric of the culture, something of a deep structure.[3] These deep structures are embedded at the core of culture, and while some appear particularly situated to a given location, many others are common to all human experience and thus express a shared humanity. This latter category of deep structures we will term cultural existentials, and includes among others our relational nature and our desire to hope—our temporal orientation to the future.

Popcorn, Cinema, and Cultural Interpretation

As a medium by which culture is conveyed, film can be "read" on a variety of levels (passively enjoyed or actively interpreted). Film communicates culture in the images that are portrayed through the camera lens of the director's eye. The effective reception of this message (or intent) by the viewing audience depends on several contributing factors but is ultimately pinned upon the director, who has responsibility for giving the film its final expression and conveying his or her vision for the film to all of the contributing components. The film, then, is an act of communication by which the director as "author" conveys a specific vision or perspective, perhaps even a worldview.

Searching Behind-the-Scenes: The World-Behind-the-Text

The world-behind-the-text is most simply viewed as the background for a film, which may include the genre, social context, cinematic influences, and most importantly the director. To discern the genre is to locate the type of film by identifying certain stylistic conventions and expectations. *Gladiator*, for instance, stands in the genre of historic epics, or period films, particularly in the "sword and sandal" epics, whose heyday was primarily the 1950s and 1960s.[4] Such classic epics as *Spartacus*, *Ben-Hur*, and *The Fall of the Roman Empire* were attempts to "lure back the crowds" from the box-office decline caused by the rise of television.[5]

Similarly, contemporary social context may often exude significant influence on a film. For *Gladiator*, some reviewers found the scandals of

TOOLKIT FOR THE

If you spend much time in the interpretation of concrete texts such as film, music, literature, and art, you will quickly see that many "texts" are a cumulative product of a tradition built upon prior texts. Some works are so significant that they shape the next generation of works within that type or genre. For instance, as soon as a particular type of television show is successful, it is often mimicked. Take, for instance, the plethora of crime scene shows in the early 2000s or the abundance of law shows in the late 1990s. Identifying the ancestry (or textual indebtedness) of a particular text may be quite helpful in discerning the world-behind-the-text.

the Clinton years relevant, while others suggested references to various political issues of the day, including the 2000 presidential campaign.[6] The purported effect of such context (the behind-the-scenes of the world-behind-the-text) influences and, to some extent, depends upon the particular interpretation given to the film, though it appears unlikely in this case that the social context truly influences *Gladiator*.

Given the director's role in casting the vision of a film, it is also important to examine his or her other films for trademark qualities or plotlines. *Gladiator* is directed by Ridley Scott, who distinguished himself in filming commercials by focusing upon the impact of the visual, often filming shots himself.[7] As a result, he is known primarily for his use of imagery, "his aesthetic imprint" and "keen photographic instincts."[8] While Scott is no stranger to period films, having directed, among others, *1492: Conquest of Paradise* (1992) and *Kingdom of Heaven* (2005), he is more renowned for his early science-fiction movies: *Alien* (1979) and *Blade Runner* (1982). Other signature films include *Thelma & Louise* (1992) and *Black Hawk Down* (2001). Attempting to discern a coherence in the diversity of Scott's films, critics have proposed such common threads as a general concern "with the marginalized and powerless in society,"[9] or heroes "who put their necks on the line for corrupt organizations that don't deserve their loyalty," both of which partially resonate with *Gladiator*.[10]

Another aspect of the world-behind-the-text includes cinematic influences. Several commentators note a similarity with an earlier film by Anthony Mann, *The Fall of the Roman Empire* (1964).[11] The content of Mann's film also centers on Marcus Aurelius, Commodus, Lucilla, and a Roman general of the northern armies, whom Aurelius desires to inherit the throne. There is a discernable correspondence of action sequencing and numerous parallels between the two films, though Scott himself denies a direct reliance.[12]

Reading Cultural Texts

Gladiator is peppered with historical figures and practices, altered for the sake of creative license. The emperors Marcus Aurelius and Commodus were historic father/son figures; Lucilla, their daughter/sister, was a historic figure as well.[13] Commodus—a particularly immoral ruler—was known to have entered the arena on several occasions as a gladiator,[14] and while *Gladiator*'s Maximus represents a purely fictional addition, it is of note that Commodus is said to have killed a Maximus with a "great reputation for . . . military skill."[15]

T FOR THE OOLKIT

Just as authors must use syntax, grammar, and literary and stylistic elements in written texts, so too must the director bring together the multiple human and technological factors to achieve the intended vision for the film. Since the director's use of the camera, sound, lighting, special effects, and a variety of other components all contribute to communicating the message to the audience, advanced interpreters may be interested in pursuing competency in the technical aspects of cinematography and how these advanced tools would enhance understanding of the film. For the sake of simplicity, the author of this essay has refrained from commenting on the technical aspects of the film, but this would be a fruitful area of further inquiry.

Finally, the Roman practice of adoption in imperial succession—a common practice by which the Caesar chose an individual outside his bloodline as the appointed heir, adopting him into the royal family—is important for understanding the tension between Commodus and Maximus. Historically, Commodus is the first bloodline heir of the throne after four generations of adopted rulers, from Trajan down to Marcus Aurelius. Ironically, Marcus Aurelius, whom history has recognized as a Stoic philosopher, unwisely abandoned a tradition that had worked so effectively and thus precipitated the decline of the Roman Empire.[16]

And Now Our Feature Presentation: The World-of-the-Text

The world-of-the-text involves the formal features of the text and, from a technical standpoint, is the most difficult section to analyze. Though initially inspired by a painting of a gladiator standing over his vanquished competitor,[17] Scott, in his attention to detailed imagery, uses several interpretive versions of Rome, liberally mixing diverse periods, to recreate his own version of Rome in its glory. Of particular interest is his use of the Nazi re-creation of the Roman aesthetic,[18] which adds an interesting twist to the cultural interpretation of this film, particularly as one begins to discern the extent to which politics and power are the core themes.[19]

The plot revolves around three primary characters: Maximus, general for the northern armies; Marcus Aurelius, Caesar; and Commodus, Aurelius's son. After a protracted campaign to establish peace throughout the empire, Aurelius wants to appoint Maximus as his heir to rule until the Senate is ready to assume leadership. Maximus, however, seeks only to return to his family, though in the end he obediently submits to Caesar's wishes.[20]

Anxiously awaiting his own ascension to the throne, Commodus learns that Aurelius intends to appoint Maximus and kills his father in a jealous rage. His jealousy is fueled by the realization that Maximus possesses everything Commodus has desired: power, fame, and the love of both his father and his sister. Commodus forcefully assumes power and orders Maximus and his family executed. Though he narrowly escapes, Maximus is unable to prevent the slaughter of his family.

Weakened from injuries, Maximus is abducted and forced into slavery as a gladiator. Although reluctant, he fights for survival. He is advised that if he not only fights for survival but also learns to gain the crowd's favor, perhaps the emperor may one day grant his freedom. Eventually, his victories lead him to the Roman Coliseum where he becomes the crowd favorite.

Meanwhile, Commodus has cunningly consolidated power in order to disband the Senate. Yet, as Maximus gains favor with the crowd and defies Commodus, the senators are emboldened. Lucilla plots with a few senators to rescue her beloved Maximus in a bid to remove her brother from power. Despite foiling the escape, Commodus is manipulated by his advisors into fighting Maximus to prove his supremacy over this "rebel" and is subsequently defeated. In a final sequence alternating between this world and a world-beyond, Maximus releases his fellow gladiators and hands leadership of Rome over to the Senate.

Gladiator is filled with a variety of themes, the most important of which include the ideals of freedom, honor, and family. Freedom, especially the ideal of a republic, is highlighted through the contrast of the dictatorial reign of Commodus against Marcus Aurelius's idyllic vision of Rome. The dream of freedom is embodied by the gladiators—slaves with the improbable possibility of being released. The character of Maximus strongly validates the importance of honor. In striking contrast to Commodus's official authority, Maximus has authority by virtue of the respect given him first by the soldiers of his armies, later by the gladiators, and ultimately by the Coliseum crowd. The film also presents the importance of family, portrayed positively through Maximus's commitment to his family, a commitment that extends even beyond the grave. Its foil is the dysfunction of the royal family, in which a son murders his father and lusts for his sister.

Commentators have noted that this film differs from earlier works in this genre by its lack of Christian content. By Scott's own admission, he purposefully avoided any reference to early Christians—intentionally cutting a scene of martyrs being devoured by lions.[21] This has led some to argue that Maximus should not be seen as a Christ-figure.[22] Yet Scott comments that prior to the final fight scene, the outstretched, chained arms of Maximus depict him as a Christ-like image who dies as a martyr and becomes the "savior" of Rome.[23] Thus, at best, the role of Christianity is ambiguous in *Gladiator*. Religion, however, remains important. One cannot miss, for example, the frequent allusions to the afterlife; likewise, Maximus demonstrates a deep commitment to his religion, conveyed through prayers to his god(s). This faith carries him to the end, and as I argue later, it is this faith, as it is picked up in the structural orientation of hope, that provides the key to interpreting this film.

From the emotionally neglected Commodus to the reflective Marcus Aurelius to the noble Maximus, the humanity of the film is evident. The film privileges the viewpoint of Maximus, placing the audience behind his eyes. The use of this perspective helps the audience to identify with him, thus elevating his noble character as a model for their experience. Maximus is the hero, a farmer caught in the political storms of his time, manipulated by others, yet he remains noble in character, faithfully committed to the idyllic vision of political hope for Rome entrusted to him by his ruler.

Around the Water Cooler: The World-in-Front-of-the-Text

The world-in-front-of-the-text has to do with the perlocutionary force or the suggested response, or proposal, for our world today. The content of the perlocutionary force here, as intended by the director, depends heavily upon the deep structure(s) expressed. The meaning—the complex interchange between the actual symbols of the text and the intention of the author—influences the response that the text generates by suggesting alternative ways of living and being.[24] If, for instance, one assumes a meaning that expresses deep structures related to politics, perhaps this film is calling for a commitment to virtuous character or even idyllic democracy. My suspicion is that there is something more profound—a deeply embedded, future-oriented structure of culture—expressed in this movie that was ignored, or perhaps went unrecognized, in the reviews. This suspicion will force us to return to the issue later, after we have examined in more detail an interpretation of this movie.

Finding the Meaning

Whatever the exegetical method employed to interpret a cultural text, one will need to establish some basic criteria to discern between competing interpretations. While various interpretative strategies remain viable options, the question surfaces as to whether some interpretations are "better" than others. Basic criteria for discernment may include the largest in scope (the explanation that most adequately covers the largest amount of data), the simplest explanation (given two seemingly equal explanations, the simpler explanation is preferred), the explanation that takes the data most literally, and/or the explanation that appears to be the most likely. This comparative analysis is directed toward discerning a unifying interpretation of the text that emerges from those structures embedded at the core of shared humanity.

Many have affirmed a political interpretation by finding support in the use of Nazi renderings of the "Roman aesthetic" and the prevalence of the theme of power. The dictatorial reign of Commodus stands in contrast to his father's desire for the Senate to rule Rome. The common man is manipulated by the political powers of the day. A political interpretation may even fit with the 2000 presidential campaign and the ethical failures of the Clinton administration in the social context of the world-behind-the-text. A variation of the political interpretation focuses on the Nietzschean "will to power" and finds support in Commodus's power grab to subvert the will of his father. Other evidence includes the power of the mob, the anxiety of Commodus over Maximus, as well as the power struggle between the Senate and Commodus.

Aside from the recurring other-worldly visions of Maximus, these political, or "will to power," interpretations are quite persuasive. Yet, the limitation of many political interpretations lies in their inability to move beyond material issues to encompass adequately the complexity of texts. Thus, they are deficient with regard to the criterion of scope, failing to explain and account for enough of the movie.

A more promising interpretation proposes an alternative that resembles the biblical story of Joseph. Marcus Aurelius's love for Maximus is paralleled to Jacob's love for Joseph. This love leads to the jealousy of his "brothers," here Commodus. The favored "son" ends up in slavery but rises to power through his nobility of character. "Like Joseph, Maximus the merciful clings to hope that his god will vindicate him, even if his hope is reduced to being unified with his wife and child in the next life."[25] This reviewer predicts that as we shift from a modern to a postmodern mindset, "we will see more movies . . . where a hero is a hero only because he knows the gods are watching and that another world lies beyond this one: a world where merciful warriors embrace their children and an end is put to the reign of every Commodus."[26]

This is an interpretation worthy of consideration, but in the end it is not one faithful to the cinematic text. Here the criteria of the most literal and most likely reading should be employed. The comparison of Maximus and the biblical Joseph is interesting but ultimately forced. The increasing tension between Commodus and Maximus, so central to *Gladiator*, has no parallel in the biblical story, where Joseph is reconciled to his brothers. Consider the contrast in the characters' responses to the father's death. In Genesis, Jacob's death causes the brothers to fear Joseph's revenge. Instead, Joseph resoundingly affirms God's sovereignty and his continued care for them, which likely provides the climax and emotional high point of the narrative. In stark contrast, when Aurelius dies, Commodus unjustly exacts vengeance upon Maximus. Thus, it is difficult to maintain this parallel given the importance the continued tension carries for the film as a whole. Here lies a warning against moving too quickly and simply between a film and the biblical worldview. In the end, this interpretation is helpful, however, by attempting to move beyond the world-of-the-text to envision how this film might influence the world that views it, providing us with a world-in-front-of-the-text interpretation.

Scott himself has argued for mortality as the central theme.[27] Given the privilege we accord to authorial intention, we should take this suggestion seriously. Scott pairs the themes of home (a metaphor of heaven) and family, which are tied together through the visions of Maximus walking through a field. Undoubtedly, these themes run throughout the film. Yet, while mortality seems to grapple with the limits of finite human experience (death and meaning), it fails to address openly that which is beyond a this-worldly experience and, therefore, demands a "thicker" interpreta-

BEHIND THE TEXT

The way this author puts forward his own interpretation of the film is worth emulating. He carefully surveys various interpretations, assessing them according to clearly defined criteria, and then he proposes his answer and provides the evidence. This approach ensures that the competing perspectives are treated charitably, and ultimately strengthens the author's own position, since it is obvious he treats others with fairness.

tion that yields a cultural existential capable of encompassing the entire cinematic text. Thomas Doherty catches a flavor of this by noting that despite the intent to avoid reference to Christians, Maximus still "emerges as a kind of proto-Christian," in which the "glimpses of the afterlife" allow Maximus to stride "into the cultural arena with an alternative vision for a body politic beset with callow leaders and a citizenry all too easily diverted by bread and circuses."[28]

What Doherty relegates to an interesting footnote, I propose as a guiding interpretation that expresses an important cultural existential. One may immediately contend that I am "Christianizing" something that is inherently sub-Christian. While Scott may have intended something less than Christian, the expression of a deep orientation toward the future may undercut that intention. If mortality were the cultural existential expressed, the question begs to be asked why meeting his family in the afterlife motivates his actions in this world, as Scott himself argues.[29] In the end, I propose, Scott directs better than he knows. Through the cultural existential of hope—our structural orientation toward the future—one is able to give coherence to the entire film, permitting a guiding thread through which one can understand the sequencing of the film from beginning to end, in effect superseding politics and power and subordinating them to the overriding orientation of hope. Purely material (this-worldly) interpretations ignore the otherworldly visions that appear in the opening and closing moments of the film as well as at key points throughout. Maximus is guided by the vision of his home and his family, and this vision continues beyond the death and destruction of the physical grounds for it. This vision orients Maximus to the day when he is reunited with his family and can "go home." It motivates his subsequent actions and continued integrity of character. The words of his initial speech to his cavalry continue to ring throughout the movie, "What we do in this life echoes into eternity." Material interpretations ignore these visions because they tend to reject anything that is outside the purview of a naturalistic worldview. This orientation to the future opens a perlocutionary moment that speaks to the world-in-front-of-the-text.

How does hope run through the film? The movie opens with a dialogue of the "promise" of peace in the empire, into which flashes a vision of Maximus walking through a field. Back in this world, he prepares for battle, telling his men, "Imagine where you will be when you go home, and it will be so. What we do in life echoes into eternity." Afterward, the victorious Maximus expresses to Marcus Aurelius his desire to go home now that the campaign has ended. Aurelius asks Maximus to describe his home and responds that it is truly a home worth fighting for. He then requests that Maximus perform a final task to preserve the dream of Rome by eventually handing over control to the Senate. The hope is shifted to the whispered dream of Rome, a light in the darkness of the world. Some scenes later, after the murder of his family, Maximus says that "all else is dust and sand, but to hold them again." Commodus later presents his own vision for Rome and defines greatness in terms of vision. The remainder of the film involves a number of sequences in which there are glimpses of another world, one in which Maximus's family is alive and well. The film culminates with a sequence in which Maximus's mortality is contrasted with this other-worldly home, and he fulfills his final act of faithfulness.

By keeping in mind the trifold occurrence of mortality, home, and family under the rubric of hope, one begins to see a guiding thread that draws together the entire film. And yet at the same time, this sampling reveals several competing visions of hope—a political hope of power, of the people, of the republic; a hope rooted in the home and family; a hope of rekindled relationships. Part of the difficulty in interpreting *Gladiator* is the realization that there is no one, clear root metaphor, but only partial, competing construals. Similarly, it is never clear in the film on what basis we should hope, or even in which vision we should hope. The ambiguity of the existential of hope requires that we explore what it might mean and how that influences our response.

Articulated Hope as Living-Futurely

Hope is a concept with many possible objects. As a structural orientation deeply embedded in culture, hope may be expressed through a particular institution or person, but it primarily refers to an orientation, often signifying *telos* (i.e., a goal or purpose). Theologically this *telos* finds its fulfillment in the eschaton—the new heavens and new earth—and as a result, hope is most often expressed theologically in the doctrine of eschatology (literally the study of last things). Under a secular understanding of hope, one can find a sort of eschatological minimalism oriented toward relationships, love, community, children, social reform, etc. Indeed, many people when asked what they hope for would respond with any number of these worthy, this-worldly hopes. Hope is a broad experience of humanity, possibly an essential quality of human experience, and thus serves as a cultural existential. One could even conceive of culture as articulated hope, suggesting that all interpretative frameworks have elements of hope as either a specific theological or a generic teleological orientation. Not surprisingly, a theologian researching expressions of hope found that having children was itself a sign of hope.[30] Something so inherent to our humanity as childbirth has become an articulation of hope. It is, therefore, common to begin examinations of hope—philosophically, sociologically, or even theologically—with these everyday experiences of it.

The exploration of everyday experiences of hope is not new. Ernst Bloch, an atheist Marxist philosopher, wrote a multivolume exploration of hope as it assumes its everyday forms that has greatly influenced even theological models of hope, particularly the work of Jürgen Moltmann. Appropriate to our discussion, Bloch investigates the relationship between the arts and hope; he particularly mentions film and its powerful ability to convey images of hope.[31] While impressive in the scope of his study, Bloch never moves beyond a materialist (this-worldly) understanding, and to that extent is unable to articulate the "thick" theological understanding of hope afforded to the Christian. Indeed, biblical scholars and theologians, such as Richard Bauckham and Trevor Hart, have spoken to the "decline of secular hope" by demonstrating the ultimate futility of such models, based as they are on mere secular themes of progress or technological advance.[32] In this sense, there are a variety of alternative hopes—"hucksters of hope"—that compete for our attention.[33] In one sense, huckster is a bit harsh. There are true hucksters, such as those who peddle hope in various diet approaches, but there are also those who appeal to laudable goals or purposes. They are hucksters only insofar as they seek to become ends in themselves. Saving the environment is a worthy endeavor, but it is not a proper end of hope unless it is more adequately rooted in a grander narrative.

Real hope, in direct contrast to these imitators, stands at the core of the Christian life. Theologically, hope orients our very being. A Christian does not stop at a being-toward-death (Martin Heidegger's existential), but proceeds to a being-toward-life (Paul Ricoeur) and even a being-toward-resurrection (Kevin Vanhoozer). In fact, an increasing number of theologians have proposed hope as the key hermeneutical framework for theology.[34] If eschatological hope is such a key aspect of the Christian life, it behooves us to discern its biblical contours.

Several key elements quickly emerge from a biblical analysis of the concept of hope, including promise, covenant, fulfillment, and a strong impetus toward the ethical implications of hope. Beginning with the Old Testament, one immediately realizes the inadequacy of traditional word study approaches for understanding hope; instead, these key concepts span several words and ideas. Hope is initially understood in relation to covenant and promise. In Genesis, Yahweh covenants with his people and makes certain promises to them. With each of these covenants—which include successively the creation, Noahic, Abrahamic, Mosaic, and Davidic covenants—promises of blessings and curses were attached, and the hope of Israel rested in the positive fulfillment of these promises.[35] The exodus experience of being delivered from slavery in Egypt and receiving the promised land was the backdrop against which the drama of Israel's anticipation and experiences of the hope unfolded. One can easily see the desire to return to the idyllic setting of the Garden of Eden in which humanity openly related to God. This exodus experience and return to the garden anticipates the Sabbath rest to which the New Testament author of Hebrews appeals, echoing the new exodus and the promised land of the kingdom of God (Heb. 4). The hope of the people of God was twofold: for a restoration to the relationship with God as idealized in both the garden and the patriarchs and David, but also increasingly for a messianic future, where God would do a new thing in the establishment of a relationship with his people.

For whatever reasons, though, Israel's worship of Yahweh eventually came to rest in an objectified understanding of these promises rather than an embodiment of the covenantal relation in the life of the chosen people. The people exchanged true relationship with Yahweh for empty rituals. As a result, Israel also lost sight of the ethical implications of their hope; they failed to see not only how the covenants made promises of God's redemptive work, but that these promises carried moral entailments for how they should live. With the coming of the prophets, this hope began to emphasize an explicitly ethical quality as the prophets called the remnant—the faithful worshipers—to be the true Israel. The prophets returned to the covenants and saw that Israel had rested upon the promises of blessing but had come to ignore promises of curse. The prophetic hope unambiguously emphasized action, calling the people to live as the true Israel and to await expectantly the coming of Zion, the New Jerusalem, which was framed eschatologically. Likewise the hope of the prophets echoed the rise of the messianic expectation, which found its conception in the Davidic covenant but took on particular significance in light of the decline and eventual exile of Israel and Judah and the latter's return.

In the New Testament, hope finds a specific focus in the person of Jesus Christ. Whereas hope previously had been directed to a general desire for God's action, now the attention of hope is focused on a single person whose

TOOLKIT
FOR THE

This essay features extended theological reflection, more than most of the others in this book. Moreover, rather than focus on one or two passages, the author traces the concept of hope as it unfolds through redemptive history, from Genesis to Revelation. When a cultural text raises central biblical themes such as hope, it is good to follow this pattern and spend enough time in theological study before returning to the text and applying what you have learned.

life, death, resurrection, and ascension are the fulfillment of all the promises of God. This focal point is balanced upon a backward and forward orientation: backward in remembrance of the reality of his resurrection, and forward to his promised second coming. Moreover, the backward orientation to the resurrection of Christ anticipates, and actually contains within itself, the future hope of our own resurrection (1 Cor. 15). Hence, Jesus' resurrection is a past event that anticipates our own future resurrection. We remember something that happened to Jesus that directs us forward.

The emergence of the kingdom of God, beginning with the life and teachings of Jesus, becomes an important characterization for describing the tension of living in a time of overlapping ages—this sinful world, which is passing away, and the eschatological kingdom of God, which has already emerged but not yet fully. Jesus models to us a practice (or *habitus*) of hope in the Lord's Prayer. The second petition of the prayer solicits "your kingdom come." Prayer for the coming kingdom has been recognized throughout the ages as a model of hope.[36] As many have commented, to pray this prayer is to enter into the overlap of the ages in which the kingdom has come while at the same time hoping that it will come. Furthermore, to pray this prayer is not only to invite God's action in the renewing of all things, but to commit ourselves to embody this as well, lest we become like the Israelites in the time of Amos, calling for the Day of the Lord while hastening our own destruction.

Similarly, the hope of the apostle Paul is one that requires action, not complacency. Paul finds in the ascension of Christ and his return grounds on which to call the Colossians to set aside such things as anger, rage, sexual immorality, lust, greed, and slander and to clothe themselves with the new self, "which is being renewed in knowledge in the image of its Creator," setting aside all social and economic barriers and putting on humility, compassion, gentleness, and patience (Col. 3:1–14). In the Thessalonian correspondence, Paul appears to directly connect their misunderstandings of eschatological hope with their improper behavior. Likewise, the apostle

Peter directly links the preparation of our minds for action and self-control with the proper orientation of hope (1 Pet. 1:13).

Even a brief survey of biblical hope would be incomplete without some comment on apocalyptic in the Bible, particularly the book of Revelation. While specific interpretations are wide-ranging, an interesting theme of overcoming recurs throughout the book.[37] For instance, in the letter to the church in Ephesus (Rev. 2:1–7), the saints are admonished to return to their first love, to stand firm against a heretical sect, and to continue persevering in the name of Christ. The traditional refrain of "He who has an ear, let him hear" emphasizes the need to respond and is followed closely by the phrase "To him who overcomes." Intriguingly, readers of Revelation are to develop an "overcoming" character from the language of apocalypse, dare we say, a *habitus* of hope. This *habitus* of hope is marked by its rightful orientation upon the *eschatos*—which is Christ—rather than some preoccupation with the *eschata*—the events at the end—and eschatologically anticipates our identity as more akin to that of our future resurrection than to our old past habits of sin.

This ethical dimension of Christian hope is expressed well by Bauckham and Hart when they speak of "living expectantly," or, living a life orientated by hope.[38] Criticizing hope manifested in "triumphalistic appeals," Christian hope is steeped in "faithfulness to God's eschatological kingdom, participating in the Spirit's renewing work."[39] It is this living expectantly that creates a mode of being in us that spreads throughout our ethical interactions with the world. This hope is to be conceived against the common understanding of hope as just a political virtue. Recall that purely political hopes see as their chief aim the construction of some ideal social state or government. Directly attacking the limits of material conceptions of hope (which are focused entirely on elements of this world), Craig Gay argues that political and social conceptions do not do justice to Christian hope,[40] for a biblical hope turns them on their head and "turns out to be a profoundly important political resource," which rests upon the resurrection of Christ himself.[41] Christian hope is "attended by the virtues of humility and patience," which stand in stark contrast to the two kinds of hopelessness engendered by the contemporary world: either the "presumption that we are masters of our own fate" or despair, by which one "neglects the question of destiny altogether" and therefore lives only in the immediacy of the present.[42]

If hope is such a central aspect of the Christian narrative, then Heidegger's description of authentic existence as a resoluteness in being-toward-death factors in only half of the equation of what it means to be human. Hope is a second and more authentic mode of existence because of its relation to our created way of being, which is as beings-toward-life. This hope is grounded in the eschatological expectation of the Christian, which fixes the believer in a redemptive history that culminates in a *telos* in which God makes all things new. Finally, a proper Christian hope makes demands upon those who hope. These demands work themselves out in the way Christians who hope live, in their actions and in their decisions. Hope entails certain ethical and moral practices now. It involves actively and prayerfully entering into the petition "Your kingdom come." If indeed the Christian narrative describes the true reality of existence, culture must in some ways attempt to articulate this hope.

Gladiator and Visions of Hope

We are now able to return to the interpretation of *Gladiator*. I believe that the interpretation that best explains this cultural text is the cultural existential of hope—the structural orientation toward the future. It is possible, though unlikely, that Ridley Scott would agree that this is the intended message of the film as he struggles with the limits of his concept of mortality to give coherence to the film. Yet the movie opens itself to—and in some sense demands—a more complete theological interpretation because of its recurrent theme of Maximus's religion and visions of home (especially in the context of the afterlife). Scott's proposal of mortality factors in only part of the human experience, the mode of being-toward-death. I am cautious of "imposing" hope as an interpretation, but am not left with better alternatives that encompass the totality of the film. As such, I appeal to the interpretation I believe to be the most comprehensive and yet simplest, as that which resonates with the cultural existentials expressed in this cultural text. Quite possibly, Scott himself may have lacked a full vocabulary of hope to express his own vision and intention, even if this was at a subconscious level.

We have seen the hope of the thoroughgoing materialist Ernst Bloch, and that Christianity offers a different vision; but what of *Gladiator*? What sort of hope is projected by this film? By means of the intentional exclusion of Christianity, the film embodies a post-Christian sentiment in that it has moved beyond Christianity.[43] The irony is that just as Scott has intentionally excised reference to Christians, vestiges of Christianity remain, the clearest of which is the symbol of hope. But the question remains to be asked, a hope in what? The world that is projected in *Gladiator* invites the

BOOK LINK

Plowing in Hope:
Toward a Biblical Theology of Culture

As this essay makes clear, Maximus is a soldier who would like to be a farmer. He is just the kind of person for whom Isaiah delivered his prophecy: "They will beat their swords into plowshares" (Isa. 2:4; see also Mic. 4:3). The two implements were common symbols for war and peace respectively in the ancient world. The plowshare is the sharp digging end of early plows. In Scripture, Elisha was a plowman before he became a prophet, and in the church plowing became associated with the preaching of salvation, just as the sword became associated with the word of the Lord (Heb. 4:12). Augustine saw God himself as the plowman and the church as his field.

All this forms the background for the present book link to David Bruce Hegeman's *Plowing in Hope: Toward a Biblical Theology of Culture* (Moscow, ID: Canon Press, 1999). Beating swords into plowshares connotes a time of peace (for which we can hope), the preaching of the word, and perhaps the apocalyptic plowing under of the old order so that the seed spread by the word of God can come forth. In Hegeman's book, however, plowing is a metaphor for what humans do with the raw resources of creation to make it into a habitable culture. It is what humans do in response to the cultural mandate (Gen. 1:28).

Why are we here? Hegeman answers: to plow in hope, working the ground (i.e., building culture) according to the divine purpose in order to produce a glorious garden-city (15). Hegeman's is one of only a very few books that attempt to set forth a biblical theology of culture. Consistent with the Method in the present volume, Hegeman offers a thick description of culture, setting it within the creation-fall-redemption framework of the Bible. He argues that alongside the redemptive history that receives most of the church's attention is a properly *culturative* history. This history also calls for theological reflection.

The bulk of *Plowing in Hope* sets forth a positive theology of culture that sees culture not merely as a site of conflict with the gospel but as a stage on which God's purpose for humanity is played out. In the four tasks that make up the cultural mandate—to *rule* and *fill* the earth; to *work* and *keep* the garden—we see culture "in seed form" (26). Christians today need to recover their original calling as culture-makers (29). Specifically, men and women have been given the privilege and responsibility, as the crown and stewards of creation, to develop the potential that God has invested in the created order and ourselves.

Kevin J. Vanhoozer

viewer to enter into the character of Maximus, a character with a vision that is fueled by his hope—a hope leading him to obedience and a desire to achieve the dream of Marcus Aurelius and empowering him to live expectantly, waiting for the day when he will once again be united with his family. This leads into the perlocutionary moment of the speech-act, which is the world-in-front-of-the-text. Into this world is projected—or better, narrated—hope: a hope full of ethical implications, a hope that takes up the present world into a vision of the future. In terms of Aurelius's vision, it is the dream of freedom and democracy. Yet Maximus's hope is even greater, for it is a hope in the afterlife that orients him in this life. This begins as a minimalist hope that looks to a reunion with his family. Yet even this hope creates an orientation that motivates Maximus's character.

The film juxtaposes conflicting visions of hope, which resonate with our own experiences of hope: for power and position; for family and children; for acceptance and tranquility; for just societies standing in stark contrast with the corrupt nature of governments. But moving beyond pie-in-the-sky hopes that have no residence on the ground, Maximus models a hope that matters in the way we live now. Thus the world being addressed is called to respond with this same hope—a hope that can look beyond this life to orient itself, which gives coherence to the whole film by exposing a deeply embedded orientation of culture that also opens the text to a critique only possible within a Christian framework of existence; a hope that resonates with Maximus's battle cry, "What we do in this life echoes into eternity."

As Christians, we are confronted with the so-what of eschatological hope. How do we develop a *habitus* of hope? At a basic level this involves triangulating our position in the drama of God's redemption. In the overlap between times there is a strong tension in embodying resurrection values and properly respecting this world. The first task is, then, to reclaim a biblical notion of hope that stands against contemporary alternatives and does not fall captive to the contemporary infatuation with immediacy. A *habitus* of hope therefore cannot be an abandonment of this world, for this would negate the nature of the incarnation. At the same time, a *habitus* of hope recognizes that renewal is ultimately the work of God, and thus resists the urge toward presumption, toward power grabs that attempt to bring about the kingdom by force. By involving ourselves in the petition for the coming kingdom, we pray as and for an embodiment of hope. As those developing a *habitus* of hope we must be daily embodiments of the kingdom of God advocating justice in society, protecting the oppressed, providing acts of mercy for the needy, and petitioning the Father to finish his kingdom in hastening the return of his Son.

Reading Cultural Texts

Suggested Readings

Bauckham, Richard, and Trevor Hart. *Hope against Hope: Christian Eschatology in Contemporary Context*. Grand Rapids: Eerdmans, 1999.

Farley, Edward. *Deep Symbols: Their Postmodern Effacement and Reclamation*. Valley Forge, PA: Trinity Press International, 1996.

Moltmann, Jürgen. *Theology of Hope: On the Grounds and Implications of a Christian Eschatology*. Minneapolis: Fortress, 1993.

Part 3

Interpreting Cultural Trends

Editorial Introduction

We now turn from cultural texts, like the Universal Declaration of Human Rights or the movie *Gladiator*, to cultural trends. Although trends can be less straightforward to interpret, they offer a potentially greater reward, since they often have a more direct connection to how we live. Such is the case with busyness: it is a pervasive experience for many Americans, and yet it is hard to nail down exactly what it means. This essay offers a clear example of how all three steps of cultural hermeneutics—understanding the cultural work, assessing it theologically, and formulating our response—can apply to a trend.

7

The Business of Busyness
Or, What Should We Make of Martha?

CHARLES A. ANDERSON

"I Do
Therefore I Am."

—Nextel Billboard

Considering the Trend of Busyness

"I'm Late! I'm Late! For a Very Important Date!"

The business of America is busyness. Everywhere people feel rushed, weighed down by their to-do lists and overflowing in-trays. Nearly all of us experience busyness at some point. Consider our choice of words: "We talk of no time, lack of time, not enough time, or being out of time. Trying to get more time, we borrow time only to incur a time debt and end up with even less time. . . . Then, it's crisis time."[1] Through the last forty

How does my background influence my interpretation? The author reflects: "When I first wrote this essay, it was probably because I was feeling busy and wanted to know how to make sense of it as a Christian. I was in graduate school and working twenty hours a week as an administrative assistant, while my wife's job regularly required sixty hours a week. Other people seemed just as interested in the topic as I was: whenever I mentioned it to someone, they almost always asked to see a copy, which doesn't usually happen with seminary papers." We often have a personal stake in cultural interpretation, and that naturally influences our perspective. The overall balance, of course, is to see how our own vantage point (rightly) influences our interpretation, while still trying to understand the text or trend fairly.

years, between 70% and 80% of Americans have consistently indicated they sometimes or always feel rushed.[2]

Many facets of life reorient themselves to help us survive, though often they also serve to further our busyness. Stores and the Internet stay open 24/7 for shopping. Starbucks coffee offers double the normal caffeine to fuel our hectic pace. The drive-through enables us to order an extra-value meal, mail letters, drop off dry cleaning, withdraw money, and fill prescriptions. I once even attended a drive-in church in Florida: we picked up communion bread and juice in sealed, plastic containers as we drove in, and then listened to the service from our car. Similarly, the ideal Bible for busyness has appeared, condensed into one hundred minutes of reading.[3]

This frantic pace does not suddenly emerge once we reach adulthood. College students find time to chat only by scheduling it in: "I just had an appointment with my best friend at seven this morning," one student explained. "[You have to do that] or else you lose touch."[4] But such habits begin even earlier. The time children spend on school and studying has increased 25% in the last two decades,[5] and elementary school students often carry planners to keep track of homework and activities. Many children maintain exhausting schedules that include volleyball, basketball, swim lessons, dance, music, enrichment exercises—what one expert calls "scheduled hyperactivity."[6] Children become a busy reflection of the parents who raise them.

We commonly attribute this frantic pace to how much we work. The evidence, however, is more complicated. The Census Bureau's American Time Use Survey calculates the average workweek at 37.6 hours,[7] which actually represents a decline since the 1960s.[8] Time spent on paid and unpaid work (i.e., housework and childcare) has decreased, while leisure time has increased—yet, paradoxically, Americans feel the opposite.[9] However, these numbers, important as they are, fail to tell the whole story. For while the average total work hours have slightly decreased, who works them and how they work them have changed. Recent decades have witnessed a significant increase in married families in which both spouses work, from 36% in 1970 to 60% in 2000, as well as a dramatic rise in single-parent families, from 11% of total families in 1970 to almost 25% of total families in 2000.[10] Moreover, 40% of employed Americans now work outside the traditional 8 a.m.–5 p.m., Monday-through-Friday schedule.[11] Work hours may not have increased, but their distribution has changed—thus they feel different—and so for many people the time pressures have risen.

How do we respond to these pressures? One way is to turn to different kinds of time management. One type concentrates on "wonderful timesaving tips, techniques, ideas and strategies" to make the most of things.[12] The problem, however, is that this approach focuses too much on "management" without stopping to ask what is being managed and whether it is worth it.[13] Better is the type of time management that—while not neglecting technique—encourages people to reflect on their values and line up activities accordingly.[14] Another way to respond is to advocate a slower pace: the annual Take Back Your Time Day, for example, calls for balance between work and the rest of life.[15] Thirdly, almost all of us, even if only subconsciously, find small ways to respond. We practice "time-deepening" where we double up on activities or squeeze more things into the same period.[16] Similarly, we build what one expert calls a family infrastructure of communications and planning, as in the quick call on the mobile phone from husband to wife to double-check who is picking up the kids from soccer practice.[17] Many of us feel busy and use a variety of strategies to cope, but how do we define what is actually happening? For that, we must incorporate the world behind busyness.

Too Many Choices But Not Enough Boundaries

How did we come to feel so busy? A little historical perspective should remind us that people have always faced many demands. Even Jesus needed to get away with his disciples "because so many people were coming and going that they did not even have a chance to eat" (Mark 6:31). Having a lot to do is nothing new. Yet, busyness today seems widespread; it goes beyond a seasonal occurrence and has become for many the default rhythm of life. Why is that? At least three factors help explain our state: the condition of overchoice, the blurring of boundaries in our lives (largely through technology), and the influence of work on psychological time. What unites

TFOR THE
TOOLKIT____

For cultural texts like music or movies, the world-behind includes authorial intent: What did the creator of this text intend it to mean? With a trend like busyness, though, this question is not as helpful, since what we hear is not really the design of one person but rather the collective voice of the culture. With a trend, historical and sociological factors often weigh more heavily in deciding how it took its present form.

these factors is that they all occur within the context of our economy.[18]

"Overchoice" refers to the stress we feel from having more options than we can handle or actually need.[19] The supermarket, for example, enshrines overchoice. Certainly, we benefit from having such a wide variety of afford-able items in one place, but it takes time to navigate the proliferation of choices that often make no real difference. Does it really matter if I buy the shampoo with mint and tea tree or the one with rose and aloe? Overchoice also encompasses fields like health care and air transportation, where deregulation places the onus on individuals to research and make decisions.[20] What a travel agent once did, we now spend hours doing for ourselves on websites like Travelocity or Expedia. More fundamentally, we encounter overchoice in terms of deciding who we are. There are so few limits on our existence and experience that we face difficulties in identity formation.[21] Because of the increasing number of things we *can* do, many of us *want* to do them and *try* to do them.[22] But this nearly limitless range of options inevitably makes us feel busier, since time does not expand to accommodate all the new choices and we often lack the ability to navigate among them.

The blurring of boundaries between different areas of life is a second factor behind busyness. The distinctions that formerly characterized work life versus home have receded.[23] One anthropologist looked in a workplace and saw a whiteboard filled with reminders about family activities while the home had a desk organized for work after hours.[24] As these boundaries blur, we feel always on call in each area. Yet, at the same time, we should remember this phenomenon is nothing new. It represents, in some ways, a reversion to a preindustrial model: in agrarian societies, home and work constituted virtually identical sites. What is new is the role of technology in blurring these boundaries. Ever available via mobile phones and instant messaging, we can never put ourselves out of work's reach—at least as long as our gadgets stay on. Moreover, technology allows us to cram even more into a day than before.[25] Thus, rest from our responsibilities becomes difficult as we remain constantly "on."

A third factor behind busyness comes from the relationship between work and psychological time. Psychological time refers to our qualitative judgments about how time is spent.[26] The type of work we do has always influenced our perception of time. In an agrarian context, work proceeded according to the natural rhythms of day and night and the seasons. Moreover, it tended to be measured by tasks accomplished rather than time spent.[27] With a change in work, though, came a change in psychological time. Due in part to the increasing sophistication and availability of clocks, the Industrial Revolution could coordinate factory operations according to precise time measurements.[28] The economic ability to run machines continuously led to work being based more on the capabilities of machines than of people. Thus, the perception of time was industrialized and came to be seen as standardized segments governing when people started and stopped. Moreover, with the move toward an information economy, time becomes further detached from natural rhythms. In a 24/7 economic world, virtually no "downtime" exists. Indeed, one of the tenets of globalization is that time is universalizing: when people in Tokyo and New York can experience a business meeting or news event at the same time, then time differences have faded.[29] How work is done shapes our experience of time.

This insight leads us to consider how we view time. One possibility is the "container" view, where time is a neutral medium in which each segment is self-contained and unaffected by what happens in any other period. The "content" view, though, more accurately reflects our day-to-day lives.[30] Our experience of all time is shaped by what takes place during any one part. There is a carry-over effect, and thus "it is very difficult to leave behind the modern world's planned, strictly utilitarian attitude to time, as well as its hyperactive rhythms and routine character."[31] The industrialization of work time spills over and shapes the rest of time as well. The content view of time implies that to change how we experience time in any one area will require addressing the entire framework. Piecemeal solutions will not get us very far. The fact that all three of these factors are intimately connected with our market economy demonstrates, however, that such change will not prove easy.

We can now attempt to define busyness. At one level, busyness is a combination of activity and speed. It is having much to do and performing those activities at a high rate.[32] Basic busyness, therefore, encompasses what we do and how we do it. When most people say they are busy, however, they do not just mean lots of activity at high speed. They implicitly refer to the experience of psychological time, where boundaries dissolve and more re-

T FOR THE
OOLKIT _____

sponsibilities seem pressed upon them. For them, busyness means "a kind of work that consumes more and more time and attention."[33] Busyness is about both our perception and what we do. In this sense, the cultural trend of busyness operates at a literal level of activity and a symbolic level of time pressure.[34] Busyness operates at multiple levels, and we must tease out what it means in a given instance.

Busyness as Virtue or Vice

As a cultural trend, busyness shapes who we are, a fact that parents implicitly recognize. Consider two examples. The Zeiss family of Los Angeles pushes their children to work hard in school and enrolls them in tennis, fencing, and hockey lessons, commuting through rush-hour traffic to and from the activities.[35] They have purposefully chosen to acclimate their children to busyness in order to prepare them to succeed in a hectic world. In contrast, Phil Lancaster counsels families to do all they can to avoid busyness.[36] He and his wife homeschool, the only individual activities they allow their kids are music lessons, and the emphasis is on plenty of unstructured time together as a family. Both the Zeiss and Lancaster families grasp that busyness can form identities, but they have taken very different paths in response.

Busyness is not monolithic, with only one possible meaning.[37] It can stand as a virtue or a vice. First, all of us have undeniably benefited from what busy people accomplish. The economic prosperity we enjoy has come about, in no small part, from long, hard work. Few among us would willingly forsake the advantages gained. It is not just economic gains either—many scientific and cultural advances have resulted from the labor of diligent men and women. Busyness can lead to good things.

If defined as a high pace of activity at a good speed, busyness as a virtue may reflect an acknowledgment that life imposes inevitable limits on what is possible. We cannot accomplish all that we would like. People who accept this conclusion, therefore, may resolve to use well the time they do have, and thus to be busy. Busyness, so oriented, represents a right response in recognizing the limits inherent in all things.

Busyness as vice comes when this driven pace implicitly refuses to remain tethered by such constraints. The way many people practice (and are overtaken by) busyness actually bucks against these limits rather than accepting them. Such people work hard, seemingly believing it is always possible to do more. A study conducted in the 1990s concluded that "we have come to expect hassle-free personal relations, limitless material possessions, and a world unfolding to meet our personal agendas, timewise and otherwise. We then feel more rushed than we would prefer when the world does not respond as we expected."[38] Under this mindset, the allure of busyness can convince us anything is achievable—it just takes a little more effort or ingenuity. Limits fade away, and the highest good comes from what a person does—and the more, the better.

The new standard response to the question "How are you?" is "Busy!" As we complain about the spreadsheet to prepare for tomorrow's meeting or the quick drive from clarinet lessons to soccer practice, we may fall prey to the trap of "actually making a kind of boast: 'I'm so busy, I must be important'. One's busyness is worn like a badge of honor, a measure of one's status."[39] It is possible to become a people defined by what we do. In sum, busyness can bring about good, but it can also be symptomatic of a life oriented toward how much one can accomplish.

Busyness in Light of Christian Wisdom

Brief Biblical Reflections on Living in Time

In order to interpret busyness from a Christian perspective and act accordingly, we begin with a brief sketch from Scripture about how we live in time. The first point is that *God is the Lord of time*. He is its author (Gen. 1:3–5), and all other considerations must begin here.[40] God's sovereignty over time includes night and day (Jer. 33:20–21), the seasons (Ps. 74:17), all our times (Ps. 31:15), and the end of our lives (Luke 12:16–20). His lordship over time is complete. Psalm 127 illustrates the implications for us. The psalmist chides, "In vain you rise early / and stay up late, / toiling for food to eat— / for he grants sleep to those he loves" (v. 2). God sets boundaries of time for our activities, and our submission to those limits represents our trust in him to take care of us. One entailment of God as Lord of time is that we are to recognize time as a gift. We do not control the time we have—God has given it to us and can do with it as he pleases (Job 1:21). James rebukes planning that presumptuously fails to account for our lack of control over time (James 4:13–16). We are stewards of however long God grants us. We can only humbly receive time from him. He is its Lord, and our Lord, as we live in the time he gives us.

The second key point concerns the *progressive and yet cyclical movement of time*. The overarching framework of time is that God moves history toward its appointed end, which is the headship of Christ over all things (Eph. 1:10). The prophets speak often of the day of the Lord, a final time of judgment (Amos 5:18) and deliverance (Zeph. 3:9–20). Revelation 21–22 concludes the story by showing where we, and the entire creation, are going: God will usher in a new heaven and new earth, and time as we know it now will end. Time, therefore, is finite. Moreover, what happens in time has ramifications in eternity. In light of the impending day of the Lord and his wrath upon sin, Zephaniah exhorts the people to righteousness and humility (Zeph. 1:14–2:3). Given a content view of time, where what happens in one part affects our experience of the whole, the fact that God will draw time to a close in the future should affect how we live now.

While history moves toward this goal, it does not move straightforwardly. This progression contains periods both of repetition and of irregularity, in which God varies the pace at which he acts. For example, there is often a polarity between slowness and suddenness in the way God moves.[41] Israel languishes in Egypt four hundred years, then God delivers the people in the exodus. Biblical history is punctuated by this pattern of waiting and then God acting definitively. Indeed, even the day of the Lord will come suddenly (1 Thess. 5:2–3), after many have scoffed at its delay (2 Pet. 3:4). The most basic sense of repetition in time is the cycle of days and seasons that God guarantees (Gen. 8:22). Human life also experiences cycles, as Ecclesiastes 3:1–15 famously teaches: everything under the sun has its time.[42] The interpretive key comes in v. 11: "He has made everything beautiful in its time. He has also set eternity in the hearts of men; yet they cannot fathom what God has done from beginning to end." God as Lord of time has these cycles of planting and uprooting, of tearing and mending, in his control. In their appropriateness and completeness, they are beautiful. Moreover, he has placed in the human heart a longing for what lies beyond time. But none of this comforts Qoheleth, the preacher of Ecclesiastes, because of the inscrutability of what God does. We may live through these times, but we lack God's knowledge of them. What caused despair for Qoheleth, though, should remind us that trust and humility are essential for how we live in time.

Interpreting Cultural Trends

The third key biblical point revolves around *our responsibility to redeem the time*. Time is short, and we should live in the eschatological tension. Already we live in the last days because Christ has come and proclaimed that "the time is fulfilled" (Mark 1:15 ESV). Peter interprets the giving of the Holy Spirit at Pentecost as the fulfillment of Joel's prophecy that we live now in the last days, inaugurated by Christ's death and resurrection (Acts 2:17, 33–34; Joel 2:28–32). The end toward which all time moves has entered into time. Only it has not yet arrived. We still await Christ's second coming when we will be delivered, judgment will be levied, and creation will be redeemed (1 Cor. 15:20–28). We live, therefore, in this "already–not yet," between the times as people upon whom the ends of the ages overlap (1 Cor. 10:11), with the gift of the Spirit as down payment (Eph. 1:14).

Paul, in particular, often employs this eschatological tension as motivation for how we should live. In Romans 13:11–14, he envisions the night as nearly over and the day as almost here. In this in-between time, believers must turn away from evil and put on Christ Jesus. In Colossians 4:5, he exhorts the church to "live wisely toward outsiders by redeeming the time."[43] Wisdom is taking every opportunity and fully using the time granted us. Here, that means making the most of evangelistic opportunities, whereas in a parallel passage it means to seek God's will and cultivate holiness (Eph. 5:16). To redeem the time means to fill it with divine purpose, not just with any and every activity.[44] Christ has come and inaugurated the end of time; we should find motivation for godliness in this.

These three truths—God as Lord of time; the way in which history moves toward its end; and our responsibility to redeem the time in the midst of this tension—should serve as our foundation for interpreting the trend of busyness and responding as cultural agents.

The Importance of Discernment in Busyness

Discernment is vital for interpreting cultural trends because no trend is all good or all bad. The world-in-front-of-the-trend-of busyness demonstrated the possibilities of virtue or vice. How do we assess which it is in a given case? We must look at the orientation of busyness, which includes the beliefs and motives behind it as well as the way it is practiced. Does busyness orient itself toward achievement for its own sake, always driven to do more, and never believing there is enough time? Or does busyness orient itself toward God as Lord of time and thus make the most of opportunities in a way that recognizes time as the arena in which salvation and judgment play out? These choices may seem overly stark, but they show the ultimate aim of busyness as vice or virtue. Earlier, we distinguished between busyness as much activity at high speed, and busyness as time pressure. If busyness is defined as doing many things at a fast pace, it can be good or bad and fit into either orientation. When it comes to busyness as that pressing feeling that we should always be doing more, then discernment becomes more difficult. But on the whole, that kind of busyness, the feeling of time pressure, belongs to the achievement orientation.

Idolatrous busyness. The busyness oriented toward achievement is exemplified in a presentation by two companies on how they approached high-tech reengineering. The second presenter

> explained that, in order to keep costs to a minimum, reengineering duties were added to existing workloads. When asked by the previous presenter whether this situation didn't cause an increase in stress, the speaker casually replied that, in fact, two employees had recently suffered heart attacks, one fatal. "It's unfortunate," she said, "but it's a cost of doing a business."[45]

This "cost of doing a business" is actually the price of exploitive choices made by company executives in a society "whose main criterion for its own health is economic success."[46] Busyness oriented toward economic gain at the cost of human life should be called what it is—greed. Such a story shows the need to unmask the powers that may stand behind busyness.[47]

This kind of busyness understands itself in terms of how much it can accomplish, whether individually or corporately. Its motives may be for economic gain, recognition from others, or something laudable like social justice. Whatever the case, it feels pushed by not having enough time to accomplish its goals. This busyness, driven by achievement and frustrated over a lack of time, ultimately reflects patterns of idolatry. People allow themselves to be defined and regulated by this perceived lack of time, the very definition of idolatry.

Moreover, those who practice this busyness, who implicitly define themselves in terms of how much they do, are only a short step away from denying the gospel. Call it justification by busyness. That probably sounds like an overstatement, but here is the implicit mindset: If I can work just a little harder, do a little more, then I will be successful. The gospel tells us there is nothing we can do to be successful. Our hope is not in any self-constructed deliverance but in reliance upon God: "in repentance and rest is your salvation, / in quietness and trust is your strength" (Isa. 30:15). We do not usually connect this kind of busyness explicitly to such weighty spiritual consequences as idolatry and denying the gospel, but this is the logical outworking and ultimate destination of such an orientation.

Holy busyness. Holy busyness, oriented toward God in motive and practice, is exemplified in Paul. He characterizes his apostolic ministry as working "harder than all of them—yet not I, but the grace of God that was with me" (1 Cor. 15:10). His work included manual labor, evangelism, church-planting, teaching, and discipling, all while undergoing persecution and suffering.[48] Through it he maintained a profound awareness of the motive and source of his busyness: "We proclaim him, admonishing and teaching everyone with all wisdom, so that we may present everyone perfect in Christ. To this end I labor, struggling with all his energy, which so powerfully works in me" (Col. 1:28–29). Paul is busy so that, by bringing people to maturity in Christ, he can glorify God (cf. 1 Cor. 10:31). His strength to work hard and redeem the time comes from God's grace.

How can we distinguish holy busyness from the idolatrous kind? When are we working hard as a manifestation of trusting God and when are we trying to justify ourselves by busyness? Both of them include doing much. So what makes them different? Holy busyness is grounded in the gospel: God has saved us by grace and created us in Christ Jesus to do good works (Eph. 2:9–10). Who we are comes before what we do. Being grounded in the gospel means that relationships—with God, others, and creation—precede activity. Often, it is activity that expresses and helps build such relationships, but who we are remains primary. So, holy busyness does not begin with what we do but with what God does.

When it comes to what we do, holy busyness is confident that God has already accomplished his purposes and now invites us to participate in realizing them. It does not complain, therefore, about not having enough time, for ultimately such grumbling is directed against God—after all, who else has given us our time? Because God has provided us the gifts of time and work, we can trust that each is sufficient for the other.[49] Furthermore, when it comes to *what* exactly we do, holy busyness carries a sense of eternal priorities. It recognizes that time will end and that this

BEHIND THE TEXT

Historical perspective can often make an important difference in interpretation. The author confesses, "I did not realize the big hole in contemporary Christian reflection on busyness until I read material from earlier centuries. Once I saw what people like Jonathan Edwards had said, the difference was obvious, and I was embarrassed I had not seen it earlier." His admission points to how we may have blind spots that only become apparent in contrast to earlier eras. When you interpret a cultural text or trend, try to incorporate historical perspective, if possible, in order to help illuminate the present.

world is the stage on which the drama of redemption plays. Because we will all face judgment, time must be used to prepare ourselves and others to stand before God.

Earlier Christian generations knew this better than we do. Very little contemporary Christian writing on busyness (and there is a lot![50]) talks about eternity or final judgment. In contrast, Jonathan Edwards considered time precious mainly because eternity depends upon it.[51] Similarly, a nineteenth-century British tract urged people "to use time in reference to its true end—eternity."[52] Because we will have to answer to God for how we have used our time, Christians must profitably employ the time available.[53] The tract suggests that waking up an hour earlier each day will provide enough time over the course of a year to memorize a Gospel, or read several Christian biographies, or study apologetics.[54] Granted that the life situation of these audiences was different from ours, the contrast is still striking. They had their eyes fixed on eternity, and that decisively shaped how they approached the use of time.

Finally, because time is God's gift to us, holy busyness stewards it wisely. That involves working hard at what is important *and* cultivating times of rest. Holy busyness is difficult to maintain—the pace of activity tends to crowd out those disciplines like prayer and rest that we need for cultivating long-term fruitfulness. We can easily slide into an unbalanced approach in which our motives remain right but our practice is no longer in line with Scripture. We must heed the example of Jesus, who withdrew for times of solitude and prayer (Mark 1:35; Luke 5:16, 9:10). We should find satisfaction in our work, recognizing it as a gift from God (Eccles. 3:13). In a culture gone mad for how much it can do, a good night of sleep becomes a subversive, countercultural activity.[55] When it comes to rest, we must remember that God made us creatures before he made us Christians.[56]

Spiritual Formation in Holy Busyness

Our reflections on the characteristics of holy busyness have already moved into spiritual formation. Just as a right orientation for busyness involves beliefs, motives, and practices, our response as Christian cultural agents must encompass the same. Many good ideas have been proposed for how to be rightly busy; the key is to integrate them into a holistic response. How we cultivate holy busyness should include our heart, individual practices, and church practices. The proposals here represent a starting point for how that might look.

The Heart

Questions of our heart and character are the appropriate foundation of cultural agency, since one of the functions of culture is to cultivate identity. Who we are begins with the heart. To grapple with this trend means to discern why the busyness in our lives exists. What drives us? Taken together, Colossians 4:5 and Psalm 127 encapsulate how we should relate to God in busyness: we are to redeem the time as we trust him within the boundaries he has set. Such faith is possible, however, only when we believe God to be both sovereign and loving in our lives. He truly does control our time and wants what is best for us. What ultimately shapes whether busyness is holy or idolatrous, therefore, is how we see God and relate to him.

One character trait for cultivating holy busyness is patience. We are a patient people because we trust that God has given us our vocation and our time, and that each is sufficient for the other. We are a patient people because we know God often takes his time in forming us. Moses spent forty years in Midian before God appeared to him at Sinai (Acts 7:30). We are a patient people because we live between the times. The end has begun, so we wait eagerly; yet the consummation has not occurred, so we wait patiently. Our examples are the patriarchs who "were still living by faith when they died. They did not receive the things promised; they only saw them and welcomed them from a distance" (Heb. 11:13). We have witnessed the decisive beginning to the fulfillment of God's promises but wait for their completion. In the interim, we live by patient faith, just as they did. With this perspective, ending up in the slow-moving lane in a traffic jam becomes a divine means of grace, a small way God can shape our character to learn to wait on him.

The Individual

Most suggestions for busyness focus on the individual. For example, one writer attributes 100% of busyness to a person's own choices and declares that the solution is simply to say no.[57] This advice, however, is incomplete. It avoids matters of the heart as well as the question of why we are busy in the first place. It also fails to grapple with larger societal trends that shape our perception of time and thus neglects the need for communal practices. Concern for how we as individuals make decisions about busyness is necessary but not sufficient.

One individual practice for cultivating holy busyness is to turn off the TV. Because time is finite and eternity depends on it, we should devote

For Further
REFLECTION

This essay shows how our response as cultural agents should strive for holism. It offers concrete proposals for our character and practical steps we can take as individuals and as a Christian community. It could even incorporate public policy ideas for busyness-related proposals like mandatory minimum vacations. Too often, our suggestions can be shallow because they look only to what we should do and not who we are and what we believe, or they remain individualistic and fail to encompass the church or society.

ourselves to what is important. Under that rubric, we could stand to watch much less TV than we do. Nearly 50% of free time in America goes toward the television, and the average person watches over 2.5 hours a day.[58] Moreover, it is not just how much time we spend with the TV but the nature of what we watch. Gene Rodenberry, creator of *Star Trek*, once confessed, "TV does not exist to entertain you. TV exists to sell you things."[59] Watching 2.5 hours a day of a medium intent on promoting consumption is not a recipe for holy busyness. We do not necessarily have to banish the TV altogether, but turning it off a lot more will free up time for real rest and productive activity. We can pursue holy busyness more effectively with less TV.

The Church

Our interpretation of busyness has provided good reasons why cultural agency must go beyond individual responses. The historical and social forces behind these feelings of time pressure ensure the difficulty of responding on just our own. Likewise, a content view of time reminds us that we must wrestle with the framework in which we experience time; for such a large task, communal practices are necessary. One anthropologist remarked that field studies of families show that coping with busyness always involves more than just the individual.[60] So, a right orientation for busyness requires a communal response, and for Christians that means the church. We have the opportunity as the church to set an example to the world of another way of living in time.[61]

One church practice for cultivating holy busyness is sabbath-keeping. As considered here, a sabbath is the principle of having a weekly time dedicated to corporate worship and rest.[62] There is something about a sabbath that makes it particularly suited for the church as a whole, rather than just individuals—the fact that a group has set aside a day for worship and rest enhances the power and appeal of the practice itself.[63] Keeping this day allows us to remember we are both creatures and Christians. We need time to rest physically and recharge our batteries from our varied

BOOK LINK

A Geography of Time

We have already looked at how church buildings shape space; the present essay examines shapes of time. According to the philosopher Immanuel Kant, space and time are the forms of all human experience. Kant, following Isaac Newton, believed that time and space were absolute—always the same for everyone, everywhere—and thus subject to measurement and mathematical specification. David Harvey disagrees, claiming that whatever else it may be postmodernity is a condition that names new ways that we experience space and time (*The Condition of Postmodernity* [Oxford: Blackwell, 1990]).

Time is connected not only with space but also with *place*. This, at least, is the fascinating argument of Robert Levine's *A Geography of Time: or How Every Culture Keeps Time Just a Little Bit Differently* (New York: Basic Books, 1997). Levine's working assumption is that to understand a culture is to know the time values it lives by, its "tempo" or speed of life. This musical term is apt: North Americans live by the metronome of "clock time" (e.g., time measured in hours and minutes). Other cultures, however, live by "event time," where things begin to happen not at a particular o'clock but when people start doing something. In event time, an activity begins because people feel the time is right or because something else has happened (e.g., the train leaves the station because the cars are filled with passengers).

Levine, a social psychologist, has conducted extensive research into the way people in different cultures experience time. In one experiment he compares the pace of life in thirty-one different cities by measuring such things as the average walking speed of randomly selected pedestrians and the time it takes postal clerks to respond to a request for stamps. He concludes that people are prone to move faster in places with vital economies, a high degree of industrialization, larger populations, cooler climates, and a cultural orientation toward individualism (9).

To avoid misunderstanding about, say, why people don't show up for meetings at the appointed time, Levine counsels "temporal literacy," which is learning how to "read" a culture's views regarding activity and inactivity. He also encourages his readers to live in "middle time," somewhere between fast-paced clock time and slow-paced event time and between the tempo extremes of stress and boredom. In terms of the present work: the Christian cultural agent has to take every time captive to the time of Jesus Christ.

Kevin J. Vanhoozer

labors, and we need time to worship God publicly with other believers and to give heed to our spiritual state.

Keeping a sabbath offers significant benefits for holy busyness. It represents a countercultural practice, counter to the world and—truth be

BOOK LINK

Under the Unpredictable Plant

The apostle Paul twice exhorts his readers to "redeem" or "make best use of" the time (Eph. 5:16; Col. 4:5). How can we do that if, as the author of Ecclesiastes says, everything is vanity and if "it is an unhappy business that God has given to the sons of men to be busy with" (Eccles. 1:13 RSV)? What is the use of working if one's works neither last nor are remembered?

Eugene Peterson's *Under the Unpredictable Plant: An Exploration in Vocational Holiness* (Grand Rapids: Eerdmans, 1994) is a helpful tonic to all those who are busy with the unhappy business of mortality. The book is not really about either busyness or time, however; in fact, it is a study of the prophet Jonah. It's a book written for ministers who may be tempted to run away from what God is calling them to do in search of a more glamorous ministry.

What is relevant, however, is Peterson's distinction between "career" and "vocation." A career is the trajectory for one's work life that aims at self-advancement. What we could call "career time" is the time for us to get things done and to make a name for ourselves. Career time watches the clock and waits for no man, woman, or child.

Christian ministry, however, is not a career but a vocation. A pastor should seek not to promote his or her own name but only the name of Jesus Christ. Peterson asks his readers to think of holiness—that which is set apart for divine service—as something that pertains not only to individual and social morality but to one's work. What God has given us to do with our lives, whether we are Christian ministers or not, is best viewed in terms of vocation, not career. To set apart one's work is to do it "as unto the Lord." To see one's everyday work in terms of a response to God's call rather than as a way of advancing one's own name is to view time not as a disposable resource—a means to an end—but as a gift from God to be enjoyed and placed at his service. Only then can we say with the Preacher: "He has made everything beautiful in its time" (Eccles. 3:11).

Kevin J. Vanhoozer

told—counter to much of the church too. It steps away from the drive for achievement and consumption by marking off space from such pursuits. Perhaps one reason we struggle to keep a sabbath comes from a fear that doing so allows others to work more and get ahead of us. Indeed, the fear may be reasonable, yet holding to a sabbath despite this demonstrates faith that God gives us sufficient time for our work. Given how people complain about not having enough time for Bible study, prayer, and other spiritual disciplines, a sabbath offers an answer to such problems. A sabbath also

Interpreting Cultural Trends

reasserts, in the face of an increasingly globalized economic landscape, the importance of boundaries for how we live in time. Our goal should be to allow the sabbath to act as an optic lens for how we see the rest of the week.[64] Instead of letting the busyness of the week frame our time, we should allow our enjoyment of a sabbath to frame the week.

So What Do We Make of Martha?

In the midst of revising this essay I described what I was doing to a friend, who replied, "Oh, you're trying to rehabilitate Martha." My response is well, no, but yes. The story of Mary and Martha, and the latter's pique at her sister's unwillingness to help (Luke 10:38–42), is often taken as a condemnation of busyness. Jesus commends Mary because she makes listening to his teaching her priority over work, even over service to him. Seen in its literary context, between the parable of the Good Samaritan (10:30–37) and Jesus' instructions on how to pray (12:1–13), this story teaches that "our service to others is best set in the context of being in contact with God."[65] Holy busyness affirms the same thing. Priority belongs to relationship with God, and out of that should flow our activity. Too much busyness today is not rightly oriented, even if it has good motives, because it has lost sight of the primacy of knowing God. All the same, it should be said for Martha that what she did was not wrong in and of itself, but only in comparison to what she should have done.[66] She should have served but done so by subordinating her service to sitting at Jesus' feet. In the midst of a world so often frustrated over not having enough time to do what it wants to do, may God make us into a faithful church that lives in holy busyness as we wait expectantly for the Lord of time to draw time to an end.

Suggested Readings

"Busyness." *Social Research: An International Quarterly of the Social Sciences.* 72 (2005).

Chester, Tim. *The Busy Christian's Guide to Busyness.* Leicester, UK: Inter-Varsity, 2006.

Edwards, Jonathan. "The Preciousness of Time, and the Importance of Redeeming It." In *The Works of Jonathan Edwards*, rev. Edward Hickman, 233–36. Carlisle: Banner of Truth Trust, 1972.

Robinson, John P., and Geoffrey Godbey. *Time for Life: The Surprising Ways Americans Use Their Time.* 2nd ed. University Park: Pennsylvania State University Press, 1999.

Editorial Introduction

This next essay explores blogging, a recent trend in online interaction. Often, we may encounter a trend that itself is "of the moment," but the values it manifests will continue after the trend has become passé. Like other Internet technologies, blogging may soon be yesterday's technology, but its values of transparency and participation will endure. Thus, sometimes there is value in interpreting ephemeral trends that nonetheless capture a particular cultural moment and articulate larger realities.

8

Welcome to the Blogosphere

JUSTIN A. BAILEY

Every year Merriam-Webster releases a list of the top online definition requests. In 2003, the most sought-after definition was "democracy." The following year, however, the most requested word was not even *in* the dictionary. The demand prompted a provisional definition: "a Web site that contains an online personal journal with reflections, comments and often hyperlinks provided by the writer."[1] The word? Blog.

Like the online definition service, I was oblivious to the word until a friend invited me to visit his brand-new personal blog. All it took to get there was a simple click of the mouse: I clicked the link in my friend's email and found myself in the world of the weblog—or, as it is more commonly known, the blogosphere.

The region of the blogosphere in which I landed is known as Xanga: an online community with thousands of web diaries, most of them written by adolescents. As a youth pastor, my interest in the blogosphere was more than passing, especially when I discovered that nearly all of the students in my ministry had sites they updated on a regular basis.

The day I discovered Xanga was the day my youth pastoral naïveté died. I learned what was really going on in the lives of the kids in my youth group. While I was taken aback at the profane content on many of their sites (some

T FOR THE OOLKIT

This essay exemplifies how to interpret a cultural trend in which we ourselves participate. The author has been a blogger and reflects on what blogging signifies, then considers what the church can learn from and teach the blogging community. The most effective cultural interpretation we do is often of the texts and trends with which we are most familiar.

of the kids I considered leaders), the level of disclosure in the journals was truly astounding. One girl related how her boyfriend had just sneaked out the back window as her parents were arriving home. She was obviously not concerned that her parents might find this out by simply logging on and reading it, evidenced by the fact that in a previous post she revealed that her father had been unfaithful to her mother early in their marriage. Things were not all bad, however; in a later entry she wrote of breaking up with her boyfriend out of a desire to "grow closer to God." For better or for worse, her life was all there—uncensored, unedited, and waiting to be read by anyone who knew how to find her site.

The discovery was revolutionary for me. I made blog reading a daily part of my life, used the concept of blogs to teach the psalms, and even tried to use the medium myself by setting up a daily devotional blog for the youth group. My initial attraction to blogging was that of a youth pastor: I wanted to be in the blogosphere because that was where my kids were. I was struck by the fact that while these young people were uncomfortable revealing these things to their parents or spiritual leaders, they had no inhibitions about sharing them with the online community. The more I read, the more it became clear to me that the blogosphere deserved concentrated thought. Discovering the blogosphere was like being dropped headfirst into another world—a "world and work of meaning" composed almost entirely out of electronic text. But if the blogosphere is another world, where did it come from? What are the rules that govern it? And what does its emergence mean?

A Brief History of the Blogosphere

The blogosphere did not emerge *ex nihilo*, nor is it the final stage in the evolution of communication technology. Blogging bears definite similarities to older cyberspace architecture—billboard services, listservs, and instant messaging—and has already aided the rise of new media, like wikis and podcasts. But as a subculture of cyberspace, the blogosphere is itself a "complex whole" with unique values and conventions.

The blogosphere is much larger than the Xanga community, but its rapid growth is a relatively recent phenomenon. While the label wasn't applied until 1997, the first weblogs began to appear as early as 1994.[2] These original sites were frequently updated pages listing links to interesting corners of cyberspace that a weblog editor found while surfing the web. As more people began making their own lists and linking their sites to one another, a small community emerged; yet the number of people who could actually publish weblogs was limited to the web-savvy. One longtime blogger explains: "The promise of the web was that everyone could publish, that a thousand voices could flourish, communicate, connect. The truth was that only those people who knew how to code a web page could make their voices heard."[3]

That changed in July of 1999. Andrew Smales, a twenty-nine-year-old Toronto programmer, envisioned an "online diary community" where people could browse personal web pages without having to click blindly through Internet search engines. While working on a module that would enable common people to bypass technical web-writing code, he discovered the nascent blogging community, and *Pitas*, the first do-it-yourself blog-building tool, was born.[4] *Blogger* and *Groksoup* were launched a month later, and suddenly people had the tools to build their own blogs without needing to know any specialized programming languages or web-scripting codes. The tools were just what many were waiting for: with the new technology in place, blogs began multiplying by the thousands. Software companies rushed in to capitalize on the new trend, and today's prospective bloggers have hundreds of options for publishing their thoughts.

TAKING IT *FURTHER*

One of the difficulties of interpreting cutting-edge trends such as emerging communication and information technologies is that they are still in flux in terms of their development. At some point one has to try to anticipate coming changes while not wedding oneself to the exact manifestation of the current form of the trend. This is especially true in technology where the concept of planned obsolescence creates a shelf life for all products. The technology we have today will not be the same as what we will have in six months, let alone the next six years. Yet if we are careful, we can tap into things that are at the core of these technologies and then say things that are meaningful despite their constant development and sophistication. For instance, acknowledging the place of blogging in a long line of development of information and communication technologies—including electronic bulletin boards, chatrooms, instant messaging, and listservs—allows the individual to anticipate emerging developments such as podcasts and other innovations like VOIP (Internet phone).

The Form of the Weblog

While this rapid influx into the blogosphere has produced a diverse number of weblog types, two general styles typify the medium. "Filter-style" weblogs continue to be link-driven and follow the original formula. A blogger will link to unique websites or news stories that she has found, typically accompanied by commentary offering her own take on the link. These weblogs are often an attempt to interact with the mainstream media: by providing alternative perspectives, criticism of sources, and related links, they allow weblog editors to play a unique role as filters and interpreters of the news for their readers. They represent what bloggers call "participatory media," and they have generated a firestorm of exclusion and embrace within the traditional journalistic community.

New software developed by programmers like Smales led to a second style of weblog. Pyra Labs' *Blogger* software, for example, dropped the requirement of links and provided a would-be weblog creator with nothing more than an empty box in which the blogger could type anything she pleased. This meant a shift in definition; a weblog was no longer defined by its links but rather by frequent posting of new material. These new weblogs became something like the "online diary community" that Smales had envisioned, although that is a rather narrow description of their diverse content. Whereas filter-style weblogs are built around links, these "free-style" weblogs can be built around anything. Epitomizing individual expression, they can include anything from musings on the human condition to the mundane account of a visit to the grocery store.

A critical component that both styles of weblogs include is the opportunity for reader feedback. Readers can link to, comment on, or participate in weblog discussion. Xanga, for example, also gives its readers the opportunity to reward good or insightful writing with "E-props," an Internet currency of goodwill. Other weblogs provide "trackbacks," which allow readers to participate in the buzz surrounding a particular entry by following the trail of like-minded blogs that have linked to it.

Participation is the key word, since without it the blogosphere cannot perpetuate itself. A piece in the *New Yorker* entitled "You've Got Blog" captured this process memorably: "Other people who have blogs . . . read your blog and if they like it they blog your blog on their own blog."[5] Through interaction and participation the blogosphere expands and cultivates, resulting in estimates of as many as 53.4 million blogs at the end of 2005.[6]

Interpreting Cultural Trends

Practical Blogology

Style and substance vary widely throughout the blogosphere, yet there are several values that define the medium. The first is *transparency*. Bloggers tell you exactly who they are, what they think, and what they feel—with a level of disclosure that is, at times, shocking. Blogger Leila Fast explains: "When I started this blog, I did so on the premise that I would be painfully honest. I decided that this would be a place, perhaps the only place, where I would bare it all."[7] Such vulnerability is not, however, without consequences. Some may remember the notorious "Washingtonienne," who was fired from her Capitol Hill job in 2004 after thirteen days of blogging about her sex life.[8] In one survey, 36% of bloggers confessed that their postings have gotten them into trouble; 6% said that this happens on a regular basis.[9]

Related to the value of transparency is the value of *immediacy*. While all entries are archived for later reading, blogs always display the most recent information at the top of the page. A blog entry thus captures a particular moment by portraying how one is feeling at a particular point in time. To preserve the feeling of immediacy, many bloggers write without using spell-check or editing their prose. If their writing is sloppy today, they will write better tomorrow. The point is that they continue to write.

Thirdly, and most importantly, bloggers affirm the value of *intellectual self-reliance*. By virtue of their decision to post their thoughts publicly, bloggers are saying that their point of view is important, valuable, and deserves to be heard. For many, blogging becomes a journey of intellectual self-discovery. The more a blogger writes, interacting with the deluge of data she encounters, the more she becomes aware of her own interests and opinions. Blogging is thus a means of cultural agency. With its blend of reflection, reaction, and ranting, the blogosphere has provided "new possibilities for the Internet as a rhetorical space."[10] At their best, bloggers are thoughtful cultural critics who are able to articulate what they believe even as they evaluate the information they receive. One well-known blogger speaks for many when she writes: "Weblogs are no panacea for the crippling effects of a media-saturated culture, but I believe they are one antidote."[11] In their self-reliance, bloggers have an aversion to buying what the establishment is selling, choosing rather to process information critically and reflectively—all in the context of a friendly and equally self-aware blogging community.

Indeed, there is no shortage of reflection on the practice of blogging by bloggers themselves. Every blogger's first entry seems to be something of an explanation or apology for why they are starting this particular weblog. Perhaps it seems a bit presumptuous when one begins; after all, starting a blog presupposes the fact that there is an audience who wants to read what you have to say. While bloggers have bypassed editors and publishers, no one seems to want to bypass the audience.

Writing for an audience, however, can be a temptation to vanity, and the medium frequently has been criticized as narcissistic. One traditional journalist levels this critique:

> What began as the ultimate outsider activity . . . is turning into the same insider's game played by the old establishment media the bloggerati love to critique. . . . They've fallen in love with themselves, each other and the beauty of what they're creating. The cult of media celebrity hasn't been broken by the Internet's democratic tendencies; it's just found new enabling technology.[12]

The argument is that the blogosphere frequently confuses the value of information with the "cool quotient" of the person spreading it.[13]

Blogging has certainly produced its own celebrities, who are known as "The A-List." One such superstar, Jason Kottke, was featured in a *New Yorker* piece. Kottke is widely admired among bloggers as a thoughtful critic of Web culture. In February 2005, Kottke's popularity led to a bold career move: he quit his job as a web designer in order to begin receiving patronage from his readers. He explained the career change as an attempt to "revisit the idea of arts patronage in the context of the Internet."[14] For many, the equation of blogging with the arts is a stretch. Paying Michelangelo to paint the Sistine Chapel is one thing; paying Kottke to list his top ten movies is quite another.

Nevertheless, in the blogosphere it is not what you know but who links to you that counts. Getting blogged by a high-profile blogger like Kottke "is the blog equivalent of having your book featured on 'Oprah': it generally means a substantial boost in traffic."[15] If the traffic is significant, a blog may earn a spot on Technorati.com, a sort of blog best seller list. Technorati, which tracks more than twenty million blogs, lists not only the top one hundred blogs but also the most-discussed news stories, movies, and books.[16] Each category is measured in how many pages are linking to a particular blog, story, or book. With the top blogs garnering well over ten thousand links, all blogs, it would seem, are *not* connected equal.

This growing sense of inequality has worried idealistic bloggers ever since the tools became widely available in 1999. As early as 2000, long be-

Interpreting Cultural Trends

fore most were even aware of blogging's existence, a group of bloggers calling themselves "BLOGMA 2001" issued a tongue-in-cheek call for a regime change within the blogging community. Complaining that the "A-List" celebrities had nothing better to talk about than themselves and were no longer inter-

ested in good links and content, they called for "all true webloggers" to rise up and overthrow "the bourgeoisie" and reinstate "virtuous and pure weblogging."[17] Their tone, while ironic, already represented real concerns that the blogosphere had been compromised and would no longer be able to deliver on the promise of egalitarian opportunity of expression. More recently, critics have complained that minorities lack a real voice in the blogosphere, and that while blogs are evenly written by men and women, the overwhelming majority of A-Listers are men.[18]

Some have even wondered if the blogosphere's rapid expansion will cause it to collapse upon itself. While Technorati estimates that a new blog is created every 7.4 seconds, a 2003 study found that over two-thirds of all blogs are abandoned within four months of their inception.[19] Undoubtedly, much of the new blog activity is faddish; but the high abandonment rate could also be representative of the generational restlessness of the blogging majority. An astounding 90% of blogs are written by teens and twenty-somethings.[20] Whether this is the logical outworking of the cliché "never trust anyone over thirty" or simply another case of tech-savvy youth leading the way, the blogosphere remains the province of the young. As such, it is difficult to forecast where the blogging revolution will lead. But for some in that remaining one-third of disciplined bloggers, the emergence of the blogosphere has already set in motion some exciting cultural shifts.

The Rise of Participatory Media

The struggle between citizen's media and conventional media is not a new one. But since 2001, bloggers have dramatically recast this struggle in cyberspace by flooding the mainstream with "random acts of journalism."[21] While news organizations like ABC News, FOX News, and MSNBC have begun to publish multiple news-based blogs, many traditional journalists question the worth of the bloggers' contributions. Bloggers are, after all, amateurs: their reporting is limited, their writing mediocre, and their blogs filled with bad spelling, confirmation bias, and overconfidence. What excites bloggers, however, is not the belief that citizen's media is inherently more credible or valuable, but the fact that the "professionals" have lost sovereignty over who gets to participate in the conversation.

This movement is "participatory journalism" because it is an attempt to redefine media as a public, participatory endeavor. Instead of simply consuming the news as reported, bloggers question, interpret, and fact-check it. Bloggers become co-creators of the news process, filters who decide what is important, what is spin, and what needs greater examination. As amateur journalists, bloggers have the freedom to write with uninhibited personality and may pursue issues from which mainstream editors shy away. And what one blogger may lack in professional expertise, the blogging community makes up for in collective intelligence. Instead of one or two professional editors, bloggers are able to mobilize an army of fact-checkers just waiting for a generalization, exaggeration, or piece of skewed research to pounce upon. Moreover, bloggers have repeatedly turned the question of credibility on its head, embarrassing the mainstream media, most notably in 2004 when CBS went public with the infamous National Guard memos.[22]

It is for reasons like these that many serious journalists are beginning to see bloggers as not competing with but complementing their own work—creating a conversation that is redefining journalism.[23] One media critic explains that the "smokescreen of polling" has been mainstream media's sad excuse for interactivity, and bloggers are not buying it. He writes that there is a new movement in journalism that sees it as "a conversation, not a lecture . . . the new breed [believes] that ongoing feedback—and interaction with that feedback—advances the story."[24] It is the sign of a shift from the audience as passive consumer of the news to participative co-creator.

A Shift in Authority

The blogging revolution also represents signs of a shift in the location of authority. In postmodern fashion, authority has been decentralized from the handful of experts who hold the truth, to include anyone who wants to participate in the conversation. This is the conclusion of one well-respected blogger as she evaluates the various blog forms: "Each is evidence of a staggering shift from an age of carefully controlled information provided by sanctioned authorities (and artists), to an unprecedented opportunity for individual expression on a worldwide scale."[25] Blogging, then, is a statement about epistemology. To the question, "Who holds the truth?" bloggers answer: "We do—all of us."

The result of the shift is that people are increasingly sensitive to spin and suspicious of truth claims. Or at least we like to think that we are. The ironic success of slogans like "Don't Buy the Hype" or Sprite's "Image Is Nothing" marketing campaign shows that we live in a world where people want to think that they are no longer automatically buying what the establishment is selling—whoever the establishment is.

So in a spin-sensitive world, how do we choose whose products to buy, whose information to believe, and whose truth to live? One way we choose is on the basis of the relationships we have developed with the people recommending the product, disseminating the information, and proclaiming the truth. And the blogosphere is an ideal place to develop these relationships. One columnist for *Wired* writes that the Web is increasingly becoming a space not of connected documents, but of connected minds:

> What happens when we start seeing the Web as a matrix of minds, not documents? Networks based on trust become an essential tool. You start evaluating the relevance of data based not on search query results but on personal testimonies. ("This information is useful because six minds I admire have found it useful.")[26]

In other words, rather than a naïve ignorance of spin, there is an individual choice to tolerate a certain spin from people whom we trust.

This has at least been the conclusion of the business world. Companies are learning to use blogs to connect to customers by harnessing the human voice that blogs provide, which inspires trust and personalizes their products.[27] It is not that there is no longer salesmanship involved; rather, the kind of interaction facilitated by blogging gives the customer a broader basis for evaluating trustworthiness. Once customers are connected to a company via virtual relationship, they are much more likely to buy whatever the company is selling.

The same can be said of truth claims. People are more likely to decide that something is true based on the testimony of people they trust than they are in response to depersonalized information, which for all they know could be nothing more than smoke and mirrors. Trust, of course, does not equal truthfulness; but the "believer" is at least making her faith act based on relationships she has cultivated, even if they are only virtual ones. The blogging revolution is thus a sign that people are seeking a community of trustworthy interpreters to help them decide what is true.

A Shift in Ecclesiology

A community of trustworthy interpreters: that sounds a bit like a church, doesn't it? So how are Christians responding to the blogosphere? As with many mainstream trends, a distinctively Christian blogging subculture has emerged. As of summer 2005, Blogs4God.com listed 1,250 Christian blogs in its search engine, and this reflects only those who choose to register their blogs.[28] Christian blogs are so numerous that one Christian blogger from the Philippines releases an annual list of nominees for what he calls the "Superblessed Christian Blog Awards."[29] Other popular Christian blogs belong to Beliefnet's Blog Heaven, a place "where faith blogs go if they're good."[30] It seems that "God-bloggers" have an A-List as well.

Many in the Christian blogosphere, however, try to resist categorization. Tim Bednar represented the sentiments of many Christian bloggers when he explained to *Leadership* that "in the blogosphere, labels matter little; reputations mean everything. Spiritual bloggers often take an incarnational approach; we bring Christ into our conversations on *The Da Vinci Code*, Janet Jackson, theology, or politics. We let the reader decide whether we are spiritual."[31] Bednar's answer is symptomatic of the label-defying decentralization in which bloggers seem to revel. It leads to an important question: If authority is being taken from the hands of the "sanctioned authorities" and placed in the hands of the public, could this mean that the authority structure of the church is changing as well? For Bednar, that is exactly what it means. He recently posted a paper with the most serious theological evaluation of the blogosphere to date. The title of his manifesto? "We Know More Than Our Pastors."[32]

Similar to the way a network of journalism blogs tries to bring collective intelligence to bear on the news, Bednar believes that a network of spiritual blogs exceeds the reach of any single pastor. He writes that bloggers value the medium because "they can participate without being filtered by church structures, denominational restrictions or even doctrinal impurity." Bloggers, who "have grown tired of pastors being the gatekeepers of what is important," are now taking the priesthood of the believer to its Internet extreme.[33]

A former pastor himself, Bednar is the founder of e-Church.com, which is a representative site of what he and others call the cyberchurch: an online community of believing bloggers who use Internet technology. Using blogs to chronicle their faith journeys, encourage one another, and post prayer requests, they see blogging as a spiritual discipline. As they participate in online spiritual formation, they "link the cyberchurch into existence."[34]

While the cyberchurch is for Bednar and others the most exciting part of their spiritual lives, a place where they share life and care for one another, it is not their final aim. Bednar believes that bloggers are the vanguard of a coming transformation in the structures of the traditional church: "The phenomenon of blogging is transforming our expectations of church. Soon this meme—this product of our online spiritual formation—will emerge from our cyberchurch and transform the traditional church."[35] Bednar believes that this grassroots revival will result in what he calls the "participatory church."[36]

Take Up and Blog

There is much in the blogosphere to affirm. The transparency on display in the blogosphere, for example, should remind us that the church must be a place where people are transparent before the Lord as well as among the redeemed community (James 5:16). John reminds us that confession of sin is the prelude to walking in the light, which in turn leads to true fellowship with God and neighbor (1 John 1:6–10). The prevalence of online diary communities is an indication that people are longing for fellowship and need a place for honest confession. The more I read adolescent Xanga

As with the earlier essay on Eminem, we here come across another medium that seems to serve as a confessional. Perhaps one of the oddest aspects of blogging is the transparency and raw honesty that marks many of the entries, laid bare for the entire world to see. Those who are familiar with this trend note that this has led to individuals being dismissed from companies and overlooked for employment, not to mention the implications for others' personal lives. Perhaps here the words of Proverbs may give some guidance. "When words are many, sin is not absent, but he who holds his tongue is wise" (Prov. 10:19; see also 17:27–28; 18:7). Is it fair to say that in some cases this might be a form of confession without repentance?

sites, the more they strike me as confessionals—not to a pastor or priest, but to whoever will listen. They are a cry to be known and accepted. Many times the comments on these sites are nothing less than encouragement, exhortation, and forgiveness, oftentimes from people who have never met the "penitent." In a society that avoids personal responsibility (a problem made worse by the anonymity of the Internet), public journal entries are an invitation for *someone* to hold the writer responsible, yet to do so in a way that permits self-discovery.

This empathy is laudable but limited by the medium because it lacks the intimacy of embodied presence. Yet, we need to admit that one of the reasons why so many have gone online in search of community is that they have not found it in our churches. One such seeker left a heartbreaking comment on a popular Christian blog:

> There is the real world where I live which is broken, messy, scary, profane, filled with risk, sadness, loneliness, sickness, hate, fear, doubt, death, love, hope, mercy, grace, friends, faith and faithlessness. . . . Then there is the church world. I haven't talked to anyone in that world about what is real in many, many years.[37]

It is a tragic testimony to the state of our churches that many people experience virtual community as more real than that of the offline world. People need embodied relationships and real space to build true intimacy. Without this intimacy, concentrated disembodied interaction breeds emotional promiscuity. The church should be a place where vulnerability is welcomed in redemptive relationships, a reconciled community that listens to each other's stories and engages one another with the hope of the gospel.

Bloggers are not, however, the first to alert us to the centrality of building community in our churches. From the mega-church to the meta-church,

Interpreting Cultural Trends

evangelicalism is full of programs designed to build community. But the fact that body life remains so fragmented suggests that the wound is deeper than we think. We need to evaluate seriously the organizational architecture of our churches and ask if they are filtering our congregations apart instead of fostering true community and conversation. Do our church structures distance people in the congregation from one another? Do our recruiting drives, step-by-step discipleship programs, and Sunday school curricula encourage passivity or participation? Are we fostering intellectual self-discovery with vigor equal to that of the blogging community? If the "smokescreen of polling" is mainstream media's sad excuse for interactivity, could we also say that the church's spiritual-gift-based recruiting practices are nothing more than smokescreens that mask a lack of opportunity for real participation in our churches?

Yet, creating a participatory church is not without serious difficulties. What happens when we begin to infuse the praxis of the church with the participatory values on display in the blogosphere? As evidenced by Bednar's weariness of pastoral gatekeeping, expertise is often devalued or even dismissed. The expertise of many pastors has been hard-won, forged from years of experience and disciplined study of Scripture. While pastors should not be the sole participants in the conversation, their perspective is crucial, especially when rooted in exposition of the Word. There is an undeniable anti-authoritarian impulse inherent in the blogosphere, which ironically can make the most meaningful voices (in the form of pastoral care and expertise) less accessible than ever, lost in the din of a hundred self-publishing, self-proclaimed "experts."

More significantly, in Bednar's vision of the participatory church, definitions begin to change. Bednar's desire is to contextualize and re-envision the Christian faith for a generation of participants. The challenge of contextualization, however, is in reinterpreting key terms without gutting them of their rich biblical meanings. For example, Bednar writes that bloggers like himself are re-envisioning preaching:

> Our audience is responsible to synthesize and discover their truth. We release ourselves from the responsibility of having to "lead someone to Christ" or disciple them. *We have no other agenda than to share the truth as we experience it*, yet it is our belief that the Holy Spirit speaks through us. Thus, we preach.[38]

What drives Bednar's reinterpretation is the fear that preaching in the classical sense is domineering like a lecture; he wants to ensure that no voices are excluded from the conversation. But can we reduce biblical imperatives like "preach the word" and "make disciples of all nations" to "share the truth as you experience it"? We share our own experiences, yes, but there is also a metanarrative—sovereign over our experiences—to which we must submit. The careful exposition of the text, then, should not dominate the conversation (to the point of excluding all other voices) so much as provide a "grammar" that keeps us rooted in truth and speaking the same language.

Moreover, in a medium that places such emphasis on participation in the conversation, we need to ask whether bloggers are guilty of "always learning but never able to acknowledge the truth" (2 Tim. 3:7). The purpose of dialogue is to arrive at truth, not simply to listen to each other speak. Yet, in postmodern fashion, bloggers shy away from objective truth claims. This is certainly not to say that all bloggers believe there is no such thing as objective truth. One does wonder, however, if they will ever arrive at it. The value of a truth statement is lessened in the blogosphere because, after all, it is just an opinion and can always be retracted or modified later. With such a focus on immediacy, what is true today may not be true for long—tomorrow's post can always change it. Bednar acknowledges this pitfall when he writes, "We need to reach a point where we jump off the merry-go-round and we begin to live the truth."[39] But what truth will they live? Since many eschew doctrinal statements, confessions, and creeds, the kind of orthodoxy that emerges from the cyberchurch will be—at its best—a very loose orthodoxy. Indeed, orthodoxy is difficult for bloggers to assent to, since it automatically excludes many (heretical?) voices from the conversation. "In the cyberchurch," Bednar writes, "there is no authority that determines what is 'in' and what is 'out.'"[40]

A Theology of Participation

The participatory shift of which the blogosphere is symptomatic demands a thoughtful and balanced response from Christians. While I am not willing to go as far as Bednar does in many of his conclusions, the question he raises is a good one, but it must be nuanced: how shall we as Christians engage an increasingly participatory culture while maintaining a healthy sense of respect for the authority of Scripture and tradition?[41]

What we need is a theology of participation, one that marshals the wealth of biblical imagery on what it means to be the church. Paul gave the Corinthians the picture of a human body, where each member has no life or purpose except in relationship with the other members. Scripture

Interpreting Cultural Trends

elsewhere describes the church as a kingdom of priests, a Spirit-built temple, and a holy nation. Biblical participation means much more than entering into conversation with one another. It means serving, suffering, and sacrificing for each other's sake. Scripture's view of participation goes significantly further than the blogosphere's and calls us to its standard whether or not we find ourselves in a participatory culture.

Our theology of participation will also need to clarify the doctrine of the priesthood of all believers. Timothy George has argued that by this doctrine, the reformers did not mean "I am my own priest," but "we are priests for one another." The former leads to unmediated private interpretation of Scripture and life; the latter means a common confession, shared life, and intentional ministry in a local, visible community of believers.[42] In the end, individuation of the truth leads away from true participation, not toward it.

Indeed, locality and visibility are critical elements of authentic participation, which must be active and lived out apart from the relative safety of cyberspace. Our theology of participation must challenge bloggers who often substitute virtual intimacy for actual intimacy. As one person writes, "On a day-to-day basis, I am more intimately aware of the latest happenings in the world of my 10 favorite bloggers than I am of what's going on with my closest friends. And of those 10 bloggers, I've only met two or three in person."[43] Blogs can give readers the luxury of knowing intimate details of a blogger's life without having to engage the person. Reading a blog can be like flipping through someone's journal. (Andrew Smales, who developed *Pitas*, actually attributes the success of the weblog to this voyeuristic thrill.[44]) Yet, even when interaction occurs, it can go only so far. Examples of virtual communities emerging into real life exist, but are rare.[45]

So why do so many find more success in maintaining ten online relationships than three offline relationships? Quite simply, it is easier. The nature of the blogosphere reduces the risk, insecurity, and awkwardness of dealing with someone face to face. Admittedly, introverts (like Bednar and myself) thrive in the blogosphere. In this way, the blogosphere can actually become an impediment rather than an impetus to true participation. A blog can become just another source of distraction from the hard work of real interaction and true community. As it has been put, "The temptation is to live in a world of simulated images, simulated commitment and thus to lead a simulated life."[46]

The critical thing missing in the blogosphere is that step into the real itself. We need an active sort of participation that transcends the online world. There is a subtle temptation in the blogosphere to be content with cyberspace fellowship. But for all its promise, the cyberchurch can never be a real church. Cyber-parishioners can never receive the sacraments or lay hands on someone. The beauty and meaning of these things is bound up in our physical presence to perform or receive them. And despite Christian bloggers' desire to engage non-believers in incarnational ministry, John reminds us that the incarnation, as well as incarnational relationships, is rooted in physicality: the Word became flesh and dwelt among us. Embodied fellowship, as one Christian philosopher writes, "is an irreducible and incomparable quality that cannot be adequately translated into any other form of communication, cyberspace or otherwise. . . . When the flesh becomes data it fails to dwell among us."[47] This is not to say, however, that blogging ought to be excluded as a means of communication. It simply means that we are aware of the limitations inherent in the medium and employ moderation in its use. For the blogosphere has much to teach us, particularly in terms of cultural agency.

Conclusion

As we seek to become cultural agents—reliable filters who give trustworthy interpretations of the world through a trinitarian lens—how shall we gain a hearing in a conversation whose participants are quick to dismiss us? The answer that the blogosphere gives us is this: transparency in the principles we hold, the processes we follow, and the persons we are.[48] Transparency in the blogosphere means an admission of bias: an understanding that everyone writes with a certain spin, and a willingness to disclose one's own starting points, intentions, and vested interests. For many, transparency is the critical first step toward building credibility with an audience.

Suggested Readings

Blood, Rebecca, ed. *We've Got Blog: How Weblogs Are Changing Our Culture.* Cambridge, MA: Perseus, 2002.

Hewitt, Hugh. *Blog: Understanding the Information Reformation That's Changing Your World.* Nashville: Thomas Nelson, 2005.

Houston, Graham. *Virtual Morality: Christian Ethics in the Computer Age.* Leicester, UK: Apollos, 1998.

Jewell, John P. *Wired for Ministry: How the Internet, Visual Media, and Other New Technologies Can Serve the Church.* Grand Rapids: Brazos, 2004.

Stone, Biz. *Who Let the Blogs Out? A Hyperconnected Peek at the World of Weblogs.* New York: St. Martin's Press, 2004.

BOOK LINK

The Search; Habits of the High-Tech Heart

Marshall McLuhan, for many years director of the Center for Culture and Technology at the University of Toronto, never tired of exploring how changes in communications media affect not only the way we send messages to one another but how we think. Culture, he believed, is shaped more by the nature of the media by which people communicate than by the content of their communication. By this standard, the advent of the Internet qualifies as a cultural revolution. The Internet has changed the way we shop, the way we learn, the way we communicate, and the way we relate to other people.

This, at least, is the thesis of John Battelle's *The Search: How Google and Its Rivals Rewrote the Rules of Business and Transformed Our Culture* (New York: Penguin, 2005). Search engines like Google allow us to monitor what people are searching for and thus provide "a fascinating summary of what our culture is looking for" (2). Every day, millions of people make known their desires, wants, questions, and fears through their Internet searches. Battelle sees the sum total of these searches as forming the single most important cultural artifact in the history of humanity: the "Database of Intentions." It is "a massive clickstream [the "exhaust" of our online lives] database of desires, needs, wants, and preferences that can be discovered, subpoenaed, archived, tracked, and exploited for all sorts of ends" (6) and, as such, is a downloadable record of everyday life.

Whereas blogging is direct communication with others via the Internet, we communicate indirectly (to whom?) through our googling: Ye shall know them by their searches. Internet searches are the database deposit of our desire to be and our effort to exist. Indeed, blogging and searching for one's own name may both be signs of our desire not only to be, but to be immortal: "Is not existing forever in the indexes of Google and others the modern-day equivalent of carving our stories into stone?" (284).

Virtual immortality is hardly bodily resurrection, and "informationism" is hardly a viable faith. Christians must say more than "In Google we trust." This is the moral of Quentin Schultze's *Habits of the High-Tech Heart: Living Virtuously in the Information Age* (Grand Rapids: Baker, 2002). As the author of this essay makes clear, blogging is no substitute for participating in a flesh-and-blood community. Yes, it's easier on the Web. It's easier to inform oneself than to be transformed. Yet Internet information in cyberspace is no substitute for moral formation in community. Schultze rightly reminds us that innovations in the cyberworld do not necessarily make us better people. The good life is not byte-sized, nor is it measured in nanoseconds. As the search engines get more powerful and the information train gets longer, we must continue to ask ourselves "whether our cyber-practices are making us better persons and our society more civil and democratic" (18).

Kevin J. Vanhoozer

Editorial Introduction

We now turn to a radicalized version of human enhancement present in the transhumanist movement. Perhaps unfamiliar to many, this movement combines an unwavering devotion to technological progress with the desire to "improve" humanity to anticipate the next stage in "biological evolution." This essay introduces a number of vital issues that span a vast area of theological, philosophical, and ethical questions that beg to be addressed by the contemporary church. In so doing, this essay represents the sort of forward thinking that should overcome the reactive mentality that often marks how the church responds to technology and cultural trends.

9

Human 2.0

Transhumanism as a Cultural Trend

MATTHEW EPPINETTE

Introduction

I WAS BORN human.
This was merely due to the hand of fate acting at a particular place and time.
But while fate made me human, it also gave me the power to do something
about it. The ability to change myself, to upgrade my human form, with the
aid of technology. To become cyborg—part human, part machine. This is
the extraordinary story of my adventure as the first human entering into a
Cyber World; a world which will, most likely, become the next evolution-
ary step for humankind.[1]

A shocking statement to be sure. No doubt straight from the inside flap
of the latest science-fiction best seller. But this is no fictional monologue.
These are the opening words of Kevin Warwick—a leading researcher
and professor of cybernetics at the University of Reading, England—as
he recounts his experience of becoming the first cyborg.

There is a group of people who, like Warwick, believe that human beings are simply a product of "the hand of fate," that the present life is all there is, and that no greater being or higher power exists. Yet, like all humans, they have a longing for transcendence. So how can this gap be bridged? Warwick and others are applying the tools of reason and technology to flesh and blood, skeleton and muscle, in order to create a new kind of humanity that goes beyond who we are today and reaches for immortality.

The World Transhumanist Association has banded together to put the tools of body and brain to work in pursuit of transcendence and immortality. Transhumanists are looking to technology to alter radically what it means to be human, to become posthuman. Just as a chimpanzee cannot conceive of what it would be like to be human, so we cannot conceive fully what it would be like to be posthuman. A posthuman is a being so completely different, so advanced, that it is difficult—if not impossible—to describe. A transhuman, then, is someone working toward becoming posthuman. Transhumanism is a small but growing cultural movement that is a logical outworking of the spirit of our age: whatever *can* be done scientifically and technologically *should* be done.

Transhumanism attempts to present a comprehensive account of human existence. It tries to answer "two of the most important universal questions: (1) 'What does it mean to be human?' and (2) 'How do I live my life in a way that brings true happiness?'"[2] Belief systems answer these questions in the way that they explain *where we are and how we got here*, and *where we are going and how to get there*. In light of this, as we will see, transhumanism presents a gospel of technological salvation with striking parallels to the scriptural message. Thus, the biblical story line of creation, fall, redemption, and consumation provides a framework for evaluating and responding to transhumanism. We will explore transhumanism as a logical extension of commonly held assumptions about technology and the physical world.

Upgrading the World

The last quarter of the twentieth century was marked by the rise of the information age with innovations such as the personal computer and the Internet. Related to this informational revolution was the growth of the field of applied biology, or biotechnology. Biotechnologies are employed in the manipulation of human and animal tissues, in the modification of plants and crops, and in the development and delivery of pharmaceuticals. Examples include DNA fingerprinting, genetically modified corn, home pregnancy tests, and synthetic insulin.[3]

This convergence of technologies has led some to refer to the twenty-first century as the "biotech century."[4] Already, the complete human genome has

been sequenced and made available for download via the Internet.[5] As of the summer of 2005, more than 170 biotech drugs were available and at least three hundred more were in clinical trials; there were 1,473 biotechnology companies in the U.S. employing around two hundred thousand people, and the 314 publicly held biotechnology companies had a market capitalization of $311 billion.[6]

While the prospect of a biotech century has encountered mixed reaction—protests have been held at the Biotechnology Industry Organization,[7] and three California counties have banned genetically modified crops[8]—transhumanists have embraced it with passion. They view biotechnology as *the* source of tools for improving the human condition. Among the specific biotechnologies they embrace are genetics, stem cell research, cloning, and nanotechnology. Transhumanists believe that progress in these areas has put us on the cusp of a colossal breakthrough—the ability to modify our very selves, to alter human nature in a fundamental way.

The "whatever can be done should be done" spirit of our age is a symptom of the belief that technology is inherently good and that it holds the solution to many, if not most, of the problems intrinsic to human existence: contingency, dependency, and finitude. Ours is an era of unprecedented technological advancement that both depends on and supports this technicism. These ideas underlie not only transhumanism but also the assumptions of many in our society. For example, the mainstream publication *Popular Science* proclaims, "Science will help us live longer, smarter, stronger" by the development of artificial muscles, smart drugs, and external wombs, which will lead to "a better brain," and "cures for everything."[9]

TAKING IT *FURTHER*

As a highly technological movement, transhumanism makes many of its important and explanatory documents available solely in electronic format. For example, *The Transhumanist Declaration, Transhumanist Values,* and *The Transhumanist FAQ* are all available online at www.trans humanism.org. In addition, the peer-reviewed *Journal of Evolution and Technology* is available only on the Internet at www.jetpress.org.

Scientific developments have set only part of the stage for transhumanism; philosophical and cultural trends such as individualism and postmodernism also contribute. Individualism is the idea that one's own needs, interests, and desires are more important than those of others or of any larger group or community. In our culture, this emphasis on individuality has, in many ways, become a radical personal autonomy under which each person is a law unto himself or herself. The term "postmodernism" is used in a variety of ways, most of which encompass the idea that any kind of universal story or metanarrative is at best suspect and more likely a tool of manipulation or control. Postmodernity thus rejects traditional religious views and values, favoring—in conjunction with individualism—personal constructions of origins, ethics, and eschatology.

One area where technicism, individualism, and postmodernism intersect is in the nascent discussions on the distinction between therapy and enhancement.[10] Historically, medicine has been dedicated to the treatment of disease and the restoration of health, but emerging biotechnologies make it increasingly possible to move beyond traditional notions of healthy toward "better than well."[11] This echoes the eugenics movement of the early twentieth century, which sought to improve humanity by careful breeding. The present incarnation is a form of private eugenics through which individuals pursue their own personal sense of betterment and wellness. Examples include the use of performance-enhancing drugs in sports and the kind of plastic surgery excesses for which (allegedly) Michael Jackson is famous.

Onto this stage, enter transhumanism. Oxford philosopher Nick Bostrom cofounded the World Transhumanist Association (WTA) in 1998 and set forth a statement of its views in a document entitled *The Transhumanist FAQ.* A second version of the *FAQ,* which will provide our primary reference point, was released in October 2003.[12]

Of Nanos and Cyborgs: Or, Whatever Happened to Mice and Men?

The term "transhuman" is a confluence of the words transitional and human. While transhumans view themselves as existing somewhere along

Interpreting Cultural Trends

a continuum between human and posthuman, they maintain that the entire notion is so fuzzy that it defies explanation. Aside from simply being an advocate of transhumanism, a transhumanist is "someone actively preparing for becoming posthuman. Someone who is informed enough to see radical future possibilities and plans ahead for them, and who takes every current option for self-enhancement."[13] In order to become a transhumanist one need only "adopt a philosophy which says that someday everyone ought to have the chance to grow beyond present human limits."[14]

James Hughes, WTA secretary, indicates that since 1998, approximately four thousand people have joined the WTA via its website. He estimates that more than one hundred thousand worldwide "would self-identify as 'transhumanist' . . . [but] since many of them are anarchists and libertarians they are difficult to organize and get on mailing lists."[15] The WTA publishes a peer-reviewed journal, the *Journal of Evolution and Technology*, and *The Transhumanist FAQ* lists a number of like-minded people and organizations. Thanks to Dr. Bostrom and the World Transhumanist Association, transhumanism is well on its way to becoming a "serious academic discipline."[16]

Where We Are and How We Got Here

Science and the scientific method are the primary means by which transhumanists come to understand reality. Physics, chemistry, and biology reveal the way in which the world operates and how it can be manipulated and improved. The universal language of logic and mathematics "enables the mind mentally to homogenize the entire world, to turn it into stuff for our manipulations."[17]

One of the main premises of transhumanism is that human beings are at a relatively early phase of our evolution. We are here because of naturalistic Darwinian evolution, and the visible material world is all there is. What they call the "human condition" receives much attention in *The Transhumanist FAQ*. While it is never defined explicitly, it is always spoken of in terms of something that needs improvement, transformation, and genuine change. Transhumanists acknowledge that "we might not be perfect" and "science has its own fallibilities and imperfections," but provide no root cause for either of these imperfections.[18] It is simply a given, a part of the human condition.

In transhumanism, as in humanism, "man and his capabilities are the central concern."[19] While humanism is interested in maximizing human development, transhumanism adds the idea that by using technology, humans can progress beyond human to become posthuman. Given the emphasis in transhumanism on the human, it is interesting that transhumanists tend to take a negative view of the human body. Human brains are referred to as "three-pound lumps of neural tissue that we use for thinking," or "that gray, cheesy lump inside your skull."[20]

Where We Are Going and How to Get There

To understand transhumanism, one must look to its ultimate goal: becoming posthuman. Posthumans are "beings whose basic capacities so radically exceed those of present humans as to be no longer unambiguously human by our current standards."[21] To be posthuman is to

> reach intellectual heights as far above any current human genius as humans are above other primates; to be resistant to disease and impervious to aging; to have unlimited youth and vigor; to exercise control over their own desires, moods, and mental states; to be able to avoid feeling tired, hateful, or irritated about petty things; to have an increased capacity for pleasure, love, artistic appreciation, and serenity; to experience novel states of consciousness that current human brains cannot access.[22]

The posthuman era will be ushered in by "the singularity," a hypothesized point in time when changes of such magnitude occur that everything beyond that point is altered in ways that are impossible to describe accurately. The singularity will occur when we are able to create computers that are smarter than humans or that possess "superintelligence."[23] The term "singularity" comes from the world of physics. Just as physics cannot explain the center of a black hole (the singularity), we cannot explain a world in which superintelligence and posthumans exist. Ultimately, proponents of the singularity hope to achieve a "positive feedback loop" such that the human mind builds a superintelligent mind which in turn builds a mind that is smarter still.[24] The quest for the singularity is buoyed by speculation that it might occur in the first half of this century.[25]

Reason and technology, particularly biotechnology, are the keys to overcoming "fundamental human limitations";[26] they are the means by which we can become posthuman. The future of humanity is indeterminate, waiting to be shaped and molded. The posthuman goal, therefore, will require the rational application of all possible technologies to redesign or enhance the human organism.[27] It is as though, through the proper application of reason and technology, humans can become perfect people, in a perfect society, on a perfect earth. Three technologies merit a closer look: nanotechnology, uploading, and advanced genetics.

Nanotechnology, which involves the ability to manipulate matter at the level of the atom, is expected to play a key role in such areas as cryonics and uploading. Cryonics involves freezing a person's body when he or she dies in the hope that when technology and medicine are sufficiently advanced the body can be thawed out, brought back to life, and restored to health. Nanotechnology will be necessary to undo the damage done by the freezing process. Moreover, nanotechnology "will enable us to transform coal into diamonds, sand into supercomputers, and to remove pollution from the air and tumors from healthy tissue."[28]

Uploading, which is connected closely to the transhuman negative view of the body, involves transferring a person's essential self from his or her body into a computer. Nanotechnology would be required to re-create electronically or synthetically the brain states of the person. The conjectured benefits of uploading include backing up and rebooting the self when needed, living economically, thinking faster and learning better, traveling via the Internet, and escaping from physical decline and death. Transhumanists argue that it is "a common misunderstanding" that people who upload themselves "would necessarily be 'disembodied' and that this would mean that their experiences would be impoverished."[29] Instead, "an upload could have a virtual (simulated) body" or could "rent robot bodies in order to work in or explore physical reality."[30]

Transhumanists hope to take genetic techniques to a more advanced level, especially in reproduction. Parents have an implied duty to make use of genomics and preimplantation screening to ensure the health of their children. At its theoretical extreme, genomics could allow parents to make a child to order: "Would you like tall, dark, and handsome with that?" Preimplantation screening involves removing a single cell from an embryo created by in vitro fertilization in order to test for certain diseases or traits; embryos deemed insufficient are "discarded." While the realization of the full potential of genomics is, at best, many years away, preimplantation screening currently is offered at a number of clinics in the United States.[31]

Ethical Implications

Like genomics and preimplantation screening, many aspects of where we are going and how to get there are ethically charged. Transhumanist ethics are based on a combination of radical personal autonomy, defined

REFLECTION

Two values that are intrinsically held and protected by American culture are autonomy and utilitarianism. Autonomy is rooted in our concepts of individualism and freedom. Utilitarianism is an ethical theory that emphasizes the pragmatic belief that the ends justify the means, or that whatever produces the most pleasure for the greatest number is the good. As with technicism, awareness of core cultural perceptions or values gives us important initial insights to understand emerging trends.

as "the ability and right of individuals to plan and choose their own lives,"[32] and utilitarianism. Each person should be able to decide which technologies to apply to his or her own body and to what extent. Similarly, people should be free to choose when and how they reproduce and have complete say in the results of their reproduction. In practical terms, this means that people should be free to use "genetic medicine or embryonic screening to increase the probability of a healthy, happy, and multiply talented child."[33] Transhumanists would advocate restrictions on "procreative liberty" only in the case where definite harm would come to a child, or where the child's "options in life" would be seriously limited.[34]

Autonomy is also a factor in transhuman views on death: "everybody should have the right to choose when and how to die—or not to die."[35] Transhumanists further assert, "Voluntary euthanasia, under conditions of informed consent, is a basic human right."[36] The only acceptable restraint on radical personal autonomy is based in utilitarianism. For example, reproductive cloning is considered from a utilitarian view:

> When thinking about whether to permit human reproductive cloning, we have to compare the various possible desirable consequences with the various possible undesirable consequences. We then have to try to estimate the likelihood of each of these consequences. This kind of deliberation is much harder than simply dismissing cloning as unnatural, but it is also more likely to result in good decisions.[37]

A Posthuman Future?

The spirit of our age evokes a sense that whatever can be done, not only should be done, but in fact *must* be done. This is an unacknowledged assumption that many hold and upon which transhumanism plays when refusing to consider the possibility of setting aside any technology, no matter how dangerous. Several transhumanist writings and one section of *The Transhumanist FAQ* are devoted to existential disaster, the possibility that a man-made disaster might destroy or permanently damage all intelligent life.[38] Yet they will not and cannot disavow perilous technologies. Transhumanism assures that what we do *while continuing to pursue these technologies* will make the difference. The technological breakthrough most essential to their hopes of becoming posthuman is also one of the riskiest. When describing the singularity, they mention that it will probably occur, "provided that we manage to avoid destroying civilization."[39] It is all too true that "humanity's entire future may depend on how we manage the coming technological transitions."[40]

Transhumanism is, in many ways, a project that blends modernity and postmodernity. Its biotechnological pursuits rest solidly on the "modern scientific project, to which mankind was summoned almost four hundred years ago by Francis Bacon and René Descartes."[41] This has become "an almost blind faith in inevitable progress" that redefines good "as the suppression, repression, replacement, and/or total control of the 'natural' via science and technology."[42] Postmodernity supplies "the belief that there is nothing intrinsically valuable about the biological form, particularly not the human form."[43] In addition, transhumanists point to the postmodern emphasis on "explod[ing] conceptual barriers in order to widen the reach of human creativity" as at least a partial warrant for their agenda.[44] In sum, "because there are no true norms for existence or behavior, we may create any reality we desire, and change ourselves in any manner to our suiting."[45]

Transhumanists believe that the pursuit of immortality is an ancient human quest. They call attention to the fact that various philosophical systems have attempted to find meaning in the fact of death and that religions have attempted to convey a sense of hope regarding what follows death through teachings such as resurrection and reincarnation. In addition, developments in medicine, science, and technology have led to longer life expectancy. "If death is part of the natural order," transhumanists point

Part of interpreting a cultural text or trend is to see where it leads. What are the implications of the cultural work? Transhumanists are willing to risk the destruction of all intelligent life for the chance to become posthuman. This risk says a lot about how much they detest the current state of humanity. It is important to take a careful measure of the things that one believes, and the far-reaching implications that beliefs can have.

out, "so too is the human desire to overcome death."[46] A recent book asserts that the posthuman "potential to play God, to pursue immortality, pushes these issues beyond the ethical into the theological."[47] Appropriately, therefore, it is to the theological we now turn.

Toward a Christian Future-Human

Both transhumanism and Christianity attempt to offer comprehensive explanations for human existence and answer questions regarding what it means to be human and how to find true happiness. On transhumanism's view, to be human is to be infinitely malleable, to have a disposable body, to have no one to answer to but the self, to be strongly optimistic about the progress of technology and humanity. To live a life of true happiness is, therefore, to pursue various technologies and work toward becoming posthuman. For Christians, true happiness—purpose, meaning, significance, fulfillment—is found only in relationship with God through faith in Christ. To be truly human is to be rightly related to God through Christ.

The Christian account of where we are and how we got here is that we are created in the image of God yet are born into a fallen world (Gen. 1:27; 3). Because this is a fallen world and we are fallen creatures, we are estranged spiritually from God and subject physically to despair, disease, and death. In addition, we are in active rebellion against God. We suppress the truth, and are subject to spiritual blindness (Rom. 1:18; 2 Cor. 4:4). For this, we rightly bear a measure of guilt that we cannot assuage. Yet we desire redemption (the restoration of relationship with God) and consummation (permanent dwelling in the City of God). While the reality of these desires may be unknown to us due to our suppression of the truth and spiritual blindness, they are nonetheless real.

The good news (gospel) about where we are going and how to get there is that God sent his only son, Jesus Christ, to take on human form (a body), live among us, lay down his life, and rise again (John 3:16; 1 Cor. 15:3). Through faith in the completed work of Christ, the relationship with God for which we were created is restored. It is only in the New Jerusalem (a real, physical place) that we will experience total relief from the effects of the fall in resurrected bodies (Rev. 21).

To state it another way, the root cause of our troubles is sin and the resulting estrangement from God. The symptoms manifest themselves in many ways, not the least of which is the desire for freedom from despair, disease, and death—in a word, for immortality. Rebellious truth suppres-

Interpreting Cultural Trends

sion and spiritual blindness often cause us to seek treatments for the symptoms of the fall rather than for the underlying disease of sin and guilt. An additional effect of the fall is that we rely solely on human reason and human means in our attempts to alleviate the effects of the disease of sin. As a result, human solutions are often distortions of the reality defined by Scripture and the person of Jesus Christ.

Transhumanism constructs a noteworthy antithesis between itself and religion. While its adherents acknowledge that "transhumanism might serve a few of the same functions that people have traditionally sought in religion," they maintain, "there is no hard evidence for supernatural forces or irreducible spiritual phenomena, and transhumanists prefer to derive their understanding of the world from rational modes of inquiry, especially the scientific method."[48] When talking about the earliest roots of their thinking, transhumanists point to ancient Greek philosophers such as Socrates who relied on logic rather than faith. They lump together "religious fanaticism, superstition, and intolerance" and label them "weaknesses."[49] The transhuman position is reminiscent of a line from U2's "The Wanderer": "They say they want the kingdom, but they don't want God in it."[50]

Despite transhumanism's disavowal of religion, many of the driving forces behind transhumanism can be defined properly as religious. Transhumanism distortedly mirrors, in some ways, key Christian doctrines, particularly in areas of eschatology. The singularity represents a kind of apocalypse, and the idea of posthumanity, or of a posthuman era, in many ways mirrors Christian teaching regarding resurrection and consummation. Consider the parallels between the description of the posthuman condition—"resistant

For Further REFLECTION

The truth that God has created humanity in his image has emerged repeatedly in these essays. Pope John Paul II often said the key question facing the world was what it means to be human, and these texts and trends reflect that. Whether we are in God's image is significant for the Universal Declaration of Human Rights, transhumanism, and fantasy funerals. For a Christian cultural hermeneutic to move forward, therefore, we must continue to think biblically and creatively about what the image of God means. How does seeing human beings as God's image-bearers play out in the controversies of our day, such as in bioethics? What points of contact with the wider world does this doctrine offer? Working hard in this area will have a multiplying impact in our ability to respond to cultural texts.

to disease and impervious to aging; unlimited youth and vigor"[51]—and Revelation 21:4—"He will wipe every tear from their eyes. There will be no more death or mourning or crying or pain, for the old order of things has passed away."

Christian beliefs about resurrection involve genuine improvement, transformation, and change of the body, and offer an answer to the transhuman hope of uploading. Christ's resurrection was a physical, bodily resurrection. Because Christ rose from the dead, Christians believe that they will rise from the dead. In the same way that Christ's resurrection was a bodily resurrection, Christians trust that we too will undergo a bodily resurrection (1 Cor. 15). This resurrection will be a genuine transformation of our bodies in such a way that bears both continuity and discontinuity with our present bodies. While we do not know the precise nature of such bodies, it is clear that they will be physical, and that we will be recognizable to one another. While the resurrection body will not be subject to death, decay, and despair, the Christian view of immortality is of a very real physical existence. In our earthly, fallen bodies we "groan" for our future, immortal bodies. Christians and transhumanists share the view that death is unnatural and an enemy, yet Christians believe that Christ has overcome—and will one day destroy—death.[52]

The Christian doctrine of the fall is visible in transhuman discussions regarding the human condition. While the human condition in transhumanism appears to involve fundamental aspects of what it means to have been created by God—contingency, dependency, and finitude—as well as factors attributable to the fall—despair, disease, and death—no root cause (i.e., Satan, evil, sin, or rebellion) is given. In many ways it seems that the human condition covers only unintentional sorts of failings, and that if only everyone were given a proper chance, all would be well. Indeed, transhumanism sounds at times as if it denies the reality of evil. The implicit claim is that people basically are good and technological advancement will somehow purify the human condition.

When transhumanists state, "In some ways, human minds and brains are just not designed to be happy," they unknowingly acknowledge humanity's estrangement from God.[53] A central Christian claim is that human beings were designed in God's image and thus for relationship with God and only there is found true and enduring joy and happiness. Transhumanists also assert, "There is no reason why pleasure, excitement, profound well-being and simple joy at being alive could not become the natural, default state of mind for all who desire it."[54] Christians would counter that it is only due to Christ's atoning work on the cross and bodily resurrection

Interpreting Cultural Trends

that profound well-being and simple joy are available through faith in the risen Christ.

Distorted correspondence with other biblical themes can also be found. In a way, transhumanists look to scientific revelation to find a biotechnological savior to bring them into a posthuman kingdom. Inasmuch as humanity and its potential are the ultimate concern of transhumanists, humanity has replaced God; their theology is anthropology. In the same way that Christians look to Scripture as the source for knowledge of God, transhumanists look to science as the source for knowledge of human life. Reason has replaced faith; existential disaster is damnation. If human beings have a God-given yearning for significance beyond space and time as we know it, could it not be that human beings have the ability to subconsciously replace God-ordained structures with those of our own making?

In the same way that a transhuman is a transitional human, Christians are also humans in transition, living in a kingdom that has come and yet is coming, "strangers in the world."[55] Could we not, in fact, go further? Could it be that to be truly human is to be, in a sense, posthuman? Perhaps to be truly human is to be *post-fallen-human*, to have a resurrected body, to dwell with the Triune God in the New Jerusalem, to return to the fully or truly human state in which humans were created. To be transhuman then would be to live in the tension between the "already" and the "not yet," to be in the world but not of the world, to be a new creature in Christ. As this is possible only because of the finished work of Jesus Christ, who as the firstfruits of the resurrection sent the Holy Spirit as guarantee, perhaps Christians should appropriate and fill out the terms "transhuman" and "posthuman" with the gospel of Jesus Christ.[56] At the very least, this brief foray may help reveal specific points of dialogue with transhumanists and others who would look to technology as "the sole and ultimate solution to the problems of the world."[57]

Conclusion

As Christians, we can easily miss the way the world must look to those who are convinced that the present life is all there is and that no greater being or higher power exists. Examining transhumanism through a theological lens reveals that with which transhumanists are ultimately concerned as well as the structures and methods constructed in order to address these concerns. *The Transhumanist FAQ* represents the very real beliefs of an increasing number of people. The world that it projects is the very world in which they see themselves. They are striving to live out the way of being human that the *FAQ* describes.

Twenty-first-century Western civilization is in real danger of allowing our technological abilities to become an "unquestioned commitment to technological control of the body for the sake of eliminating 'misery and necessity.'"[58] The result will be that science, medicine, and technology focus solely on "efforts to eliminate suffering and expand human choice."[59] This view stands in stark contrast to the fact that contingency, dependence, and finitude are inescapable aspects of the human body specifically and life generally. Rather than trying incessantly to remove all suffering, we should instead seek a correct orientation to our limitations. We can do that best "by recovering the moral significance of the body" specifically, and the material realm in general.[60]

Christianity and transhumanism both acknowledge the transitional nature of our current bodies. Yet, for Christians that does not lead to devaluation of the body; rather, there is regard for its place, even as we look forward to a resurrection body. This is an important realization for those who traditionally have tended toward an underdeveloped theology of the material realm. As Christians, we need to consider "what our bodies are for, how suffering relates to these purposes, and how technological medicine assists or hinders these purposes."[61] Rather than trying to cure every disease and overcome every obstacle, recognizing the contingency, dependency, and finitude of our bodies will ultimately enable us to care better for others.

Christians should be involved in discussions over science, technology, biotechnology, and medicine with all of their potentials and pitfalls. We have a role to play in shaping the future, and can be involved in technological discussions in a number of ways. We can study to work as scientists and researchers who develop technologies while recognizing the sovereignty of God over all things. Christians must model appropriate and God-honoring utilization of technology, and we can engage the designers and developers of technology to argue for its wise creation, implementation, and use. As citizens, we can participate in the political processes surrounding the regulation and oversight of technology.[62]

It is important that we recognize not only the threats that technology presents, but also the opportunities for obeying the cultural mandate that humans have been given by God. One theologian asserts, "the problem is not with technology itself but our lack of a moral framework that can tell us how rightly to resist and appropriate it."[63] We must strike a balance

Interpreting Cultural Trends

BOOK LINK

Begotten or Made?

Recent developments in pharmacology, neuroscience, and genetic engineering not only affect the practice of medicine but raise important theoretical questions about what it is to be human. Oliver O'Donovan's *Begotten or Made? Human Procreation and Medical Technique* (New York: Oxford University Press, 1984) tackles these questions head-on in an insightful book whose small size belies its importance.

New technologies raise the possibility of the ultimate makeover. Sex-change operations that go against the natural given encourage the transgendered to think that gender is artificial rather than something determined and given by God. If the term "revolution" signals the moment when a community assumes responsibility for its own future, then we are indeed in the midst of a technological revolution. It is a fact of more than lexical significance, O'Donovan suggests, that the word "revolution" entered the vocabulary of the West only when its faith in divine providence was weakening.

O'Donovan sees into the soul of our technological culture when he identifies "making" as a key category in modernity's interpretative framework. Indeed, "making" may be one of the most important root metaphors in contemporary culture. Much of what we do—everything from dinner to sex ("lovemaking") to cars to public opinion—is viewed in terms of instrumental making. When every activity becomes "artifactual," however, technical intervention becomes appropriate everywhere and everything comes to be seen (by postmoderns, for instance) as "artificial."

What our technological culture needs, O'Donovan contends, is a good dose of trinitarian theology. To be precise: we need to recover the distinction between "making" and "begetting" that was the keystone of Nicene orthodoxy. The church fathers at Nicaea declared that Jesus was "begotten, not made" of the Father. Why? Because that which we make is fundamentally *unlike* us; it is the result of human will and human work and is therefore something to be used rather than loved. That which we beget, by contrast, is beyond our ability to determine or control; we do not make what we beget but we receive it as a gift from God to be cherished, not manipulated or made over. According to O'Donovan and the church fathers, only God can "make" human beings. It is the better part of human maturity and wisdom not to chafe against the givens (including our being male or female) but to accept them as God's gifts.

Kevin J. Vanhoozer

between completely rejecting technology and viewing technology as the solution to all of humanity's problems. Ours is an age of unprecedented technological development, which fuels and is fueled by the belief that technology is inherently good and that it holds the solution to all of our problems, and the resulting belief that whatever can be done must be done.

Is it possible that in our actions and attitudes we are overly optimistic about technology? Most people, including Christians, are not aware that they hold these assumptions, yet these assumptions shape nearly every public debate regarding new technologies. These are not scientific beliefs but philosophical and moral presuppositions to which Christians need to call attention. It is all too easy to get swept up in the message our culture sells about the "need" for the latest and greatest gadget and forget where our ultimate solution lies. Instead, "the prophetic witness of Christians must challenge the assumptions of technicism and offer a more realistic and fruitful alternative."[64]

Finally, Christians must appropriately model the biblical idea of community. We are the body of Christ, joined together and functioning in concert. This contrasts starkly with the cultural notions of individualism and radical personal autonomy upon which transhumanism relies so heavily. We are not our own, nor do we live for ourselves alone (1 Cor. 6:19; Rom. 12). The biblical emphasis on neighbor-love should motivate us to cultivate biblical communities, to care for one another, and to engage technology.

Transhumanism is a logical extension of assumptions about technology and the physical world that many, even some Christians, hold. Seeing ostensibly innocuous assumptions pressed to their logical conclusions should stimulate reconsideration of the ways in which we look at, think about, relate to, and live in the world. Then perhaps we can begin to more fully bear one another's burdens and better offer our own bodies as living sacrifices. What all of us need, Christians, transhumanists—whatever label we choose to wear—is the gospel. We need to hear and proclaim the good news that God became man in order to restore us to the relationship for which we were created.

Suggested Readings

Alcorn, Randy. *Heaven*. Wheaton: Tyndale, 2004.

Houston, Graham. *Virtual Morality: Christian Ethics in the Computer Age*. Leicester, UK: Apollos, 1998.

Kass, Leon R. "*L'Chaim* and Its Limits: Why Not Immortality?" *First Things* 113 (May 2001). http://print.firstthings.com/ftissues/ft0105/articles/kass.html (accessed January 12, 2004).

Interpreting Cultural Trends

Kurzweil, Ray. *The Singularity Is Near: When Humans Transcend Biology.* New York: Penguin, 2005.

President's Council on Bioethics. *Beyond Therapy: Biotechnology and the Pursuit of Happiness.* Washington, DC: President's Council on Bioethics, 2003. http://www.bioethics.gov/reports/beyondtherapy/index.html (accessed September 21, 2005).

Pullinger, David. *Information Technology and Cyberspace: Extra-connected Living.* Cleveland: Pilgrim, 2001.

Editorial Introduction

This essay examines a trend that has recently emerged in the funeral industry—fantasy funerals. By examining the motivation of this macabre trend, the author highlights the struggle of coming to terms with death in a post-Christian America. In so doing, the author opens the door for reflection on the proper grounds for a Christian conception of death and assesses the contributions that this trend offers for personalizing the celebration of life.

Fantasy Funerals and Other Designer Ways of Going Out in Style

Ben Peays

When Jack Faria died in April after a long bout with lung disease, his wife threw him a party. To honor her late husband—a passionate Miami sports fan—Carole Faria asked the funeral home to re-create a stadium setting with Marlins, Heat and Dolphins paraphernalia. Jack's favorite putter, pool cue and family photos surrounded his coffin. The song "As Time Goes By," from his favorite movie, Casablanca, *played in the background.*[1]

No staid, generic, one-size-fits-all funeral for Jack Faria—his final gathering distinctively represented who he was. The race to keep up with the latest trends has extended into death as people seek the most fashionable ways of going out in style. As America's view of death continues to evolve, a $17 billion industry is changing—which promises to alter the way we bury our dead—as people design elaborate and fanciful fantasy funerals.

In an increasingly secularized landscape detached from traditional Judeo-Christian rituals, many Americans have found a new freedom in creatively rethinking funerals. Imaginative expressions and celebrations replace the traditionally solemn funerals of past generations. Cultural texts and trends testify to the deep structures of a people by revealing their true convictions and values. As a result, these fantasy funerals can be seen as a cultural trend, projecting one way we interpret the world. So what does this developing trend say about us? What is causing the shift in our approach to death? Moreover, what does the Bible say about death? And is there such a thing as a Christian funeral? These questions will guide us as we interpret the trend of fantasy funerals.

The New Trend of Fantasy Funerals

In the summer of 2003 one woman ordered a "gaming theme" funeral when her husband died, complete with "authentic slot machines discreetly positioned around the neon-lit casket, gambling chips the size of manhole covers, and a jumbo deck of cards in lieu of a flower spray covering the deceased. Instead of folding chairs, jumbo dice . . . serve as ottomans, cocktail tables or the perfect surface for a memorial craps game."[2] This sort of themed funeral is just one of the new phenomena laying to rest the traditional American funeral.

No longer interested in the practices of past generations, some are beginning to look to ceremony designers for a unique twist to their final farewell. Fashion an all-night theme party, an elaborate interactive service, a crazy stunt, an environmental statement, an online memorial, and more. While you are at it, choose a custom casket, funeral caterer, costume and prop rentals, lighting design, make-up service, even special souvenirs. For a long time, the survivors themselves tended to be removed from the process of funeral planning, leaving the details to professionals like funeral directors and clergy who tended to craft impersonal ceremonies. Many people, however, no longer want the standard program and instead either do it themselves or turn to different kinds of professionals, such as event coordinators and design specialists, as one-stop shops for all their funeral planning needs.

After trying to plan the funeral for his deceased aunt, Pat Fant was frustrated at the lack of options available to capture her uniqueness. He responded by starting a business that specializes in unique caskets that help express and celebrate the deceased's life in a manner that actually reflects who they were. Fant says,

> This is the generation that permanently changed a lot of ways we do things. This generation put the father in the delivery room. That same influence over

the way birth occurs—that influence is being felt in the way death is being celebrated. . . . They're saying, "let's go out with some style. For heaven's sake, make a statement."[3]

Today, for roughly $1,000 to $3,000, people can buy predesigned themes, such as the "rodeo" theme offered by Palm Mortuary in Las Vegas, "complete with a plastic horse, bales of hay, wagon wheels, cacti and a cowboy boot."[4] For those feeling especially creative, you can construct your own theme using props from favorite hobbies, such as fishing, classic cars, sailing, model trains, quilting, or football. For a more personal touch include family photos, keepsakes, favorite personal belongings, and special souvenirs from trips. The only apparent boundary is your credit limit.

Not to be outpaced by funeral services, coffin manufacturers have also entered this new creative world of expression as people search for unique alternatives to the basic black box. Fant's company offers a photo-laminate process in which a picture collage of the person's life covers the entire eighteen-gauge steel casket. One Texas-based company offers a design the NRA would love: a rust-resistant metal casket painted in hunter's camouflage and fitted with gun racks and camouflage netting. Or one can choose "The Cowboy Western," with its "classic pine box in blazing Western motif" with horseshoe-shaped handles.[5]

Another significant change in the funeral industry is the increased popularity of cremation. The Cremation Association of North America predicts that cremation rates will jump from 28% in 2003 to 46% by 2025.[6] Hawaii, Nevada, and Washington already report rates higher than 60%. People are drawn to the improved hygiene and psychological sentiment of cremation, as well as a low-cost alternative to burial. A traditional funeral costs on average $5,800 along with an additional $2,000 in burial fees, while cremation costs around $1,000 and gives the family the option of scattering the ashes in a meaningful ceremony or storing the urn in a significant place.[7]

Cremation appeals especially to mobile families who find it difficult to visit a cemetery. No time to visit grandma? Why not bring her with you wherever you go? LifeGem in Chicago uses new technology to compress several ounces of your cremated loved one into a high-quality diamond, which can then be treasured as a beautiful piece of wearable memories.[8] So go ahead and get that great-aunt Linda pendant to match the first cousin earrings. Another company incorporates ashes into an abstract watercolor painting for a "lasting artistic expression of how much you care."[9]

This definitely is not your grandmother's funeral. The decisions are no longer simply which kind of flowers to have, but should we launch them into space or put them in a coral reef? For those who love astronomy and exploration, Space Services will launch their cremated remains into the stratosphere. The company advertises, "On launch day families gather at the liftoff site to share the experience of seeing their loved ones' dreams of space flight realized. With a roar and a fiery streak across the sky, the rocket lifts its precious load higher and higher into the peaceful solitude of space."[10] And for the scuba diving enthusiast, a company in Georgia will combine your ashes with concrete to create a "reef ball," which mimics a natural coral reef on Florida's Gulf coast. Customers can choose all the way from "the top-of-the-line 'Atlantis' [which] is four foot high by six feet wide," weighs almost four thousand pounds, and costs $4,995, down to the low-end community reef model, where their "ashes are mingled with many others."[11]

Our culture is pushing the limits on what has traditionally been a serious event designed to commemorate a person's death. How far will this new trend of fantasy funerals go?

On the Surface: Celebrating the Individual

So what was *wrong* with traditional funerals? Why are so many people seeking new alternatives? On the surface, the trend of fantasy funerals suggests people are searching for more personal and therefore meaningful ways to bury their dead. Social commentator Jessica Mitford, in tracing the history of American funerals, has concluded that their evolution has had more to do with quick-paced cultural development than Christian ideals or traditional religious doctrine.[12] Mitford notes that seventeenth-century Puritans had little interest in the physical remains of the dead. Bodies were hurried into the ground after death with little ceremony. It was not until the eighteenth century that some funerals became elaborate by including more extensive ceremonies and displays of public mourning. It was here that a shift began toward survivors placing significance in the funeral service on who the deceased had been as a means of remembering them.[13]

Another historian notes that from colonial days until the nineteenth century, the American funeral was mostly a family affair. Family members and a few close friends performed most of the tasks associated with the corpse, including washing and wrapping, ordering the coffin from a local carpenter, transporting it to a graveyard, and digging the grave. During

Interpreting Cultural Trends

the time between the death and burial, the body was usually displayed in the family's house for visitors. The church was the usual place for the funeral service, with a brief religious service often performed at the gravesite as well.[14]

The use of a casket is a relatively new concept that was not introduced to America until the nineteenth century. Mitford explains that prior to this time it was not standard practice for Americans to embalm their dead or even bury them in any sort of container. Plain coffins were built by local cabinet makers as a structure for transporting the body. This soon turned into an industry in itself, and the linguistic shift from *coffin* to *casket* provided evidence of a new trend. The development of industrial technique in the nineteenth century set the stage for new designs and mass production of caskets made of marble, metal, glass, and bronze that inhibited decay.[15]

In the middle of the nineteenth century, the factors that made up a *respectable* funeral began to change under the influence of wealthy and prominent members in society. Dark clothing became a unifying theme at funerals, especially for the purpose of identifying the funeral party, particularly in a long procession. Flowers became a symbol of condolence, despite the opposition of church leaders.[16]

Eventually the private, post-death services that had been performed by family members began to be hired out to local trades. For example, midwives and nurses offered to lay out the dead, livery-stable keepers began to offer transportation services for coffins (the original hearse), carpenters were continually making standard coffins to add to their inventory, and the church sexton began to offer grave-digging services.[17] By the end of the nineteenth century, the undertaker emerged as a full-time position for handling the dead, developing eventually into the funeral director who could take care of all funeral responsibilities. This has, in turn, led to the contemporary funeral designer who adds a little glamour, creativity, and style to the service.

A consistent emotional tone throughout this evolution of American funeral customs from family-run to professionalized affairs has been one of solemnity and grief. By nature, funerals are sad because the community is experiencing the loss of a friend. Many people, however, increasingly question this need for sorrow. Many funeral homes are receiving requests for funeral themes that are more like celebrations rather than serious or sad events. Why not memorialize that special someone who loved the music of Jimmy Buffett with a "funeral party" where mourners can celebrate with margaritas on a seashell-lined beach?[18] Rather than a depressing event, a funeral becomes a colorful commemoration of a life well lived. Eagle Custom Caskets epitomizes the emphasis on celebration with its appeal to Harley-Davidson fans:

> Don't put your loved ones through the agony of a typical memorial service where no one knows what to say to the surviving family. Break tradition! Lighten the moment! Give them something to talk about that may bring back a happy memory, a smile through the tears, or maybe even give those tough-guy biker brothers of yours a way to make it through the receiving line without crying over you.[19]

We are undergoing a redefinition of what it means to honor the dead. Along with the change (in some quarters) from sorrow to celebration, there is also a shift from culturally shared traditions to customization and innovation. Given the broader cultural emphasis on individualism, many consider it a shameful misrepresentation for everyone to be buried the same way. The best way to honor the deceased is to give them funerals as distinctive as they were. It means celebrating what made the deceased unique and having the freedom to conduct funerals outside churches, outside religion, and outside the ordinary. It is to want guests to walk into a funeral and say, "This is the way they would have wanted it to be," or "This is the way we all remember them." One wife had her late husband laid out next to a soda-packed cooler and his beloved barbecue pit:

> He would barbecue at every holiday, the Super Bowl or for no reason at all, just to invite the neighbors over. . . . He always told me he didn't want a sad funeral; he said he wanted something people could remember. People were laughing and joking. Everybody said it was different, but that it was L. C.[20]

Below the Surface: The Secularization of American Funerals

Why does our contemporary culture increasingly choose fantasy funerals? What do such changes communicate about the American mindset? Below the surface, the secularization of mainstream America has led to the removal of God from death and funerals. The historical context for American funerals was undeniably Christian, at least broadly so. For the Puritans, death represented the two stark options of heaven or hell. As a result, services featured Scripture readings and prayer, appropriately intended with these options in mind. One historian observed that by the middle of the eighteenth century, perceptions of death and the afterlife began to vary as Protestant theology encountered alternate interpretations from the rise of new religious influences such as evangelicalism, Arminianism, revivalism, and millennialism. Social changes brought on by urbanization, expanding markets, increased migration, and Jacksonian Democracy also altered the thinking of this traditionally Protestant nation. The nineteenth century marked the time in which American funerals began to shift away from possessing a standard Christian framework. New industries, religious influences, consumer options, social standards, and cultural advancements fractured the idea of a broadly *Christian* funeral. Funeral ceremonies were simply an expression of the underlying mindset of a nation that was experiencing an explosion of growth in unprecedented ways. The Christian funeral maintained its place among Christian believers, but for an increasingly diverse American population it became simply one religious option among many.[21]

With the broader secularization of American culture, a Christian context no longer shapes what a funeral means. This is visible in the changing physical spaces for funerals and burials. Most funerals have made their way out of the church into funeral homes, and public cemeteries, separate from church properties, are now the norm. A representative from one funeral home claims that services without ministers are quite popular today: "People just want to stand up and talk about the deceased. . . . There's laughter. It's more up-lifting."[22]

Into this void have stepped other ways to give definition to funerals and, by extension, the lives for which they are the culmination. These elaborate, often individualized services, complete with gaming chips or camouflaged casket, are supposed to sum up and express the values for which that person's life stood. Similarly, meaning for the deceased comes through being remembered or making a statement. Perhaps the most striking way for

For Further REFLECTION

Several essays have pointed to how American society has become increasingly post-Christian and, in the process, contains interesting contradictions that are vestiges of Christian practices and beliefs. According to the Nietzschean image, the idols should be tested (with a hammer) to see if they have any content to them, with the assumption being that if they are empty they will be smashed. In the same way Christian cultural hermeneutics may test these same vestiges, not in an attempt to destroy, but rather to see if they might serve as a fruitful means of opening dialogue between culture and Christianity.

people to ensure that their funeral carries the meaning they want is to host it themselves! Pre-death funerals are growing in popularity.[23] They allow the would-be "deceased" to make sure the ceremony proceeds according to their wishes, to enjoy personally the kind words usually shared after they are gone, to have the chance to say goodbye to friends and family, and to reminisce about the good old days, all before they die.

This quest for meaning affects the gravesite. Whereas traditionally tombstones primarily marked a grave and secondarily communicated a few facts about the deceased, digital technology can now ensure that future mourners will be able to know so much more about the dearly departed and what they accomplished in life. A Los Angeles cemetery called Hollywood Forever now offers flat-panel TV screens on tombstones where a personal video message or photomontage appears at the push of a button. Visitors have the opportunity to view short documentaries about the deceased and even take home a DVD.[24]

This idea was taken to a whole new level in the 2004 sci-fi thriller, *The Final Cut*. The film merges this idea of capturing the lives of loved ones with the technological idea of memory devices that parents implant in their children prior to birth in order to record every thought and action. In the film, Robin Williams plays a "cutter" whose job is to use the memory device to create a highlight clip of the person's life which is viewed by family and friends at a funeral-type event called a "rememory." One of the most interesting features of the film is the ethical struggle the cutter faces as he attempts to portray a person's life positively, despite seeing his or her most despicable moments recorded in the memory device. Williams's character felt the obligation to put a positive spin on the lives of clients even with his knowledge of their darkest behavior. The role of the cutter is similar to the task family members encounter in the process of planning a funeral, namely, how does one represent or summarize another's life? Who were they? In one sense, the work of the cutter represents judgment day for the deceased in that his or her life is reviewed and evaluated for the purpose of a final effect. Family and friends also feel the obligation to produce a final effect that characterizes someone's life, and increasingly this is being played out in the form of the fantasy funeral.

In an age particularly predicated on accomplishment, where "whoever dies with the most toys wins," people can go to creative measures to represent (and even maintain!) their social status postmortem. Many of America's largest cities are building the opportunity to house your precious remains in new upscale crypts, mausoleums, and luxury columbarium vaults. Green-Wood Cemetery in Brooklyn, for example, has built a two-thousand-five-hundred-crypt mausoleum designed to look like an office tower complete with a glass roof and "two four-story waterfalls that flow into reflecting pools."[25]

The quest to impart meaning to our deaths through funerals leads to the glorification of certain "goods," especially personal accomplishment. The emphasis in remembering a person's life is inevitably on what he or she did and cared about. The in-charge, autonomous individual always in control of his or her life is praised for his or her self-confidence. Large public gifts to charitable organizations and educational institutions are lauded (as opposed to the anonymous giving that Christ instructs). The slothfulness of the avid sports fan who rarely leaves the recliner is transformed into commendation for being a loyal, die-hard fan. In keeping up with the Joneses, the self-indulgence of American consumerism is celebrated for trying to achieve the "good life" rather than for the selfish ambitions that inhibit the biblical virtues. Thus, in an increasingly secularized culture, the very virtues that are often praised are actually spiritual vices.

Above the Surface: Death in America—Accepting and Denying the Mystery

An American view of death is difficult to define, as death is both overstated and understated in our culture. On the one hand, people are fascinated by death. They view it as an exciting mystery surrounded by questions: What happens to us after we die? What does it feel like? Stories of bright lights and tunnels, reincarnations, positive energy forces, harps, clouds, and pearly gates are images that represent our thinking about what really happens. While people hold a diverse array of beliefs about what happens when we die, most want to see it as something positive. They look to some kind of continued existence. They assume, or hope, that their loved ones live on as spirits or energy forces; they picture them playing poker in the skies, or hovering over their favorite football stadium, still enjoying in heaven the things they loved on earth.

Some American subcultures have an odd fascination with death, or at least with its trappings. One casket company owner reported that people sometimes rent caskets to use for birthday parties or as beer coolers; some even buy them for furniture: "I had one kid come in, ask if we could turn a casket on end and turn it into a home entertainment center."[26] Perhaps the idea is to spend a lifetime enjoying the furniture before being buried in it.

TAKING IT *FURTHER*

This simultaneous denial of death and yet attention to what lies beyond it makes explicit the importance of eschatology for cultural hermeneutics. Many essays address this topic: the different visions of hope in *Gladiator*, the absence of eternity from most contemporary Christian writing on busyness, the way transhumanism seeks the resurrected body in this world. What is striking is that this emphasis on eschatology runs counter to the place it has in much of our thinking. Beliefs about what comes after death are a part of our mental furniture, but they are in a corner of the room, a little lamp stand we usually ignore in our everyday lives. These essays demonstrate that what we hold to in eschatology should significantly shape our cultural interpretation and witness.

American culture and media encourage and manifest the interest in death by using it as a recurring theme in cultural texts like *Six Feet Under*, *The Lovely Bones*, and *The Dogs of Babel*.[27] Perhaps death remains a popular topic because it is the one universal experience. Our lives, and the lives of those around us, steadily approach an end, which naturally may attract our interest, especially as that end becomes more imminent (witness the aging Baby Boomer population). What used to be something that happened just to grandparents begins happening to our parents, then to our peers, and then maybe even our children. It is the one possibility we must all realize.

But what do we do when death becomes impersonal? How does the average American react to a report of slaughter totaling five thousand deaths? How do we grasp the reality of a natural disaster that claimed the lives of ten thousand people? Unless we are forced to deal with death in a personal way, we usually choose not to dwell on it. For many, death is somewhat of a taboo topic. It is seen almost as one of those things that if you dwell upon it, it will more likely find you. Some people choose to pretend death does not exist by avoiding the topic altogether. It is these people who are the most stunned when eventually faced with planning a funeral service for someone they love. This inability to come to grips with the reality of death has led many to confusion and shock when death finally appears.

Thus, we see that despite this fascination with death, mainstream American culture at the same time denies it, or at least denies that we personally will die. Many of us act as though just enough plastic surgery, trendy diets, and trips to the gym can stave off death, preferably indefinitely. We are given ways to look and feel younger, while we try to forget we are inevitably getting older. In this light, fantasy funerals culminate a lifetime

Interpreting Cultural Trends

spent denying death by distracting ourselves through mass media, sports, and other forms of entertainment. Who has time to notice the corpse or mourn when there is a craps game to be played?

Our denial of death and ensuing quest for immortality can most dramatically be seen in the increasingly popular science of cryogenics, which attempts to preserve the body by freezing it in liquid nitrogen. David Ettinger of The Cryonics Institute says, "In the future, there are going to be tremendous medical advances that people dying today can't take advantage of. . . . We like to call it the 'ambulance to the future.'" This ambulance does not come cheaply—it can cost nearly $30,000 for the annual maintenance of one's body.[28] Cryogenics represents the wealthy Western quest for immortality—shorn of any religious considerations—ready to wake up, be cured, and go on living the good life forever.

Theological Engagement

Perhaps all these examples have begun to raise a few questions for us. What, if anything, does the Bible say about death? The Bible says quite a bit about death, which makes it difficult to summarize scriptural teaching on the topic. One scholar suggests that at least for the Old Testament, death is seen in three ways: (1) biologically, it is the common end to life; (2) metaphorically, it represents life apart from the way God intended, i.e., spiritual death; and (3) theologically, it is a power that has invaded the created order due to Adam's sin.[29] For our purposes, we are interested in the way the Jewish people dealt with the cessation of life and how they practiced burial as a result of their understanding of death.

The Hebrew people saw death as an unavoidable reality but believed God was ultimately in control of both life and death.[30] In fact, on two occasions God showed his power over death and the natural order by taking people into heaven directly.[31] Death is sometimes seen as something brought about by God as punishment for sin, while at other times it is simply the natural end to life, despite obedience to God.[32] In the Psalms and various portions of the Wisdom literature, death is mourned and even feared. Death is sometimes violent and other times peaceful. Old Testament believers lacked a fully developed understanding of the afterlife, so as a result they often simply saw death as the opposite of life.[33]

By the beginning of the first century BC, Jewish understanding of the afterlife began to change. The Sadducees denied the resurrection (Acts 23:8) because it is not mentioned in the Torah, while the Pharisees believed resurrection was God's plan for the restoration of Israel. Death in the New Testament saw a shift in mentality. A stronger emphasis began to be placed on eternal life as a result of Christ's sacrifice on the cross. Christ emphasized that God is a God of the living, and his covenant with humans is not broken by death (Matt. 22:31–32). Christ's death on the cross conquered death and offered the way to maintain relationship with God even after humans experience biological death.

As a result of Christ's death on the cross, as well as a more developed understanding of the afterlife, Christian funerals evolved out of traditional Jewish burial customs and incorporated new aspects of their own. For example, Jewish practice included hiring professional mourners to wail and lament during the funeral procession, whereas Christian funerals tended to emphasize a triumphant note of celebration based on Christ's victory over death.[34] The New Testament contains several stories that give insight into Christian burial practices. For example, after someone died, the body was washed (Acts 9:37), anointed with oil, spices, and perfumes (Matt. 26:12; Luke 23:56), and wrapped from head to toe (John 11:44). Since embalming was not practiced at the time, decomposition necessitated timely burial of the body (Acts 5:6). The burial was usually preceded by a procession that consisted of family and friends carrying the body outside the city to be placed in a tomb or cave of some sort.[35] Luke records a story in which Jesus approaches such a procession and touches the coffin while commanding the dead man to rise (Luke 7:11–17). Most people were buried during this time since cremation was seen as a pagan practice. What Scripture does not contain, though, is a set of programmatic instructions on how to have a funeral. Instead, we witness how people in those times held such ceremonies. These customs may shape our practice, but there is no explicit biblical mandate to follow them.

Should we think theologically about death, and if so, how? First, we should note that death is not a part of God's natural design for humanity. We were originally created to live in fellowship with God as perfect beings forever. The story of creation in Genesis tells how Adam and Eve disregarded God's warning that eating from the Tree of the Knowledge of Good and Evil would result in death (Gen. 2:17). By this disobedience, sin spread to the entire human race as an unnatural corruption (Rom. 5:12). As a consequence to sin, God determined that all people would die: "The wages of sin is death" (Rom. 6:23). Humanity had fallen from its glorified state and encountered a lethal obstruction. Just as we were created from dust, to dust we were also now to return (Gen. 3:19). This is the first theological truth about death that we should note: its unnatural universality. Death

Interpreting Cultural Trends

comes to us all, but not ultimately as a result of natural life processes, as if it were the normal default setting for humanity. Rather, it represents a perverse intrusion into God's original design for his creation.

From the unnaturalness of death, it follows that God must have his purposes in allowing it to enter the creation. The Bible shows that death represents God's judgment over his creation for sin (Gen. 2:17; 5:5). Death is the end of the gracious gift of life and the point at which we face God's judgment and the ultimate determination of our eternal future. Death holds dramatic eternal significance for every person. During this day of judgment, both the believer in Jesus Christ and the unbeliever will reap what they have sown during their time on earth (Gal. 6:7–8). All people will stand before God in judgment, and those not included in the book of life will be thrown into the lake of fire (Rev. 20:11–15). Here, then, is the second theological truth about death: it is God's judgment on sin.

This second point about death is difficult for people to accept. It is the point at which American sentiments about death fracture into a multiplicity of options. As new religious and secular beliefs about death compete with the biblical truth, the significance behind death is lost. We do not like to believe that there will be judgment after death for what we have made of our lives. So either we dismiss it altogether, or we imagine the scales of justice to be so lenient that all but the Hitlers and Stalins of the world will be rewarded. Moreover, because we do not grapple with the seriousness of judgment, much of the fantasy funeral trend cheapens what death is—it turns this mark of God's judgment into an opportunity for Jimmy Buffett parties and urn launches into space. When we lack an awareness of what lies beyond this life, the time we use to commemorate its end inevitably focuses only on the things of this world.

There is more to the story than simply that death represents a crossroads for the soul. Death stands in the way of humans spending eternity with God. In this way, Paul characterizes it as the last "enemy." But the good news for creation is that God has declared victory over death (1 Cor. 15:26). The death of Jesus Christ on the cross satisfies the wrath of God and serves as the atonement for human sin. Furthermore, the resurrection of Jesus is the promise of a resurrection for those who are in him. In sending Jesus, God publicly acquits us and effectively says "Yes" to creation, where sin had previously said "No." Jesus is the resurrection and the life; whoever believes in him will live, even after they die (John 11:25–26; 3:16). Here is the third major point about death: as Christians move toward death in this world, they also move toward life in another. God has taken what is unnatural and used it for his good purposes to unite us to himself.

Christian hope is not in the immortality of the soul, but rather in the resurrection of the body as a new creation that will spend eternity with God. At the time of death, believers will be with Christ (Luke 23:42–43), and eventually they will find their place as a part of the restored creation in the new heaven and new earth (Isa. 65:17–25). Unless we understand death as a part of God's sovereign plan, we are prevented from truly understanding life. What we believe to be true about the afterlife has—or at least it should have—a major impact on the way we live, including what motivates us and how we spend our time. Or, to reverse this, the way we live demonstrates what we truly believe about the afterlife. The fact that we will die and face judgment, with the opportunity to dwell with or apart from God, should radically shape how we live now and even what kind of funerals we hold. We must hold to this tension that death is both God's judgment on sin and the point at which we are joined with him in fellowship. Death, therefore, should be different for Christians. If we are to live the joyful life God intended, we must accept the inevitability of death and its role in our transition into heaven. Disproportionate fears of death or an outright denial of its imminence only testify to a misunderstanding of life.

Paul said that for him, "to live is Christ and to die is gain," and "I desire to depart and be with Christ, which is better by far" (Phil. 1:21, 23). Perhaps the failure of Christians to display Paul's attitude toward death has contributed to the death of the traditional funeral. After all, if Christian funerals are somber and downcast, can the non-Christian really believe in the joyful message of hope? This does not mean that Christian funerals should become glib celebrations that mask true grief. Christians rightly experience sadness at death, but it should not be in the same way as those who grieve without hope (1 Thess. 4:13). Charles Spurgeon once said,

> Well, you may weep for "Jesus wept." Do not think there is any sin in sorrowing over departed friends, for the Lord never denies to us those human feelings which are rather kindly than vicious. . . . Still, you must remember that there is a moderation in grief. . . . Sometimes grief is not a sacred feeling, but only a murmur of rebellion against the Most High.[36]

The subject of death should not be taboo in the church. When a Christian dies, the funeral should be a time where the church comes together to celebrate the entrance of the deceased into paradise and the presence of God as well as to commemorate his or her life.

Interpreting Cultural Trends

A Christian Response to Fantasy Funerals

As the trend of fantasy funerals continues to gain momentum, Christians must consider how to respond. Are there any redeeming characteristics in fantasy funerals? As discussed earlier, these new funerals do, in fact, represent some positive steps. If people choose to honor a loved one through a more creative and personal funeral ceremony, then we should celebrate with them. Many of the reasons behind the latest fantasy funeral trends are rooted in a desire to celebrate a person's life rather than only mourn his or her death. After all, why should family and friends not participate in a ceremony designed to eulogize your accomplishments and remember your true character? Themed caskets and decorative urns are a special manner of appreciating individuality. If life is seen as a continuous expression of personhood, then the funeral is the last opportunity for such expression.

The Christian, however, should remember that true personhood is rooted first and foremost in Jesus Christ. Our identity may be reflected in our funerals, but this should then be a reflection of Christ. When people die they are typically remembered for the things they loved and the passions that motivated them. Here is a major distinguishing characteristic between Christian and non-Christian funerals. Considering the implications of Christ's work on the cross and the effect that it has on our eternity, it seems most appropriate to center a funeral on this truth rather than a hobby or pastime. We must avoid the pitfall of removing the true content from a funeral and replacing it with a substitute. For example, Christians must seriously examine to what their actions witness should they decide to purchase the "Fairway to Heaven" funeral theme for the golf aficionado, the heavy-metal "Kiss Casket" for rock and roll fans,[37] or the "Gone Fishin" coffin.[38]

In some ways, one cannot be too critical of secular funerals for their creative burial stunts and design alternatives. Those who do such things are simply trying their best to honor their loved one by representing him or her as best they can. Without the hope of life after death, sadly it does make sense to center funerals on earthly meaning. However, to have one's life represented as the guy who loved to hit the links with his buddies after work is a sad and hopefully unrepresentative commentary. May a Dallas Cowboys–themed funeral—like a child would choose to celebrate a seventh birthday—never be how your life as a whole is remembered. Can the "Return to Sender" Elvis coffin really be the image that most accurately and completely characterized your life? In this way, a Christian funeral should look different. The reality is that in a moment, in the twinkling of an eye, at the last trumpet, we will all be resurrected and changed (1 Cor. 15:52). It is in this miraculous resurrection that creation itself will be redeemed and made new. This is the joy and the hope that should be the ultimate theme for all Christian funerals.

A misunderstanding of death, and the subsequent misappropriation of meaning in funerals, has promoted events that tend to place a greater significance on the physical remains of the deceased. There is the misconception that the body of the deceased may play some significant role. This is why someone may send a loved one into space or give him or her a gravesite with a lake view. The Bible, though, while affirming the continuity of this creation with the one to come, distinguishes between the physical and the spiritual body in a series of contrasts between perishable and imperishable, dishonor and glory, and weakness and power (1 Cor. 15:42–44). It is of lesser importance, therefore, what we do with the corpse, provided it is treated with the dignity appropriate for one of God's image-bearers.

What, then, should we say about burial versus cremation? Does the Bible say anything about this decision? The early church, along with the Jews, buried their dead. Among the Greeks and Romans, however, cremation was a common practice. Even though burials are documented throughout Scripture and cremation has its origin in pagan religions, burials are not the only possible moral decision for Christians. Nothing in Scripture mandates burial. Believers are free to decide on burial or cremation in light of other considerations, such as economic, environmental, or pragmatic concerns.

So what then should a Christian funeral look like? The significance of our temporal lives on earth pales in comparison with the eternal significance of our resurrection bodies. Christian funerals should include a celebration and appreciation of life, an acknowledgement of Christ's work on the cross as the conquering of death, and the hope and assurance of the deceased's ascension into heaven with God forever.

In hope, we are able to affirm God's good intentions for creation, his continued governance of it, and his loving design for its eternal, transformed future. Christian funerals should not be used to promote our personal identity above who we truly were. With Christ as our identity, the emphasis should not be on making a final claim as the hero of our life, but rather as a humble servant of God. The funeral of the Christian should reflect the same meaning in death as the person did in life. Let us

Interpreting Cultural Trends

BOOK LINK

The Denial of Death

Pope John Paul II adopted the unsettling habit of calling our Western secular society a "culture of death." To be sure, he was thinking more of abortions than of fantasy funerals. Nevertheless, the way a culture regards death speaks volumes about its values and beliefs. One helpful book that deals with this is Ernest Becker's 1974 Pulitzer Prize–winning *The Denial of Death* (New York: Free Press, 1973). Becker's book combines depth psychology with cultural anthropology, the subject of his doctoral work, and while it does not qualify as a work of Christian theology it does contain no small amount of Christian truth.

Charles Dickens opens his novel *David Copperfield* with the narrator's words: "Whether I shall turn out to be the hero of my own life . . . these pages must show." Becker believes that this desire to be the hero of one's own story is universal because "[one] must desperately justify [oneself] as an object of primary value in the universe" (4). Society is simply the theater for earthly heroism: "What the anthropologists call 'cultural relativity' is . . . really the relativity of hero-systems the world over" (5). What is significant is that this is a uniquely human need. Unlike other animals, humans can imagine possibilities and philosophize about the meaning of life. Like animals, however, humans have bodies that are subject to disease, death, and decomposition.

The fear of death, says Becker, haunts the human animal like nothing else. And the denial of death is "a mainspring of human activity" (ix). Much of what we do, we do to cover up the story of our own death. What Becker sets forth in his book is nothing less than a large-scale hypothesis about the meaning of culture. Despite the myriad variations from place to place and from time to time, at the root of human business and busyness is a single simple truth: all our activities and all our works are but tragic attempts to convince ourselves that we are heroes that will live forever.

Becker's is a hermeneutic of suspicion: culture in his view is an elaborate distraction that encourages the illusion of our heroic immortality. Had he known of them, fantasy funerals would have no doubt added further grist to Becker's mortality mill. Indeed, this cultural trend is an extreme case of the denial of death inasmuch as it provides the illusion that one will have "control" over one's own death. Christians must acknowledge death as real, though not the end of the story. A thick description of death would speak not only of decay, but of the wages of sin. Sin is itself the great denial: of God, of the world as God's creation, of oneself as God's creature. Christians have nothing to gain by participating in our culture's denial of death or of any other aspect of reality. The church is to be a culture that can acknowledge death, but only as the next-to-last word. The church is ultimately a culture of life that does not deny but affirms reality: that new order where all things are being made new in Christ.

Kevin J. Vanhoozer

glorify God, therefore, in the service of death, as we also seek to glorify him with the service of our lives.

Suggested Readings:

Bailey, L. R. Sr. *Biblical Perspectives on Death*. Philadelphia: OBT, 1992.

Johnston, Philo S. *Shades of Sheol: Death and Afterlife in the Old Testament*. Downers Grove, IL: InterVarsity, 2002.

Laderman, Gary. *Rest in Peace*. New York: Oxford University Press, 2003.

Mitford, Jessica. *The American Way of Death Revisited*. New York: Vintage, 2000.

Searl, Edward. *In Memoriam: A Guide to Modern Funeral and Memorial Services*. Boston: Skinner House, 2000.

Part 4

Concluding
Untheoretical Postscript

Editorial Introduction

Previous essays have offered examples of how a theological hermeneutic of culture actually looks by utilizing the methodology set out in the opening essay. By interpreting texts like the music of Eminem as well as trends like transhumanism, they have provided models for how to interpret all sorts of cultural expressions and respond as Christians. This next chapter invites you to do the same. We pull back the curtain, as it were, and walk through the steps of theologically minded cultural exegesis, by taking weddings as a case study (also with examples from the rest of the book). The case study is the practical counterpart to the opening essay on methodology and thus will make most sense after having read that first chapter. This case study focuses on how to apply the methodology and take steps toward becoming everyday theologians.

11

Putting It into Practice
Weddings for Everyday Theologians

CHARLES A. ANDERSON AND MICHAEL J. SLEASMAN

The conversation at the next table in the Barnes & Noble café penetrates the din of hissing espresso makers and Saturday afternoon shopping. Glancing up from your book, you are startled by the large pile of magazines on the table, each one the size of the Yellow Pages but with glossy paper. The whole stack leans precariously to one side, threatening to topple over and leave a small dent in the floor.

"I don't know where we're going to have it," one of the women says. "The place we had our heart set on is booked solid for July. And that's the only month Jason's brother can be there the whole summer."

"That's hard," her friend responds sympathetically. "What are you going to do?"

"I don't know." She pauses, and you continue to listen, intrigued. "I knew this would be a lot of work, but we've just gotten started. We haven't even set a date or found the place yet, and I'm already frazzled. I just want the perfect wedding. How hard is that?"

"The perfect wedding." You ponder that phrase. What does it mean? How does one define "the perfect wedding"? Who gets to define it? Does it differ from person to person? You've been to a number of weddings in the past year but don't know where you'd start if someone asked you to describe "the perfect wedding." As your mind thinks through all the bouquets and best man toasts and wonders how to make sense of them, you suddenly realize—you've stumbled onto a cultural text.

They're Here, They're Everywhere: Picking a Cultural Text or Trend

Cultural texts and trends are all around us. We do not have to look far to find them. Indeed, one of the points of this book has been that everyday life abounds with cultural expressions that are meaningful and worthy of our attention. They are all around us—the grocery store checkout line, busyness, *Gladiator*. They carry messages about what the world is really like and what kind of people we should be. The first step in becoming an everyday theologian is developing this awareness, learning to recognize these texts and trends. That awareness may come from listening to a favorite band and loving their lyrics, or perhaps from pondering the underlying social issues that trouble you. Or, it may be as simple as overhearing a conversation about weddings.

Cultural texts are often easier to identify than trends, since they are more tangible, particularly in the form of movies, TV shows, musical artists, and the like. What movie or website are people talking about around the proverbial water cooler? Which television show has a small but rabid fan base that cares about it passionately? What band has registered on the cultural Richter scale? All these questions are a way of discovering what texts have cultural influence.

Putting your finger on cultural trends, on the other hand, may require stepping back to look around and discern what is happening. To do this, consult key knowledge sources: look at news magazines like *Time* or *Newsweek*; consult websites like *Wired* or *Arts and Letters Daily* to find out what is going on in technology or the humanities.[1] What new trends are newspapers reporting? Perhaps a comparison with an earlier period can highlight what is distinctive now. How is today unlike the 1950s or 1970s? Look at the world from a personal standpoint for what excites you or bothers you right now. It may prove helpful to approach it as a pastoral task, finding trends in terms of what is either hindering or helping people live as Christians. It may require more effort to identify a cultural trend than a text, but often the potential benefits are greater because trends probably have more influence in shaping us.

Whether you interpret a text or trend, assess its significance. How important is it? Do not think about high culture versus low culture, but rather think in terms of influence. What kind of impact does a given cultural expression have? What can it mean in the present or perhaps in the future? The significance of a cultural work may be that it is a developing trend, a portent of things to come. Take transhumanism, for example. Probably few of us know any self-confessed transhumanists, but the larger trends embodied by this movement (e.g., faith in scientific progress and human potential) are all around us. To consider transhumanism, then, is to wrestle with one possible direction in which the culture as a whole may soon move. Since the ultimate goal of a Christian hermeneutic of culture is to cultivate men and women more faithful to the gospel in the culture in which they live, the importance of the texts and trends does matter.

On any scale, weddings are a cultural text that matters. First, they are a cultural text. Weddings carry with them certain practices and shared expectations, and so we can observe and learn how they function. Ultimately, a wedding projects a view of how the world, and we who live in it, should look. They tell a story about how life should be—a world of joy and relationships where everything is in its right place. Our responsibility as interpreters is to reflect on what that story means. Second, weddings matter. Most of us will be the featured players in at least one wedding at some point in our lives, and we usually attend and participate in many more. From a pragmatic standpoint, weddings are big business, an estimated $72 billion a year in the U.S. alone.[2] Weddings have always mattered—throughout history and across cultures, humankind has held ceremonies to mark the beginning of marriage. Most importantly, perhaps, a wedding is a central event in life, a defining moment for who we are. Weddings are a cultural text worth examining.

We will use weddings in this case study to illustrate how one might approach interpretation. The questions and ideas we raise are suggestive—certainly you will think of other facets of weddings that we do not mention. What we have done here is intended to make the whole Method more concrete, to let you in "behind the scenes."

Putting a Foot Forward: The World-Of

So if you want to understand weddings, where do you start? The key is repeated "reading" of the text or trend. There is no substitute for spending time on careful observation. This is the primary aim for the world-of.

For a text, that means repeated viewings or readings. If it is a movie, try to watch the director's commentary on the DVD and check out the disc's bonus features. If it is an album, listen to it numerous times with lyrics in hand. Pay attention to the nuances and subtle movements of the text; move beyond the passive entertainment value. More advanced interpreters may want to develop competency in the locution of the text; for example, in film, learn about cinematography and how lighting and camera angles contribute to the movie and its message.

For a trend, the approach is more indirect. If you have personal experience with the trend, start there. What is characteristic or foundational or unusual about it? Talk with friends about their experience. Type keywords from the trend into Google or Amazon and browse the results. Look through magazines at a bookstore for relevant titles or articles.

Weddings offer a rich variety of observation points. The best place to start is by reflecting on weddings you have attended:

- Start with the invitation: When did you receive it? How was it designed? What did it say? What else happens before the actual day? Showers? Bachelor party? Rehearsal dinner?
- Move to the wedding day: Where and when does it take place? How is the venue decorated? How many guests attend? How does the bride's dress look? Who participates in the wedding?
- Describe the ceremony itself: How does it begin? Who conducts it? What vows do the bride and groom make? Is there any explicitly religious content? How is it used? What is the main point of the homily? What kind of music is there? Who sings or performs it? How does the service end?
- Turn to the reception: Is it simple and low key or a black-tie formal dinner? Where is it held? What kind of food and drink is served? What other activities take place? If there are speeches, who gives them and what do they say? How long does the reception last? When do the bride and groom leave?
- If you can, compare multiple weddings from your experience. Look for similarities and differences, and even for explanations of those patterns.

Significant observation can take place apart from a wedding itself. Look at some websites like The Knot or Wedding Channel.com. Perhaps the couple has an online registry (a sign of how technological developments can influence cultural trends). What kinds of gifts are on the registry? Browse through magazines like *Modern Bride*, *Martha Stewart Weddings*, and *Wedding Dresses*. What do the articles cover? What advertisements appear? Look through a few wedding planning books. How do they characterize weddings? Where do their emphases lie? If you feel particularly ambitious, perhaps you can visit a bridal show.

A valuable resource for cultural hermeneutics is talking with other people. They allow us to probe below the surface as we ask why things are the way they are. They also help us to avoid potential blind spots created by the limitations of our own experience or presuppositions.

- Talk with engaged couples who are in the midst of planning a wedding. What are their experiences? What do they enjoy? What do they find stressful?
- Talk with some newlyweds. How do they feel now about the whole process? When they look at their pictures, what do they think? What would they do the same way? What would they do differently? What difference has their wedding made (or not made) in their marriage?
- For a more advanced level, interview a professional wedding planner or a pastor. What perspectives do they have on weddings? What patterns do they detect? What kinds of questions and concerns do couples tend to raise?

Hopefully, two points emerge from these suggestions. First, our investigation should be thorough and thoughtful. As you explore a text or trend, cover as much ground as possible. Get a feel for the surface of the text, its features and characteristics. Then, sift that knowledge and look for patterns. What connections emerge from your observations? Sometimes, a telling quote or fact can illuminate the text. For example, Eminem called his music his therapy. That admission offers an important vantage point from which to understand his lyrics. Part of being thoughtful is respecting the particularity of the text or trend while at the same time trying to identify what is universal about it. How does the text reach beyond itself, so to speak? If our foundation of knowledge is not thorough and thoughtful, our final interpretation will easily break down.

The second point is that at this stage we should do our best to suspend judgment, whether positive or negative. We should practice a hermeneutic of charity that listens sympathetically to the text or trend and withholds critical assessment. Every cultural text reveals signs of creation and the fall, markers both of God's original good design and of how those intentions have become corrupted by sin. True theological understanding will incorporate both types, but each in its time. If we rush to judgment on a text we may inadvertently muzzle part of its message to us. Taking Eminem again as an example: if as Christians we too quickly condemn his violent and profane lyrics, we may miss his implicit rebuke of our failure to reach out to the hurting and disadvantaged. A hermeneutic of charity strives to hear what the text is saying before it makes judgments.

Putting It in Perspective: The World-Behind

Once we have gained a good initial grasp of the text or trend, we broaden our scope to incorporate the world-behind. Our purpose is to understand more fully how the work came to take its present shape. This stage of the hermeneutical process examines historical and social forces, biographical details, the genre, and so on; in other words, look for factors that influence the work. It helps us not to jump straight from our observations of the cultural work to what it means. The world-behind combats the danger of reductionism in our interpretation.

The first stage of interpretation may have already uncovered potential starting points for the world-behind. If not, one way of doing so is to look at what others have said. For example, look for movie or album reviews on the Web or in major publications. Browse through more intellectual journals like *Atlantic Monthly*, *Books and Culture*, *Hedgehog Review*, or *The New Yorker*. A quick search for weddings on their websites reveals some thoughtful articles that could prove helpful.[3]

After you have read through smaller pieces, you may be ready to look at a few books, especially those that provide historical and cultural perspective. You may find the right books from the articles you have already read. Or it may require a bit more detective work. One good method is to visit the online catalog of a major university library. Enter a keyword as a subject heading and see what it produces. For example, when you type in "weddings" as a subject heading in Northwestern University's library catalog, the search yields promising results, as do the subheadings "Weddings–Economic Aspects–United States" and "Weddings–United States–History."[4] Become a bit creative and type in "Marriage customs and rites," and the United States subcategory again features relevant titles. If your library does not have a particular book, often you can obtain it via interlibrary loan.

Concluding Untheoretical Postscript

As you read, try to assess critically the arguments. Do the explanations offered seem plausible in light of what you have learned already? For those who want to go beyond basic competence, pay particular attention to footnotes and endnotes. Such details are often important for assessing the arguments, and through these the author has left a paper trail of his or her own research. Look for repeated references to a particular author or book in order to find key authorities in the field. With our case study, books like *Cinderella Dreams* or *All Dressed in White* can provide invaluable historical and cultural context to help explain how we have arrived at contemporary weddings.[5] Drawing in such perspectives ensures breadth and depth in our interpretation.

The world-behind is also the right place to look at who is involved in the creation and dissemination of cultural texts and trends. For texts, that may involve biographical information and interviews with the artistic figures behind them. How have their own stories and intentions shaped what they have made? Furthermore, every text belongs to a particular genre: it is a certain kind of book or movie or music. That genre will shape our understanding—we interpret a historical epic by somewhat different rules than we do an animated children's movie. So, for example, it helps to know that *Gladiator* is an heir of the old "sword and sandals" epics. Why? Because movies in that genre typically had a certain amount of Christian content. The fact that *Gladiator* deviates from that convention provides clues for interpretation.

For trends, questions of creator and genre are not as relevant, so we ask whose interests are advanced by the trend. Who stands to gain from it? With weddings, one answer points to the money. Remember, weddings are not just a "big day," they are big business. Lots of people have a stake in this $72 billion industry—event planners, dress makers, photographers, and the like. If we follow the money, we often will discover ways the text or trend is shaped for the economic benefit of those involved. Part of the world-behind weddings, therefore, is to examine how those economic interests, in turn, influence the shape of weddings.

Finally, we may also ponder other cultural trends that influence the cultural work. Weddings are shaped by other trends. We might ask: How does the fading disapproval of pre-marital sex and cohabitation shape weddings? In at least one small way: it has been observed that the bride and groom are more likely to stay much longer at their reception. The prospect of sex holds no unusual incentive for them to hurry into the honeymoon.[6] Similarly, the secularization of American culture has shaped how weddings are celebrated; as traditional Christian practices recede, other options, both religious and secular, emerge. The world-behind explores such trends for how they affect weddings.

The goal for the world-behind stage, and for the entire cultural herme-neutic enterprise, is not to transform you into a *bona fide* expert able to participate in scholarly discussions about the text or trend. If we all have to be experts on a subject before we can open our mouths, then very little Christian thinking and living is going to take place. Rather, the aim is for competency: you can follow those discussions, and an expert who listened to your interpretation would respect your grasp of the subject. At the end of this stage, you should have a sense of how weddings have taken their current shape and the most important contributing factors.

Putting It Together: The World-in-Front

The world-in-front is where the insights gleaned from studying the work, paired with an awareness of the historical and cultural contexts, come together to begin to answer the question of what it all means. In the world-in-front, we look at how the text or trend interacts with our world, especially in terms of its influence and ideals.

Perhaps the most straightforward place to begin is with the audience. How do people respond to the text or trend? Usually, reactions range from affirmation to rejection, with many mediating points along the way. Such is the case, for example, with the Universal Declaration of Human Rights, which has been both foundational for the human rights movement and reviled as a tool of Western imperialism. Listen to how particular segments of the audience respond. In our case study, we are interested not only in how Americans in general practice weddings, but also how it breaks down according to groups. How do men respond to weddings compared to women? Does economic status make a difference? What about ethnicity? Where is there uniformity across these groups, and where do meaning-ful variations exist? For example, if the cost of weddings across all these demographics rises, that provides a significant clue for interpretation.

More broadly, look to how the text or trend influences its culture. Perhaps it has spawned imitators or pioneered a new genre. Look for how other texts respond to yours: they may build on it or argue against it—both are signs of a text's influence. Trends may have an impact as more and more people participate. They can contribute to public policy discussions, as when feelings of busyness influence debates over parental leave and flexible work schedules. Trends may spark changes in beliefs

Concluding Untheoretical Postscript

and practices, much like the role of blogging in a more accountable mass media.

One way to understand how weddings influence American culture is to examine their impact on marriage. The connection between the two may seem obvious, but it is striking how little marriage is mentioned when weddings are discussed. After all, it stands to reason that there might be some talk about the institution of marriage when discussing the ceremony that marks its beginning. It is instructive to note that as marriage has diminished in stature and longevity, weddings have simultaneously grown in cost, production, and emphasis. Of course, it is always possible that no actual connection exists between these two trends, and thus we should explain this inverse relationship on other grounds. Either way, the world-in-front is the stage where such questions are explored. Moreover, this give-and-take, where weddings affect marriage and marriage affects weddings, points to the complexity of our task. As a text or trend influences its culture—and in turn is influenced by it—a feedback loop can result, where the process continually mutates. Thus, often our cultural interpretation provides no more than a snapshot of where things stand at a particular moment.

The world-in-front is an imaginative enterprise. It recognizes that cultural texts and trends shape human identity and project a vision of the way the world should work. Thus, our hermeneutic must ask: What kind of people do weddings envision? What kind of worldview do weddings project? Weddings make all sorts of implicit statements about human relationships, values like love and commitment, the place of community and celebration, the importance of public displays of wealth, and so on. Teasing out each of those statements is integral to discerning what weddings mean. Imagine different people and ask how they would describe the ideal wedding—what would a typical bride-to-be say? A groom? A wedding planner? A photographer?[7] The various answers help show the significance of weddings and what they mean.

Another way to approach the world-in-front is to look for a root metaphor, an image that sums up what you have learned and encapsulates it. Examples of root metaphors include the world as machine or as a living organism. Finding a root metaphor is not easy but, when done well, can powerfully express what the text or trend means. Possible root metaphors for weddings might include the party of a lifetime or the special day of a princess.

When you work at this level of interpretation, you do the hard labor of putting together what you have learned and observed. You are trying to understand the text or trend sympathetically, clearly, and insightfully. At the end, you should be able to give a sense of what it means on its own terms. When you can do that, then you are ready to move on to the explicitly theological level.

What Does the Bible Say About . . . ?

We move now into the last level of interpretation, a theological reading of the cultural work. Understanding the text or trend from an explicitly Christian point of view reflects our belief that the gospel is the true story of the world. It is the real context in which all texts and trends live and move and have their being. Often, the cultural work—or its creators—may not recognize this context, or even resist it. They might label a theological reading as naively Christianizing the work. Moving from close attention to the cultural work and then to the level of theological interpretation hopefully forces us to listen to the texts and how others read them and thus keeps us honest and avoids imposing meaning. At the same time, we may have to "expose" another level of real meaning by interpreting the cultural work in light of Christian wisdom. We can never reach a truly thick description without this theological level.

We begin by finding a biblical-theological understanding of the issues raised. To do that, we must first figure out where to look. Weddings are relatively straightforward, since they and marriage are topics directly addressed by Scripture, but this is probably the exception rather than the rule. Not surprisingly blogging, for example, gets no mention in the biblical text. But the values it champions, like participation and community as the means by which we discover truth, are topics on which Scripture speaks. So a theological analysis would begin by exploring what the Bible says about the topics that blogging embodies and expresses. Similarly, any theological interpretation of weddings should also include categories like covenant, children, divorce, and sexuality, in order to paint a full picture. It may also prove helpful to place the text or trend within a category of thought: Does it talk about what it means to be human, relationships, the world, a spiritual realm, the nature of things, the future, etc.? Correctly categorizing a cultural work may point to the right biblical points of contact.

But where do you start to look even after you have an idea about the right topics? One possibility is to read a few entries in a good dictionary, like the *Anchor Bible Dictionary*, *Evangelical Dictionary of Theology*, or *New Bible Dictionary*.[8] Their articles can provide a succinct overview, point to biblical passages, and supply key bibliography. Dictionaries, therefore, make an invaluable launch pad for theological analysis. Rather intriguingly, looking up "weddings" in such dictionaries leads nowhere. None of them include a separate entry for weddings; at most, they have a note that says, "See marriage." That omission perhaps offers a significant clue about a biblical view of weddings—they are not nearly so important as marriage itself.

Another strategy is to utilize the online library catalog of a seminary, as we did earlier. The subject heading of "weddings" in Trinity Evangelical Divinity School's library yields some promising results. Even better is "marriage," especially after scrolling through the subheadings and finding "marriage–biblical–teaching."[9] This search produces worthwhile books like *Marriage: Sex in the Service of God* and *God and Marriage*.[10]

Dictionary articles and well-chosen books offer important resources not only for getting started but also for developing substance to our understanding. But nothing takes the place of our own study of the world of the biblical text. To have a good sense of what Scripture says in relation to weddings or human rights or busyness, we need to spend time in the biblical text. Such study provides the core for theological engagement with the cultural work. So before we can say anything about a Christian perspective on contemporary American weddings, we need to examine key passages:

> **Genesis 2:18–25.** The first wedding occurs, and we learn that marriage is a one-flesh union.
>
> **Song of Solomon 4:1–15.** Sexuality and beauty within marriage are frankly celebrated.
>
> **Matthew 22:23–33.** Jesus denies that marriage has any place in the age to come.
>
> **Mark 10:1–12.** Jesus affirms the significance of God's original intent for marriage.
>
> **Ephesians 5:22–33.** Marriage is patterned on the relationship of Christ and the church.
>
> **Revelation 19:6–9.** A wedding banquet is the image for God's relationship with his people.

This list is certainly not exhaustive, but it includes some of the most important biblical passages on this topic.[11] Again, we notice how little there is about weddings themselves. No explicitly didactic passage in the Bible teaches us how to have a wedding. We can observe customs from biblical times but not instructions. Thus, when we synthesize a biblical view on weddings it will need to reflect this lack of emphasis on the structure of the wedding itself.

The goal of this stage, as you study key passages and incorporate what others have to say, is to formulate a coherent sense of the biblical view on the topic. Once you have done that, you are ready to bring those insights to bear upon the cultural work.

Seeing the World through Redemptive History–Colored Glasses

Now that you have done the hard work of understanding what the cultural text or trend means and sketching a biblical perspective, how do you bring these parts together? One method is by situating the text or trend within the world of the biblical text. Scripture reveals an unfolding story of the history of redemption, a story that begins with creation but goes tragically awry with the fall, finds its center point in redemption in Jesus' life, death, and resurrection, and will reach its conclusion in the new creation.[12] We live within this story, as God works out redemption in and through us and the whole creation. Reading a cultural work through this lens places it within its real context. It also helps keep the central focus of interpretation on the gospel. It is easy to apply biblical passages atomistically to a cultural work and subtly forget that they are part of the story line of salvation, not commentary on the text or trend. Thus, reading the cultural work through the world of the biblical text helps keep the main thing the main thing.

Start by looking for signs of creation and the fall in the cultural work. This requires discernment to tease out elements of the text or trend and assess them in light of what you have learned from theology. Signs of creation are characteristics of the cultural work that correspond to the biblical design. They are the remnants of how God originally intended things to be. For example, from the story of Jesus at a wedding in Cana (John 2:1–11) and other references to wedding banquets (e.g., Matt. 22:1–14) we get the sense that a wedding should be a special celebration. Thus, we can affirm, in some way, contemporary efforts to make weddings special, often by spending more money or putting significant planning into this one day. Finding similarities between the cultural work and the biblical perspective reminds us that we can affirm something positive about (nearly) every cultural work.

Concluding Untheoretical Postscript

Signs of the fall are characteristics of the cultural work that diverge from the biblical design. Look for clear instances where sin has deformed the text or trend, which now falls short of what it should be. Thus, while it is good to make a wedding a special event, one must question how far those efforts have gone. The average American wedding budget is around $20,000.[13] In light of the biblical mandate for mission, are such expenditures justified? Could not some of that money be better spent elsewhere in light of eternity? Is there a level of showmanship and a measure of status behind the expense of a wedding? Does the designer of the dress overshadow the designer of the occasion? That $20,000 is the *average* for a wedding seems to indicate that non-biblical priorities drive many wedding decisions.

Earlier, we cautioned against too quickly evaluating the cultural work and recommended a hermeneutic of charity. It is appropriate now to include a hermeneutic of suspicion. Who is really being served by the text or trend? For weddings, we should question the economic interests that drive such budgets. No doubt this spending is influenced, in part, by the marketing strategies of the wedding industry. Brides and grooms are told that unless the day is perfect their wedding will be a failure. What (or who) defines perfection? Apparently perfection means spending enough money to make every dream come true and safeguard against any possible mistake. Thus, an ideology of consumption lurks in the background, shaping the text. As we look for signs of the fall, we need to examine the cultural work with a certain amount of suspicion and question the way things are.

An advanced way to look for signs of the fall is to identify the theological root error. At the world-in-front level, we spoke of finding a root metaphor, an image that could encapsulate what the work means. Now, the goal is to find its theological root error. Go past problems of morality and burrow down to the core of what the text or trend professes—in what key way does it fall short of the gospel? To answer this question requires a good knowledge of both the cultural work and the biblical perspective. It would be premature, therefore, to point to a theological root error for weddings, since we have not done a full interpretation of this cultural text. Instead, we can illustrate this concept from the essay on busyness. It is possible to pursue either idolatrous or holy busyness. The theological root error is to deny God as Lord of time and submit our lives to the demands of the clock. We believe that if we just work hard enough, things will go the way we want. That is more than a moral failure—it fails to trust God and rejects grace. Thus, the core problem with busyness comes from how we see God and try to relate to him and the world. This kind of interpretation is deep analysis. Indeed, determining a theological root error addresses the cultural work at its core.

After identifying signs of the fall, it makes particular sense to turn to redemption. Here we take the text or trend and imagine how to redeem it. We may use the particular story of Jesus as a guide. If the practices and values of Jesus were applied, how would the text or trend look different? We envision how trust in his redemptive work at the cross should shape the cultural work. How can the cultural work be re-created in line with the gospel? This task requires imagination. Often it takes dreaming of new possibilities, thinking from a theological foundation and then jumping off into what could be. For weddings, we might imagine how the bride and groom, instead of being served, could actually serve their guests. Or we could find natural ways to include a presentation of the gospel in the ceremony. The goal is to generate ways to bring the text or trend in line with the gospel.

For many of us, this approach—of trying to read the work through the world of the biblical text—will be a new way of looking at things. The realm of the Bible seems so remote to us in the twenty-first century. The power of this way of seeing things, though, comes from realizing that the seemingly distant biblical world is actually the real world. As we read these texts and trends through the lens of redemptive history, we realize that we are a part of God's ongoing mission of salvation. We too demonstrate both the goodness of creation and the corruption of the fall. Because we ourselves are a part of the story of God's work in history, so too are all the texts and trends we make. Thus, redemptive history offers a truer way to understand the world. Having read the text theologically, we are ready to live out our response.

Beyond Discussion: Becoming a Cultural Agent

Too often, our cultural engagement remains a purely intellectual pursuit. Sometimes, in fact, the pursuit is not even that intellectual, especially when we make rash judgments and off-the-cuff evaluations without wrestling with the deeper issues. But even when our thinking is more rigorous, the temptation is to offer feedback and "engage" the culture at a healthy distance. How different this looks, though, from the incarnation of Christ. The ultimate goal of cultural hermeneutics is to live redemptively in response to the cultural work. We find ourselves in a world in decay and yet with the shadow and promise of glory, a world that God is reconciling to himself. Part of our ambassadorship for Christ is to imagine how he should shape our lives in light of the influences of the texts and trends around us. Only if we practice cultural agency have we truly done cultural interpretation and fulfilled our responsibility to acquire wisdom.

Theological analysis of the cultural work should already have prepared us for how to respond. Identifying signs of creation and the fall, and imaginatively reconceiving the text or trend in redemption, should yield concrete possibilities for wise living. For example, we could propose ways to designate part of the wedding budget toward mission. Or we might think of how to ensure that the elements of the wedding point prominently toward the marriage and that the ceremony does not become an end in itself. Good theological understanding of the text or trend should lead naturally into cultural agency.

Our mandate to live wisely as Christians includes all of life. Our response, therefore, should be holistic, encompassing hands and the heart, the individual and the group.[14] The type of text or trend may point to some of these areas more than others: fantasy funerals lend themselves well to a response on all four levels, whereas *Gladiator* tends more toward the heart than concrete practices—we probably would not suggest that one of the points of action from the film is to go out and fight gladiator-style for Christian hope (though maybe metaphorically!).

Proposals for the heart focus on what we believe and value. Cultural agency starts with the heart, because it recognizes this is where cultural texts most fundamentally want to shape us. Our response, therefore, must match accordingly. All other cultural agency flows from the heart. For weddings we might ask whether we are more excited about the event or the marriage. Then we might measure how we allocate our time and efforts during engagement to reflect a priority on the marriage (while simultaneously recognizing the inevitable and right demands of a wedding).

Cultural agency in individual practices is perhaps more straightforward. We might propose shorter engagements to help curtail excesses in planning the ceremony but with longer honeymoons to give more time for enjoying the first weeks of marriage and easing the transition. Remember that many texts or trends have multiple roles that people might play. So our application should also pay attention to members of the wedding party, the family, and the guests. We must be careful, though, not simply to compile a laundry list of moral do's and don'ts, but to think in terms of wise, gospel-shaped practices.

It may be less natural for us to think of cultural agency at the level of the church (largely because of cultural trends like individualism!). Nevertheless, the church's mission is to proclaim and embody the redemptive reign of God, and Christian corporate practice is actually our best means of response. The texts and trends in this volume require a group effort to act—reaching out to the marginalized to whom Eminem appeals, physically remodeling the worship area of a church to embody theological values, speaking with a prophetic voice about biotechnology. All these actions are most effective when undertaken *as the church*. So for weddings, perhaps we have older married couples in the church mentor engaged couples. Or, we have volunteer wedding coordinators who help couples navigate the maze, with *both* practical tips *and* godly advice.

This category can also include how we might offer a "Christian" way to practice the text or trend. Christian rap was a suggestion for one way to respond to Eminem's music. It will always require discernment to decide which aspects of the trend should be retained and which altered. For example, fantasy funerals show some characteristics that a more Christian approach could copy. How would a "Christian" wedding both resemble and differ from a "non-Christian" wedding? This question carries greater weight when we remember that marriage is a creation ordinance. Creation ordinances refer to God's intentions for this world, how he designed family, work, rest, and other aspects of life to function for every human being. Marriage, as instituted in Genesis 2, is an ordinance of creation and thus valid for all male-female sexual unions, whether Christian or not. So what should all weddings have in common since God designed marriage for all human beings? How might Christian weddings be distinct since we now live in a fallen creation?

Finally, because all these texts and trends originate from and move in the wider world, our cultural agency should encompass the same. The avowedly Christian orientation to our hermeneutics should not be mistaken for a call to speak only to Christians. We ought to make proposals for responding to cultural works in the world. The essay on the Universal Declaration of Human Rights suggested getting involved with organizations like Amnesty International or International Justice Mission. Part of engaging with transhumanism is participating in the scientific research that helps drive that trend. For weddings, we might encourage all couples to attend premarital and postmarital counseling as preparation for the actual marriage.

Christian cultural agency is the culmination of cultural hermeneutics. It comes after we have given a thick description of the work on all levels, including evaluation in light of Christian wisdom. Upon that interpretation, it builds a response with our lives. And so we come full circle, from being passive consumers influenced by culture to agents who competently read texts and interpret trends in order to change ourselves and the world for the glory of God.

BOOK LINK

We Are What We Celebrate

It is only fitting that we conclude our study of how to read culture with the "and they lived happily ever after" that is a distinguishing feature of the human comedy and the tacit promise of every wedding. Weddings are of special importance for our study of culture: First, they mark the formation of new families, and families are one of the chief means of propagating systems of values and beliefs. Second, weddings occupy a peculiar place between the sacred and the profane. Indeed, in our post-Christian culture, weddings may be the only time some people attend a church service. Third, weddings and other holidays—days set apart to commemorate an event of special importance, "holy-days"—are particularly important cultural texts, effective indicators of what is going on in culture. This, at least, is the thesis of a volume of essays that originated in an academic conference on this very subject: Amitai Etzioni, ed., *We Are What We Celebrate: Understanding Holidays and Rituals* (New York: New York University Press, 2004).

In our postmodern, "postsentimental" times (52), selective observance of holidays has become the norm. Increasingly, individuals feel free to uphold or adapt traditional celebrations on the basis of what seems personally meaningful to them. The way people plan their weddings, for example, says something about individuals and families as well as about the general culture. These and other holy-days reaffirm communal bonds and reinforce communal values.

Special celebrations like weddings and regular celebrations like Christmas and Thanksgiving are all rituals: solemn performances that mark important events, rule-governed symbolic activities that focus the attention of their participants on something of special significance. According to the sociologist Émile Durkheim, everyday life—our secular routine—tends toward individualism and hence to weaken the bonds and beliefs that hold society together. Rituals, he believed, are one mechanism for members of a community to reaffirm what holds them together: "Hence, when holidays deteriorate, so do moral and social order" (8).

The authors of *We Are What We Celebrate* agree with Durkheim that the ways holidays are celebrated tell us much about a culture, but they see celebrations as having more than a single socializing function. We need thick descriptions, not simple theories, if we are to understand Thanksgiving, for instance. Some holidays (e.g., St. Patrick's Day, Kwanzaa) celebrate specific ethnic groups, not the whole of society. And we must not forget the profit motive behind the increasing commodification of special days: "After about 1910 it was difficult to name a holiday or rite of passage that was devoid of all four of the most common elements—presents, flowers, cards, and candy" (45). If we are what we celebrate—as families, communities, and nations—then Christians need to be able to read the signs of these special times and to remind themselves that Christians are, or should be, what we celebrate each time we share the Lord's Supper: a communion of saints who share new life as the body of Christ.

Kevin J. Vanhoozer

Glossary
of Methodological Terms

KEVIN J. VANHOOZER

The following terms feature prominently in the Method for interpreting culture set out in the opening essay.

adaptation
> Michel de Certeau's term for describing people's ability to resist the strategy of culture's producers; the name for everyday ways of using imposed cultural systems

agent
> one who acts from freedom rather than necessity; one who uses various media (e.g., language, paint, bricks, etc.) to say or do something

cultural agency
> the outcome of cultural literacy and the opposite of passive consumerism; the ability to read and write culture by making one's own mark rather than simply submitting to cultural programming

cultural competence
> the implicit knowledge or tacit mastery people must have of their everyday culture in order to be effective cultural agents

cultural discourse
> the notion that culture and its products, like language, communicate things and, again like language, *do* things other than simply transmit information (e.g., ads not only inform but make promises)

cultural hermeneutics

in this book, the art and science of interpreting culture; the set of rules, guide-lines, or principles for interpreting cultural texts and trends; outside this book the term stands for approaches to interpretation in which the social and cultural location of the interpreter (e.g., feminist, African-American) serves as a principle of interpretation

cultural literacy

minimally, the ability to "read" or make sense of cultural texts and trends in everyday life; maximally, the ability to "write" culture, that is, to use the resources of culture to make one's own meaningful statement

cultural studies

the study of everyday or popular culture, which began to find a niche in aca-demia in the 1960s; in Britain (at the Birmingham Centre for Contemporary Cultural Studies), the study of everyday culture especially as it relates to social hierarchies, economic processes, political power, and identity formation; in North America, the study of popular culture, especially as expressed in the electronic media, with tools drawn largely from literary criticism and com-munication studies

cultural text

any human work that, precisely because it is something done purposefully and not by reflex, bears meaning and calls for interpretation

culture

the world of meaning, made by humans, in which we dwell; in contrast to nature, a comprehensive term for the beliefs, values, and way of life passed on from one generation to the next: a "web of significance" (Clifford Geertz); in contrast to economics, the sphere of producing and consuming not things but meaningful life

culture industries

a pejorative term used by the Frankfurt School to offer a neo-Marxist critique of the system in which certain industries (e.g., the movie industry, the music industry) mass-produce symbolic goods (e.g., films, CDs) for ideological or mon-etary (exchange value) rather than moral or aesthetic purposes (use value)

discourse

the act of using language by persons in concrete contexts (speech, *parole*) as opposed to language as an abstract system of signs (code, *langue*); what someone says to someone in some way about something; language in its inter-subjective, communicative aspect; pertaining to semantics (the study of verbal utterances longer than a sentence) as opposed to semiotics (the science of signs or signifying elements)

Glossary of Methodological Terms

everyday theology
the attempt to think theologically about the everyday world; faith seeking understanding of contemporary culture, its products (texts), and processes (trends)

excorporation
John Fiske's term for the process by which people make their own culture and meaning out of the resources and commodities produced by the dominant culture; a term that calls attention not to the things in culture but to the way people use them (meaning as use)

exegesis
the act of interpretation, with or without acknowledging one's hermeneutical presuppositions; in biblical studies, setting forth the meaning of the text, especially through close attention to its philological, historical, and literary features; in cultural studies, describing the form and content of cultural works

Geisteswissenschaften
German term employed by Wilhelm Dilthey for the human sciences (literally, "sciences of the mind" or "spirit"); academic disciplines that study the expression of human life in objective forms (e.g., works, texts); the knowledge humans have of themselves via interpretation and understanding rather than via causal explanation

hegemony
the domination of one culture over another; Antonio Gramsci's term for the process by which a dominant class maintains its control or leadership (Gk. *hegemon* "ruler") of a society through noncoercive means (e.g., schools, media, families) by getting subordinate groups to consent to the dominant group's ways of making sense of the world (worldview); the way in which everyday meanings serve the interests of the powerful by making those interests appear natural and common-sensical

hermeneutics
the theory and method of textual, especially biblical, interpretation; in twentieth-century Continental philosophy, the study of human understanding; in the singular ("hermeneutic"), a particular interpretative approach

hermeneutics of suspicion
Paul Ricoeur's term, employed in his *Freud and Philosophy* (1970), for critical interpretations that distinguish appearances (i.e., surface meanings) from the deeper reality (i.e., what a text is really saying or doing); the tendency to suspect that the world projected by the text may be false or otherwise hazardous to one's well-being

high vs. low culture

the distinction, dominant in the nineteenth-century West but now largely discredited and deconstructed, between the "serious" art, literature, and music favored by the educated elite (what Matthew Arnold called "the best that human beings had ever thought or said") and the mess of cultural pottage favored by the masses

ideology

neutrally, the beliefs and attitudes (worldview) characteristic of a social class; negatively, the Marxist notion that ideas are tied to materialist bases and economic conditions such that meaning is a sociopolitical construction that is always in the service of power; beliefs and ideas that are rationalizations justifying oppressive systems or the interests of a dominant group

illocution

central concept in speech act theory referring to what someone does *in* saying something (promising, warning, commanding, asserting, etc.); by extension, what someone does in using some cultural medium to express or communicate something (e.g., advertisements make promises)

interpretation

as verb, the process of acquiring understanding by making sense of or discovering meaning in texts; as noun, the result of this process; an application of hermeneutics to a specific text

locution

the act of saying something in a particular medium of communication (e.g., words, images, music, film)

meaning

a controversial notion, both as to its nature and its location (e.g., in the mind of the author/producer, in the text/product, in the reader/consumer's response); in semiotics, the referential relation between signs and things or the differential relation between one sign and another; for pragmatics, a function of use; in this book, what is shared through successful communicative interaction, whatever the medium; that which is proposed for our consideration via texts; what the author/producer is doing with his or her locutions

perlocution

what we bring about *by* saying something (e.g., by affirming something we may persuade someone); the consequence, intended and unintended, of an illocutionary act

popular culture

in contrast to high, mass, and folk culture, the culture of, for, or by the people; the library of texts—songs, ads, movies, art, gadgets, toys, fashions, etc.—from which people borrow and read in order to achieve everyday literacy; the shared environment of products and practices that comprise the everyday life of people in a given society or social group; what people do, the ways of everyday life, ways of eating, dressing, playing, working, relaxing, worshiping, etc.

reductionism

explanation of complex data in overly simplistic terms; in cultural studies, the tendency to explain away meaningful human behavior by giving causal (e.g., sociobiological) explanations; yields inadequate understanding because it offers only thin, not thick, descriptions

root metaphor

way of viewing the world *as* something that highlights certain aspects of reality and yields certain kinds of theories rather than others (e.g., world as machine vs. world as organism)

semiotics

the science of signs; an approach to culture that views meaning as an effect of differential relations in the sign system itself rather than an effect of what human users do with the sign system

speech act

approach in linguistic philosophy concerned with the use of words to perform actions (e.g., assert, promise, warn, greet, bless, etc.)

text

discourse given stable form by writing or some other medium (e.g., book, musical score, film); a structured work composed of signifying elements

theology

faith seeking understanding by (1) identifying God through his words and actions recorded in the biblical text and (2) inquiring into the relation of everything else to the God so identified

thick description

introduced into cultural anthropology by Clifford Geertz, but originally used by Gilbert Ryle to distinguish a blink (an involuntary nervous reaction) from a wink (a willed, and therefore meaningful, act); in this book, the process of interpreting cultural texts by examining multiple levels of significance, including the theological; the attempt to avoid reductionism in cultural hermeneutics

understanding

the result of successful interpretation; the grasp of the meaning of a sign, thing, or act (e.g., a sentence, a musical note, a gesture) by determining its proper context and place in a larger whole (e.g., a text, a composition, a ritual); the recognition of what illocutionary acts have been performed in some locutionary medium (e.g., words, music, film, images); the discernment of the question or concern to which a text presents the answer; the grasp of a text's subject matter

work
> something made intentionally, not by instinct, out of some material (e.g., work of art, an author's "collected works"); an object or instrument of meaningful action, especially communicative action (e.g., the action of "displaying" or "projecting" a world)

world-behind-the-text
> the actual historical world of a text's producers or authors; the material and intellectual cultural situation that serves as the context of a text's composition

world-in-front-of-the-text
> an imaginative projection of cultural texts that depicts the way the real world, or human beings, *could* be; the world of the text as it impinges on the world of the reader/user

world-of-the-text
> a possible state of affairs displayed by or included within a cultural text or work; the product of human "sub-creators" (Tolkien) who envisage the world otherwise than it actually is

worldview
> "the comprehensive framework of one's basic beliefs about things";[1] the intellectual scaffolding that supports a culture's way of life

Zeitgeist
> German term meaning "spirit of the age"; the prevailing mood or ethos that culture both expresses and reproduces; the moral, intellectual, and aesthetic instincts of people at a particular place and time

Guidelines for Everyday Theological Interpretation of Culture

1. Try to comprehend a cultural text on its own terms (grasp its communicative intent) before you "interpret" it (explore its broader social, political, sexual, or religious significance).
2. Attend to what a cultural text is *doing* as well as saying by clarifying its illocutionary act (e.g., stating a belief, displaying a world).
3. Consider the world *behind* (e.g., medieval, modern), *of* (i.e., the world displayed by the cultural text), and *in front of* (i.e., its proposal for your world) the cultural text.
4. Determine what "powers" are served by particular cultural texts or trends by discovering whose material interests are served (e.g., follow the money!).

5. Seek the "world hypothesis" and/or "root metaphor" implied by a cultural text.
6. Be comprehensive in your interpretation of a cultural text; find corroborative evidence that makes the best sense of the whole as well as the parts.
7. Give "thick" descriptions of the cultural text that are nonreductive and sensitive to the various levels of communicative action.
8. Articulate the way of being human to which a cultural text directly or indirectly bears witness and gives commendation.
9. Discern what *faith* a cultural text directly or indirectly expresses. To what convictions about God, the world, and ourselves does a cultural text and/or trend commit us?
10. Locate the cultural text in the biblical creation-fall-redemption schema and make sure that biblical rather than cultural texts have the lead role in shaping your imagination and hence your interpretative framework for your experience.

Notes

A Reader's Guide

1. *The Gospel in a Pluralistic Society* (Grand Rapids: Eerdmans, 1989).

Chapter 1 What Is Everyday Theology?

1. John Frame, *The Doctrine of the Knowledge of God* (Grand Rapids: Baker, 1987), 81.

2. The *Proslogion* offers a proof for God's necessary existence; *Cur Deus Homo?* sets forth reasons for the necessity of the incarnation as well as the cross of Christ.

3. Luther's principle of the "priesthood of all believers" was meant to stress the privilege and responsibility of having direct access to God in Scripture; it was not meant to lead to modern individualism.

4. For an earlier essay on similar themes, see my "The World Well Staged? Theology, Culture and Hermeneutics," in Vanhoozer, *First Theology: God, Scripture, and Hermeneutics* (Downers Grove, IL: InterVarsity, 2002), chap. 11.

5. Augustine, *Confessions*, bk. 11.

6. I shall return to the theme of "writing" culture in the Conclusion under the heading of "cultural agency."

7. I hasten to add that "my neighbor" is a fictional, composite figure.

8. The distinction between *what* is said (the "story") and *how* it is said (the "discourse") is especially important in the interpretation of culture. While all cultures have weather (the what), the particular discourse varies from culture to culture. See Seymour Chatman, *Story and Discourse: Narrative Structure in Fiction and Film* (Ithaca, NY: Cornell University Press, 1980).

9. Though the physical world exists apart from culture, the concept of nature is itself a human construct that has a history and that varies from culture to culture. See Neil Evernden, *The Social Creation of Nature* (Baltimore: Johns Hopkins University Press, 1992). I am indebted to Charles Anderson for this point and for the reference.

10. Kant's nature-freedom distinction eventually led to the dichotomy between public facts that are verifiable through science and private values. This so-called "fact-value" distinction is an important ingredient in modern Western culture.

11. Cf. Kelton Cobb's definition of culture as "any conversion of raw nature into a habitable world through the exercise of human labor and attention" (*The Blackwell Guide to Theology and Popular Culture* [Oxford: Blackwell, 2005], 41).

12. See Wilhelm Dilthey, "The Development of Hermeneutics," in *Selected Writings*, trans. H. P. Rickman (Cambridge: Cambridge University Press, 1976).

13. According to Paul Ricoeur, human being is characterized by the "desire to be" and the "effort to exist." See Ricoeur, *The Conflict of Interpretations* (Evanston: Northwestern University Press, 1974), 266.

14. See Lee Cronk, *That Complex Whole: Culture and the Evolution of Human Behavior* (Boulder, CO: Westview, 1999).

15. What animals do instinctively—making homes (e.g., nests, webs, cocoons); making music (e.g., birdsong); making love (e.g., mating)—humans do intentionally and thus meaningfully.

16. The human sciences include history, sociology, anthropology, and economics. Each of these disciplines studies some aspect of human behavior that is inexplicable in terms of the natural sciences only. The liberal arts, for their part, focus on artistic expressions of human creativity.

17. David Newman, *Sociology: Exploring the Architecture of Everyday Life*, 4th ed. (Thousand Oaks, CA: Pine Forge, 2002), xxvi.

18. There is a lively debate among sociologists as to whether society is an objective reality that constrains individual freedom or simply the joint product of intersubjective action (or a bit of both).

19. I am using the term somewhat differently from J. M. Balkin, *Cultural Software: A Theory of Ideology* (New Haven: Yale University Press, 1998). By cultural software, Balkin is referring to the "know-how" that is transmitted from one human being to another, through teaching or example or telling stories, and so forth: "Examples of cultural software are knowing how to operate a computer, being able to dance the waltz, or being fluent in a particular language" (6).

20. The *Matrix* film trilogy graphically illustrates how culture is like a software program into which human beings are plugged.

21. Raymond Williams, *Keywords* (Oxford: Oxford University Press, 1985), 87.

22. See his *Reflections on the Philosophy of the History of Mankind*, abridged with introduction by Frank E. Manuel (Chicago: University of Chicago Press, 1968).

23. Cited in Cronk, *That Complex Whole*, 3; for other definitions given in anthropology textbooks, see the chart on 132–33.

24. Kathryn Tanner, *Theories of Culture: A New Agenda for Theology* (Minneapolis: Fortress, 1997), 31. Tanner is describing the consensus of modern anthropologists.

25. For a fuller development of cultural moods as they are expressed in music, see my "What Has Vienna to Do with Jerusalem? Barth, Brahms, and Bernstein's Unanswered Question," *Westminster Theological Journal* 63 (2001): 123–50.

26. New York: Basic Books, 1973.

27. I make use below of Geertz's notion of "thick description," which he imports into anthropology from its original appearance in the work of the philosopher Gilbert Ryle, who uses it to distinguish a wink from a blink. My contribution in the present essay is to take the notion of thick description even further by incorporating a theological moment into the process of interpretation.

28. Geertz, *Interpretation of Cultures*, 10.

29. And as long as we are on the subject of patron saints, I should acknowledge that the philosophical patron saint of my approach is Paul Ricoeur, inasmuch as it is his theory of interpretation from which I borrow and seek to build. The final product—a theological hermeneutics of culture—is, however, ultimately mine.

30. See, for example, the work of Roland Barthes, especially *Mythologies* (New York: Hill and Wang, 1972).

31. Later I shall distinguish semiotics from semantics, the science of discourse. The former studies static systems of language, the latter systems of language put to actual use on particular occasions.

32. The seminal figure here is Ferdinand de Saussure, the father of what has come to be known as "structuralist" linguistics.

33. Tanner argues that postmodern anthropologists have rightly corrected the modern assumption that cultures were sharply bounded, self-contained units (*Theories of Culture*, 53–58).

34. For the claim that human beings are neither captives to nor sovereigns over but "citizens" of language, see my *Is There a Meaning in This Text? The Bible, the Reader, and the Morality of Literary Knowledge* (Grand Rapids: Zondervan, 1998), 202–4.

35. William Romanowski writes: "Cultural texts are human actions, events, and material works that embody meanings that are widely shared" (*Eyes Wide Open: Looking for God in Popular Culture* [Grand Rapids: Brazos, 2001], 57).

36. Paul Ricoeur, *Interpretation Theory: Discourse and the Surplus of Meaning* (Fort Worth: Texas Christian University Press, 1976), 37. See also Nicholas Wolterstorff on the phenomenon of world-projection, in *Art in Action: Toward a Christian Aesthetic* (Grand Rapids: Eerdmans, 1980), 122–34.

37. So Cobb, *Theology and Popular Culture*, 7.

38. I am here amending a similar definition provided by Raymond Williams: culture is a "signifying system through which a social order is communicated, reproduced, experienced and explored" (*The Sociology of Culture* [New York: Schocken, 1981], 13).

39. Matthew Arnold, *Culture and Anarchy* (Cambridge: Cambridge University Press, 1932), 6.

40. "The idea of *high culture* should . . . be seen as the creation of certain writers working at certain historical contexts, rather than something that is a universal and timeless cultural category" (Gordon Lynch, *Understanding Theology and Popular Culture* [Oxford: Blackwell, 2005], 7).

41. Andrew Edgar in *Cultural Theory: The Key Concepts*, ed. Andrew Edgar and Peter Sedgwick (New York: Routledge, 2002), 101.

42. Lynch, *Understanding Theology and Popular Culture*, 15.

43. As we shall see below, reading popular culture involves examining both products/texts and the actual practices of consuming/reading these texts.

44. Catherine Belsey, *Critical Practice* (New York: Routledge, 1980), 47.

45. Raymonde Carroll, *Cultural Misunderstandings: The French-American Experience* (Chicago: University of Chicago Press, 1988), 3.

46. Douglas Kellner, *Media Culture: Cultural Studies, Identity and Politics Between the Modern and the Postmodern* (New York: Routledge, 1995), 17.

47. Cobb, *Theology and Popular Culture*, 14–18.

48. I am indebted for the material in this paragraph to William Brown's *The Ethos of the Cosmos: The Genesis of Moral Imagination in the Bible* (Grand Rapids: Eerdmans, 1999).

49. John Hartley, *Communication, Cultural and Media Studies: The Key Concepts*, 3rd ed. (New York: Routledge, 2002), 51.

50. It is important to note, however, that cultural influence is often a two-way street; certain Indian terms and habits affected British civilization as well.

51. Cobb, *Theology and Popular Culture*, 36–37.

52. See the seminal 1936 essay by Walter Benjamin, "The Work of Art in the Age of Mechanical Reproduction," in *Illuminations* (London: Jonathan Cape, 1970).

53. Cobb, *Theology and Popular Culture*, 40.

54. Richard Dawkins, preface to Susan Blakemore, *The Meme Machine* (Oxford: Oxford University Press, 1999), viii, citing the *Oxford English Dictionary*. The term has become the darling of evolutionary anthropologists intent on explaining the development of culture with Darwinian concepts. Dawkins himself suggests that even religion is a "meme population" that "infects" whole societies with belief in God. My own view is that we need not subscribe to the underlying evolutionary ideology of much memetic theory if we remember that we are dealing with an analogy. Unfortunately, I have not to date been able to find any Christian critical engagement with this theory.

55. Cronk, *That Complex Whole*, 14.

56. Ibid., 84.

57. Ibid., xii.

58. Balkin, *Cultural Software*, 43.

59. Ibid.

60. Cronk, *That Complex Whole*, 87.

61. Dallas Willard, *Renovation of the Heart: Putting on the Character of Christ* (Colorado Springs: NavPress, 2002), 14.

62. Nicholas Johnson, formerly of the Federal Communications Commission, in *Life*, Sept. 10, 1971.

63. Television is a prime instance of what I call *cultural discourse*. Note that we can say and do things with images as well as words. We shall return to the question of cultural discourse and illocutionary acts below.

64. Romanowski, *Eyes Wide Open*, 31–32.

65. Just as tragic as living a simulated existence is following what Sam Van Eman calls a "SimGospel"—a message that simulates the good news of the Bible through popular media for the purpose of selling goods and ideas—in his *On Earth as It Is in Advertising? Moving from Commercial Hype to Gospel Hope* (Grand Rapids: Brazos, 2005). My thanks to Michael Sleasman for this link.

66. Paul Tillich, *Theology of Culture* (Oxford: Oxford University Press, 1959), 42. See also T. S. Eliot, who similarly suggested that culture and religion are different aspects of the same thing, "the culture being, essentially, the incarnation (so to speak) of the religion of a people" ("Notes towards the Definition of a Culture," in *Christianity and Culture* [San Diego: Harvest, 1976], 101).

67. Romanowski is not uncritical of popular culture, rightly acknowledging that this sphere of human life has been corrupted by sin and is in need of transformation as is any other (20).

68. Craig Detweiler and Barry Taylor, *A Matrix of Meanings* (Grand Rapids: Baker, 2003), 9.

69. Philadelphia: Westminster, 1976.

70. Chicago: Thomas More, 1988.

71. Lynch, *Understanding Theology and Popular Culture*, 37.

72. Ibid., 97.

73. Ibid., 98.

74. George Hunsberger, "The Newbigin Gauntlet," in *The Church Between Gospel and Culture: The Emerging Mission in North America*, ed. George Hunsberger and Craig van Gelder (Grand Rapids: Eerdmans, 1996), 5.

75. I explore the theatrical model more fully in my *The Drama of Doctrine: A Canonical-Linguistic Approach to Christian Theology* (Louisville: Westminster John Knox, 2005), esp. chap. 12.

76. For Chomsky, this knowledge is innate. My use of the term, however, need not enter this debate.

77. Note that these four functions parallel the functions of culture we examined above.

78. As far as I know, I am the first to employ Paul Ricoeur's interpretation theory (especially the notions of discourse and the three worlds-of-the-text) for the sake of cultural hermeneutics. Note the striking absence of Ricoeur from the list of "background theorists" in the annotated bibliography of works on theology and popular culture in Cobb's *Theology and Popular Culture*, 324–34.

79. I elaborate on culture as a special kind of discourse below.

80. See, for example, Irena R. Makaryk, ed., *Encyclopedia of Contemporary Literary Theory: Approaches, Scholars, Terms* (Toronto: University of Toronto Press, 1993).

81. See the discussion in John Barton, *Reading the Old Testament: Method in Biblical Study* (Philadelphia: Westminster, 1984).

82. Robert Stam, *Film Theory: An Introduction* (Oxford: Blackwell, 2000), 1.

83. One of the earliest pioneering papers was W. D. Hamilton's "The Genetic Evolution of Social Behavior," *Journal of Theoretical Biology* 7 (1964): 1–52. The most important recent advocate is Edward O. Wilson, especially his *Sociobiology: The New Synthesis* (Cambridge, MA: Harvard University Press, 1975).

84. David Sloan Wilson, *Darwin's Cathedral: Evolution, Religion, and the Nature of Society* (Chicago: University of Chicago Press, 2002), 87. Wilson devotes a whole chapter to a case study of Calvinism and interprets Calvin's church in sixteenth-century Geneva in terms of its "adaptations to its environment" (91).

85. The Frankfurt Institute for Social Research was founded in 1923 by neo-Marxist scholars including Walter Benjamin, Theodor Adorno, Max Horkheimer, and Erich Fromm.

86. Dominic Strinati, *An Introduction to Theories of Popular Culture*, 2nd ed. (New York: Routledge, 2004), xvi. Marx had earlier stated: "The class which has the means of material production at its disposal, has control at the same time over the means of mental production" (cited in Cobb, *Theology and Popular Culture*, 45).

87. Lynch, *Understanding Theology and Popular Culture*, 71.

88. Its critics accuse the Frankfurt School of portraying the masses as "dominated" by popular culture. This ignores the often creative reception of cultural texts on the part of its actual users.

89. Note the importation of Marxist economic categories into the discussion (e.g., "cultural production and consumption," the "culture industry," and "cultural capital").

90. The Center opened in 1964 and closed in 2002.

91. Hartley, *Communication*, 50.

92. Ibid., 99.

93. T. J. Gorringe, *Furthering Humanity: A Theology of Culture* (Aldershot, UK: Ashgate, 2004), 130.

94. Cf. Theodore A. Turnau: "Culture here is seen as a smoke screen to hide the real situation—that a minority controls the means of production, thereby marginalizing the majority" ("Reflecting Theologically on Popular Culture as Meaningful: The Role of Sin, Grace, and General Revelation," *Calvin Theological Journal* 37 [2002]: 283).

95. Another form of reductionism in cultural studies proceeds from the structuralist insight that language is a closed system of signs: semiotics vs. semantics. Popular culture is here read as an immanent sign-system where meaning is a function of one sign's difference from other signs rather than of a sign's reference to something outside the language system. As such, this view of popular culture as a closed sign-system is closed to the possibility that the meaning of cultural texts is related to something transcendent, something outside the sign system—God, for example.

96. Kevin Vanhoozer, *Is There a Meaning in This Text? The Bible, the Reader, and the Morality of Literary Knowledge* (Grand Rapids: Zondervan, 1998), 32.

97. The term "cultural hermeneutics" is sometimes used to refer to the approaches that focus on the social location of the interpreter (ethnicity, gender, class) as the mainspring of interpretation.

98. For an excellent treatment of this three-dimensional biblical worldview, see Albert M. Wolters, *Creation Regained: Biblical Basics for a Reformational Worldview* (Grand Rapids: Eerdmans, 1985).

99. Vanhoozer, *Drama of Doctrine*, chap. 2.

100. Tillich, *Theology of Culture*, 50–51; see also Lynch, *Understanding Theology and Popular Culture*, 103–4.

101. See the title of Lynch, *Understanding Theology and Popular Culture*, chap. 4: "Can Popular Culture Be Bad for Your Health?"

102. Detweiler and Taylor, *Matrix of Meanings*, 8. See also, along with the books by Lynch and Cobb cited above, Tom Beaudoin, *Virtual Faith: The Irreverent Spiritual Quest of Generation X* (San Francisco: Jossey-Bass, 1998).

103. David Dark, *Everyday Apocalypse: The Sacred Revealed in "Radiohead," "The Simpsons" and other Pop Culture Icons* (Grand Rapids: Brazos, 2002). This is a very helpful book, though I think he needs to do more to distinguish between apocalyptic as a textual genre and apocalyptic as a way of reading. I am in favor of apocalyptic reading of apocalyptic texts only.

104. Stanley Grenz, "The Place of (Pop) Culture in Theological Reflection," *Journal of the Evangelical Theological Society* 43 (2000): 309. Elsewhere Grenz says that culture too can be the voice of the Spirit: "Because the life-giving Creator Spirit is present wherever life flourishes, the Spirit's voice can conceivably sound through many media, including the media of human culture" (Stanley J. Grenz and John R. Franke, *Beyond Foundationalism: Shaping Theology in a Postmodern Context* [Louisville: Westminster John Knox, 2001], 162). While the Spirit does indeed "blow where it wills" (John 3:8), I think it is a mistake to identify an authoritative speaking of the Spirit apart from Christ and the Scriptures. The Spirit's activity outside the church includes restraining sin and even illumining truth, but not speaking new words.

105. Andrew Walls, *The Missionary Movement in Christian History: Studies in the Transmission of Faith* (Maryknoll, NY: Orbis, 1996), xvii, 26.

106. Cobb follows the philosopher Johann Herder who believed that the reason we have diverse cultures is because each represents one of God's "ideas" about how humanity should live (see *Theology and Popular Culture*, 42, 72).

107. Ibid., 54.

108. What Walls names the "indigenizing" and "pilgrim" principles to describe the way in which the church relates to national cultures may be stretched to describe the relation of the church to popular culture: the indigenizing principle sees every culture as a potential host for the gospel; the pilgrim principle insists that the church must be more than a reflection of the host culture.

109. See also the study of Karl Barth's incarnation-centered theology of culture as examined in Paul Metzger, *The Word of Christ and the World of Culture* (Grand Rapids: Eerdmans, 2002).

110. Turnau, "Reflecting Theologically on Popular Culture," 273.

111. Ibid., 287.

112. It is important not to confuse general and special revelation: culture is not Christ. It may, however, be one of the "little lights" of creation that Barth somewhat begrudgingly acknowledged. Paul Tillich believes that culture can in its own right mediate truth and goodness. See also Lynch, who takes a revised correlational approach in *Understanding Theology and Popular Culture*, 104–5.

113. The idea of common grace, though not the terminology, derives from Calvin. See Calvin's *Institutes* 2.2.14–15.

114. Richard Mouw, *He Shines in All That's Fair: Culture and Common Grace* (Grand Rapids: Eerdmans, 2001), 82.

115. Ibid., 36. Mouw goes so far as to suggest that God even takes delight in Tiger Woods's putts—presumably those that drop in.

116. Ibid., 50. Here we may recall Herder's idea that each culture embodies one of God's "ideas" about humanity.

117. David Bruce Hegeman, *Plowing in Hope: Toward a Biblical Theology of Culture* (Moscow, ID: Canon, 1999), 26, see also 41–47. In the context of noting that one of the first things humans did was cultivate crops, we may here recall the original meaning of *cultura*.

118. Anthony A. Hoekema takes this narrative schema into account when he distinguishes the original image from the perverted, redeemed, and perfected image (*Created in God's Image* [Grand Rapids: Eerdmans, 1986], 82–95).

119. Turnau, "Reflecting Theologically on Popular Culture," 289.

120. Cf. Hoekema's remark: "God's common grace restrains the outward manifestation of this corruption in such a way that civilization, culture . . . is still possible in this present world" (*Created in God's Image*, 63–64). Note that Hoekema places his entire discussion of common grace in a chapter entitled "The Restraint of Sin."

121. Hoekema, *Created in God's Image*, 196–97.

122. Calvin, *Institutes* 2.2.15.

123. This requirement is my chief reason for preferring a semantics to a semiotics of culture.

124. Discourse pertains to the use of language by persons in concrete contexts (speech; *parole*); the implied contrast is with language as an abstract system of signs (code; *langue*).

125. The connections between culture and language are very close. It should therefore come as no surprise that many approach the interpretation of culture with the same theories and assumptions with which they interpret language. Those who favor the semiotics model treat culture as a system of signs where meaning is a function of structural differences between one sign and another. The method employed in the present chapter proceeds differently, viewing language not as a static system of interconnected signs to which speakers are subject but as signs that acquire meaning through their speakers' use. On the distinction between *langue* and *parole*, see Ricoeur, *Interpretation Theory*, 2–9. The semiotics of culture approach is very popular in cultural studies. For a further exposition of this model, see Strinati, *Theories of Popular Culture*, chap. 3.

126. Paul Ricoeur, *Hermeneutics and the Human Sciences: Essays on Language, Action and Interpretation* (Cambridge: Cambridge University Press, 1981), 134. Ricoeur defines a text as "any discourse fixed by writing" (145).

127. Turnau, "Reflecting Theologically on Popular Culture," 273.

128. Ricoeur, *Hermeneutics*, 138.

129. Cf. Steven Best and Douglas Kellner: "A multiperspectival social theory views society from a multiplicity of perspectives" (*Postmodern Theory: Critical Interrogations* [New York: Macmillan, 1991], 263). Best and Kellner are right as far as they go, but they do not go far enough; they entirely omit the level of the spiritual and the theological.

130. For a fuller development of this point, see my *Is There a Meaning in This Text?* 328–31.

131. It is important to remember that a single cultural text may perform multiple illocutionary acts, as do many speech acts. For example, to say "God is faithful" is to make an assertion but also to make a promise, at least tacitly. Similarly, breaking the window may also count as opening it. One of the challenges in interpretation is to specify *everything* that an agent is doing in his or her locutionary medium.

132. Arthur Peacocke, *Theology for a Scientific Age*, enlarged ed. (London: SCM, 1993), 39.

133. See the helpful chart in Peacocke, *Theology for a Scientific Age*, 217.

134. Lynch devotes three chapters to a similar endeavor, one each to an "author-focused," "text-based," and "ethnographic or audience-reception" approach (*Understanding Theology and Popular Culture*, chaps. 6–8). In Lynch's work, the three approaches are complementary but not organically linked, as is the case in the present essay, where each is viewed as an aspect of cultural discourse.

135. Karl Barth, *The Word of God and the Word of Man*, trans. Douglas Horton (Gloucester, MA: Peter Smith, 1978), 28–50.

136. Mortimer J. Adler and Charles Van Doren, *How to Read a Book*, rev. ed. (New York: Touchstone, 1972).

137. Lynch, *Understanding Theology and Popular Culture*, 112.

138. There has been an ongoing debate in film studies since the mid-twentieth century, associated with the influential journal *Cahiers du Cinéma* founded by André Bazin, concerning the role of *auteurs* in film. François Truffaut and others believe that certain directors (e.g., Alfred

Hitchcock) are so proficient in their medium that they can impose their personality and vision on any film. The *auteur* may not be responsible for the "what" (e.g., story) of the film, but a true *auteur* is always responsible for "how" the story gets told (e.g., the style of discourse).

139. Nicholas Wolterstorff, *Art in Action: Toward a Christian Aesthetic* (Grand Rapids: Eerdmans, 1980), 89, as cited in Romanowski, *Eyes Wide Open*, 86.

140. Robert Gibbs, *Intentions in the Experience of Meaning* (Cambridge: Cambridge University Press, 1999), 326.

141. "We believe that texts, including those that are nontraditional such as public spaces, songs, and advertisements, have meanings that can be uncovered through the exploration of their elements" (Jonathan Silverman and Dean Rader, *The World Is a Text: Writing, Reading, and Thinking About Culture and Its Contexts*, 2nd ed. [Upper Saddle River, NJ: Pearson Prentice Hall, 2006], 2–3). The authors provide a helpful reading of the public space of a Starbucks coffee shop (9–10).

142. Cf. Bernard F. Dick's remark: "A movie is a text" (*Anatomy of Film*, 2nd ed. [New York: St. Martin's Press, 1990], 3). See also James Monaco, *How to Read a Film: The World of Movies, Media, and Multimedia*, 3rd ed. (New York: Oxford University Press, 2000).

143. On the Western, see James Kitses, *Horizons West* (Bloomington: Indiana University Press, 1969), who argues that Westerns are about a distinctly American theme: the tension between wilderness and civilization. If Kitses is right, then the Western is itself a fascinating case study in culture as cultivation. On screwball comedies, see Stanley Cavell, *Pursuits of Happiness: The Hollywood Comedy of Remarriage* (Cambridge, MA: Harvard University Press, 1981). See also Thomas Schatz's *Hollywood Genres: Formulas, Filmmaking, Studio System*, 2nd ed. (New York: Random House, 1993) for an argument that film genres may be subdivided into two kinds: those that work to reestablish social order (e.g., westerns) and those that work to establish social integration (e.g., comedies).

144. See the "book link" in chap. 3 on genres in popular music.

145. Adler and Van Doren, *How to Read a Book*, 114.

146. John Searle offers the following formula for speech acts—*F(p)*—where (p) stands for propositional content and *F* for the particular illocutionary force associated with it (*Speech Acts: An Essay in the Philosophy of Language* [Cambridge: Cambridge University Press, 1969], 31). I believe we can stretch the formula to cover what we might call "culture acts"—or, as I have here, *works* of culture—as well.

147. Silverman and Rader, *World Is a Text*, 12, emphasis mine.

148. Adler and Van Doren, *How to Read a Book*, 130.

149. For the record, Adler does discuss imaginative literature too. He agrees that such literature invites us to indwell a world but insists that the very tendering of an imaginative world makes a kind of truth claim: this is the way the world is.

150. Ricoeur, *Hermeneutics*, 177.

151. This is the thesis of Mary Louise Pratt (*Towards a Speech Act Theory of Literary Discourse* [Bloomington: Indiana University Press, 1977]) regarding literary texts. In this essay I am extending her argument toward a speech act theory of *cultural* discourse.

152. Pierre Bourdieu, *Outline of a Theory of Practice* (Cambridge: Cambridge University Press, 1977), 82–83.

153. Stephen Pepper, *World Hypotheses* (Los Angeles: University of California Press, 1970).

154. George Lakoff and Mark Johnson, *Metaphors We Live By*, 2nd ed. (Chicago: University of Chicago Press, 2003), 5.

155. Ibid., 8.

156. Metaphors are cognitive instruments, ingredients in what Lakoff and Johnson term "imaginative rationality" (Ibid., 235).

157. Adler and Van Doren, *How to Read a Book*, 340–41.

158. So Ricoeur, *Hermeneutics*, chap. 7.

159. Ricoeur, *Interpretation Theory*, 95.

160. Paul Tillich, *Dynamics of Faith* (New York: Harper & Row, 1957), 10.

161. Mark Fenske, *One. A Magazine* 1, no. 2 (1997), cited in Warren Berger, *Advertising Today* (New York: Phaidon, 2001), 10.

162. Marshall McLuhan, *Understanding Media: The Extensions of Man* (Cambridge, MA: MIT Press, 1994), as cited in Berger, *Advertising Today*, 28.

163. See Judith Williamson, *Decoding Advertisements: Ideology and Meaning in Advertising* (New York: Marion Boyars, 2002).

164. Silverman and Rader, *World Is a Text*, 17.

165. For more on the church as a performance of the gospel, see my "The World Well Staged?" in *First Theology*, esp. 331–36, and *Drama of Doctrine*, chap. 12.

166. For an excellent study from an Anabaptist perspective of how Christians can be catalysts for redemptive change, see Duane Friesen, *Artists, Citizens, Philosophers: Seeking the Peace of the City—An Anabaptist Theology of Culture* (Scottdale, PA: Herald, 2000).

167. Michel de Certeau, *The Practice of Everyday Life* (Berkeley: University of California Press, 1984), 18.

168. John Fiske, *Understanding Popular Culture* (New York: Routledge, 1991), 15.

169. Gorringe, *Furthering Humanity*, 142. See W. L. Adamson, *Hegemony and Revolution: A Study of Antonio Gramsci's Political and Cultural Theory* (Berkeley: University of California Press, 1980), 143.

170. Friesen, *Artists, Citizens, Philosophers*, 139.

171. So Slavoj Zizek, *The Ticklish Subject: The Absent Centre of Political Ontology* (London: Verso, 1999), 199, as cited in Gorringe, *Furthering Humanity*, 264.

172. Marx, "Theses on Feuerbach: Thesis 2," in *Karl Marx: Selected Writings*, ed. David McLellan (Oxford: Oxford University Press, 1977), 158.

173. J. I. Packer, "God the Image-Maker," in *Christian Faith and Practice in the Modern World: Theology from an Evangelical Point of View*, ed. Mark A. Noll and David F. Wells (Grand Rapids: Eerdmans, 1988), 28.

Chapter 2 The Gospel according to Safeway

1. Kathy Prentice, "Your Client on TV in the Checkout Line: Be Seen by Shoppers Buying the Week's Groceries," *Media Life*, January 4, 2005, http://69.20.6.242/News2005/jan05/jan03/2_tues/news5tuesday.html (accessed February 23, 2006).

2. Ibid.

3. Ibid., 4–13.

4. Indeed, lest we doubt the intentionality of the attempt to create the consumer mentality even in children, see Susan Linn, *Consuming Kids: The Hostile Takeover of Childhood* (New York: New Press, 2004). Linn analyzes the growing marketing trend of targeting children, aptly naming one chapter "Branded Babies: From Cradle to Consumer." James Farrell describes this as part of the socialization process of educating our children in consumption by "introducing" them to the supermarket in infancy and later the shopping mall. James Farrell, *One Nation Under Goods: Malls and the Seductions of American Shopping* (Washington, DC: Smithsonian, 2003), 75–91, esp. 85–86.

5. Spence Hackney, *The Point of Purchase Handbook*, Hackney & Associates, Inc., 1997, http://www.hackneyonline.com/Resources_POP_Handbook.htm (accessed September 15, 2005).

6. Janet Attard, "Get Ready to Capture Sales Now and All Year Long," Business Know-How, 1999, http://www.businessknowhow.com/marketing/holidaymarketing.htm (accessed February 23, 2006).

7. Cf. the PBS Frontline video *The Persuaders* (2003), which highlights the emotional attachment ("connection") that marketers try to establish between Americans and consumer brands.

8. John O'Shaughnessy, *Why People Buy* (New York: Oxford University Press, 1987), 9.

9. Ibid.

10. Ibid., 10.

11. Berger's dialectic of humanity and society (externalization, objectivization, and internalization) is a helpful paradigm here, although space does not allow for a more complete discussion. The key idea is that humanity is in an ongoing "balancing act" with the world, in which there is a mutual relationship. See Peter Berger, *The Sacred Canopy* (New York: Doubleday, 1967). A concrete example of this argument is demonstrated in the PBS Frontline video *The Merchants of Cool* (2001). The video traces how the creators and sellers of popular culture market "cool" to teenagers. One of its key insights is this dialectic relationship between the fashion-forward (those on the cutting edge of trendiness in the culture) and the media, which is a giant feedback loop. The media are trying to be trendy, which influences the perception of being cool in the youth culture, but youth culture likewise influences the trends.

12. Lisa Biank Fasig "Kroger to Put 'Cosmo' under Wrap: Reason Isn't Breasts, It's Risqué Headlines," *The Cincinnati Enquirer*, January 12, 2000, http://www.enquirer.com/editions/2000/01/12/fin_kroger_to_put_cosmo.html (accessed February 23, 2006).

13. Magazine headlines, unless otherwise noted, come from September–October, 2005.

14. National Association of Anorexia Nervosa and Associated Disorders, Eating Disorders Info. and Resources, http://www.anad.org/site/anadweb/content.php?type=1&id=6982 (accessed February 23, 2006). Cf. National Institute of Mental Health, "Eating Disorders: Facts About Eating Disorders and the Search for Solutions," 2001, http://www.nimh.nih.gov/publicat/NIMHeatingdisorder.pdf (accessed February 23, 2006).

15. Kevin Vanhoozer helpfully pointed out the location of the tabloids in reference to this point.

16. O'Shaughnessy, *Why People Buy*, 111–12.

17. Bauer Advertising Sales, Bauer Publishing Group, "First for Women Overview," http://www.baueradsales.com/f/overview.asp (accessed October 5, 2005), italics added.

18. For documentation of this trend, see Jeff Bercovici, "A Better Year for Magazines, but Dicier: Rising Tides in Ad Dollars Will Swamp as It Lifts," *Media Life*, January 6, 2004, http://www.medialifemagazine.com/news2004/jan04/jan05/2_tues/news3tuesday.html (accessed February 23, 2006).

19. Even here, however, the checkout-line experience is mirrored as the digital shopping cart tempts you with a few last-minute deals while you attempt to finalize your online purchase. The difference, of course, is that you do not have to wait to finalize your online purchases, whereas one cannot control the speed of the actual checkout line.

20. Tad Walch, "Y Study Shows Oprah's Influence," *Deseret Morning News*, December 20, 2004, http://deseretnews.com/dn/view/0,1249,595113603,00.html (accessed February 23, 2006). This A-list phenomenon of Oprah's book club led to the late 2005–early 2006 scandal over her endorsement of *A Million Little Pieces*. "Oprah to Author: You Conned Us All," CNN.com, January 27, 2006, http://www.cnn.com/2006/SHOWBIZ/books/01/27/oprah.frey/index.html (accessed February 23, 2006).

21. See Anthony A. Hoekema, *Created in God's Image* (Grand Rapids: Eerdmans, 1987), esp. 11–101.

22. On Christ as the image of God who reveals the Father, see also Col. 1:15; John 14:8–9; Heb. 1:3. For the idea that we are to imitate Christ, see also Matt. 10:24–25; Mark 8:31–34; John 13:4–5; 1 Cor. 11:1; 15:49; Phil. 2:5–11; Col. 3:9–10; and 1 John 3:2.

23. See Markus Bockmuehl, *Jewish Law in Gentile Churches* (Grand Rapids: Baker, 2003), 124–25.

24. Note the book review by Lauren F. Winner, "Fit or Fat? Why We Worship Slimness While Supersizing Our Lunches," *Christianity Today*, September 2005, http://www.christianitytoday.com/ct/2005/009/33.103.html (accessed September 15, 2005). This is a review of R. Marie

Griffith, *Born Again Bodies: Flesh and Spirit in American Christianity* (Berkeley: University of California, 2004), and Morgan Spurlock, *Don't Eat This Book: Fast Food and the Supersizing of America* (New York: Putnam, 2005). Winner notes the contrasting values upheld in evangelical Christianity by placing such emphasis on outward beauty and compulsive gluttony.

25. Michelle Graham, *Wanting to Be Her: Body Image Secrets Victoria Won't Tell You* (Downers Grove, IL: InterVarsity, 2005), 122–37, esp. 128.

26. This is not to say, however, that our knowledge is so perspectival that there is no possible common ground with others who have starkly different starting points.

27. See, for example, http://www.americandecency.org

Chapter 3 Despair and Redemption

1. Anthony Bozza, *Whatever You Say I Am: The Life and Times of Eminem* (New York: Bantam, 2003), 193.

2. Maureen Dowd, "The Boomers' Crooner," *New York Times*, November 24, 2002, 4–13.

3. Bozza, *Whatever You Say*, 80.

4. David Stubbs, *Cleaning Out My Closet: The Stories Behind Every Song* (New York: Thunder's Mouth, 2003), 52.

5. Ibid., 63.

6. Adam Matthews, "Eminem Opens Up," *Rolling Stone*, April 27, 1999, http://www.rolling stone.com/news/story/_/id/5921313/eminem?pageid=rs.ArtistArticles&pageregion=mainRegion (accessed November 2, 2005).

7. This song was left off the "clean" version of the album. It was included on the explicit edition and was played in concert.

8. Unlike his relationship with his mother, grandmother, and wife, Eminem has a strong relationship with his daughter, Hailie.

9. Stubbs, *Cleaning Out My Closet*, 74.

10. Ibid.

11. Bozza, *Whatever You Say*, 235.

12. Bozza, "Eminem Blows Up," *Rolling Stone*, April 29, 1999, 75. Quoted in Allen L. Oliver, "It's All the Rage: A Study of a Cultural Icon," *Psychoanalytic Review* 89 (2002): 668.

13. Stubbs, *Cleaning Out My Closet*, 77.

14. Richard Goldstein, "The Eminem Consensus: Why We Vote for Slim Shady," *Village Voice*, November 13–19, 2002, http://www.villagevoice.com/news/0246,goldstein,39833,1.html (accessed November 2, 2005).

15. Ibid.

16. The lyrics are part of "Criminal," a song from the *Marshall Mathers LP*.

17. Roger Ebert, "8 Mile," *Movie Reviews*, November 8, 2002, http://rogerebert.suntimes .com/apps/pbcs.dll/article?AID=/20021108/REVIEWS/211080301/1023 (accessed November 2, 2005).

18. James Haskins, *The Story of Hip-Hop* (London: Penguin, 2002), 11.

19. Ibid.

20. Ibid., 77.

21. Ibid., 107.

22. Stubbs, *Cleaning Out My Closet*, 56.

23. Matthews, "Eminem Opens Up."

24. The commentator is Shelby Steele, a research fellow at Stanford University's Hoover Institution. Steele is quoted in Bozza, *Whatever You Say*, 260.

25. Emphasis original. The reader identifies herself only as a sixteen-year-old girl whose initials are R. J. K. The original review is by Gerald Marzorati, "Eminem's Martyr Complex:

The Rapper Is a National Nightmare in His Own Mind," *Slate*, May 30, 2002, http://www.slate.com/id/2066292 (accessed November 2, 2005).

26. Bob Smithouser, "8 Mile," *PluggedIn*, http://www.pluggedinonline.com/movies/movies/a0000193.cfm (accessed November 2, 2005).

27. Ibid.

28. Chris Lutes, "The Shady Side of Eminem," *Campus Life*, March/April 2001, http://www.christianitytoday.com/cl/2001/002/24.30.html (accessed November 2, 2005).

29. Neil Strauss, "The Pop Life: Will the Real Voters Please Stand Up?" *New York Times*, February 14, 2001, E3.

30. Richard Goldstein, "The Eminem Shtick: What Makes a Bigot a Genius? Presiding Over Guilty Pleasures," *Village Voice*, June 12–18, 2002, http://www.villagevoice.com/news/0224,goldstein,35576,1.html (accessed November 2, 2005), emphasis original.

31. Katina R. Stapleton, "From the Margins to the Mainstream: The Political Power of Hip-Hop," *Media, Culture, and Society* 20 (1998): 229.

32. Michael Eric Dyson, "Bum Rap," *New York Times*, February 3, 1994, A21. For a similar, but more extended, version of the same line of argument, see Dyson, "Rap Culture, the Church, and American Society," *Black Sacred Musicology: A Journal of Theomusicology* 6 (1992): 268–73.

33. Shelby Steele, "Notes from the Hip-Hop Underground," *Wall Street Journal*, March 30, 2001, A14.

34. Ibid.

35. Ibid.

36. N. Lynne Westfield and Harold Dean Trulear, "Theomusicology and Christian Education: Spirituality and the Ethics of Control in the Rap of Hammer," *Black Sacred Music: A Journal of Theomusicology* 8 (1994): 218.

37. Cornel West, *Prophetic Fragments* (Grand Rapids: Eerdmans, 1988), 186–87, cited by Westfield and Trulear, "Theomusicology," 218.

38. Angela Nelson, "Text, Texture, and Context in Theological Perspective," *Black Sacred Music: A Journal of Theomusicology* 8 (1994): 71.

39. My exegesis of Luke is indebted to Joel B. Green, *The Theology of the Gospel of Luke*, New Testament Theology (New York: Cambridge University Press, 1995), esp. chap. 4.

40. Ibid., 136.

41. Ebert, "8 Mile."

42. John Webster, *Holiness* (Grand Rapids: Eerdmans, 2003), 27.

43. Miroslav Volf, *Exclusion and Embrace: A Theological Exploration of Identity, Otherness, and Reconciliation* (Nashville: Abingdon, 1996), 58.

44. Andrew F. Walls, "The Gospel as Prisoner and Liberator of Culture," in *The Missionary Movement in Christian History: Studies in the Transmission of Faith* (Maryknoll, NY: Orbis, 1996), 7.

45. Ibid., 8.

46. For a citation of the quote, see Daniel Jeffreys and Rebecca Fowler, "Public Eminem No. 1," *The* [London] *Daily Mail*, February 3, 2001, 16. For serious questions about the authenticity of the quotation, see Barbara and David P. Mikkelson, *The Urban Legends Reference Page*, June 28, 2003, http://www.snopes.com/politics/bush/eminem.asp (accessed November 15, 2003).

47. Mark Morning, "The Christian Slim Shady," *Campus Life*, June/July 2003, http://www.christianitytoday.com/cl/2003/002/3.29.html (accessed November 2, 2005).

48. Haskins, *Story of Hip-Hop*, 126.

49. Geoffrey Wainwright, "Babel, Barbary, and the Word Made Flesh: Liturgy and the Redemption of the World," *Antiphon* 3 (1998): 10.

50. Ibid.

Chapter 4 The High Price of Unity

1. Jann S. Wenner, "The Rolling Stone Interview: Bono," *Rolling Stone*, November 3, 2005, 62. The UDHR crosses the screen during the song "Love and Peace or Else."

2. Eleanor Roosevelt and William De Witt, *UN: Today and Tomorrow* (New York: Harper, 1953), x.

3. Mary Ann Glendon, *A World Made New: Eleanor Roosevelt and The Universal Declaration of Human Rights* (New York: Random House, 2001), 10.

4. John Rawls, *Political Liberalism* (New York: Columbia University Press, 1996), 133–72. Rawls speaks of the "overlapping consensus" of doctrines within societies and argues that this is the best possible meeting point for democratic nations. Cited in Jack Donnelly, *Universal Human Rights: In Theory and Practice*, 2nd ed. (Ithaca, NY: Cornell University Press, 2003), 40. Donnelly agrees with Rawls and argues that this can be extended to the entire international community.

5. Some of the significant works that examine the UDHR include Glendon, *World Made New*; George Weigel, "Are Human Rights Universal?" *Commentary* 99 (1999): 41–45; Johannes Morsink, *The Universal Declaration of Human Rights: Origins, Drafting and Intent* (Philadelphia: University of Pennsylvania Press, 1999); Asbjorn Eide and Theresa Swinehart, eds., *The Universal Declaration of Human Rights: A Commentary* (New York: Oxford University Press, 1992).

6. John C. Haughey, "Responsibility for Human Rights: Contributions from Bernard Lonergan," *Theological Studies* 66 (2002): 763–800.

7. Glendon, *World Made New*, 18.

8. Jerome Shestack, review of *The Universal Declaration of Human Rights: Origins, Drafting and Intent*, by Johannes Morsink, *American Journal of International Law* 94 (July 2000): 600–603.

9. Ibid., 603.

10. Jürgen Moltmann, *God for a Secular Society: The Public Relevance of Theology* (Minneapolis: Fortress, 1999), 119.

11. Keith Suter, "The Fiftieth Anniversary of the Declaration of Human Rights," *Contemporary Review* 273 (1995): 281.

12. Richard John Neuhaus, "Documentation: Christianity and Democracy," *First Things* 66 (October 1996): 30–36.

13. Morsink, *Universal Declaration*, 28–34.

14. Glendon, *World Made New*, 12: "The genesis of each article, and each part of each article, was a dynamic process in which many minds, interests, backgrounds, legal systems and ideological persuasions played their respective determining roles."

15. Editorial Board, "Fifty Years Ago in Monthly Review," *Monthly Review* 52, no. 8 (2001): 63.

16. Haughey, "Responsibility for Human Rights," 764–74.

17. Glendon, *World Made New*, 146. Nations such as Brazil and the Netherlands argued that the image of God should not be absent from the UDHR, but the compromise agreement required that there be no direct assertion of a particular human nature or God, but "those who believed in God, [Cassin] suggested, could still find the idea of God in the strong assertions that all human beings are born free and equal and endowed with reason and conscience."

18. Glendon, *World Made New*, 39–41.

19. Roosevelt and De Witt, *UN*, 217.

20. References to the UDHR come from United Nations, Department of Public Information, "Universal Declaration of Human Rights," http://www.unhchr.ch/udhr/lang/eng.htm (accessed November 21, 2005).

21. Glendon, *World Made New*, 58. This version, according to Humphrey, had no particular philosophical foundation, but rather it was a descriptive collection of global rights.

22. Donnelly, *Universal Human Rights*, 22.

23. Eleanor Roosevelt, "For Better World Understanding," *Pi Lambda Theta Journal* 22 (1949): 196–203.

24. Glendon, *World Made New*, 42, 89.

25. David Reiff, "Moral Imperatives and Political Realities: Response to Principle, Politics and Humanitarian Action," *Ethics and International Affairs* 13 (1999): 35.

26. Ibid.

27. John Humphrey, "The Implementation of International Human Rights Law," *New York Law Review* 24 (1978): 32.

28. Samuel P. Huntington, *The Clash of Civilization and the Remaking of World Order* (New York: Touchstone, 1996).

29. Weigel, "Human Rights," 41.

30. Elliott Abrams, review of *A World Made New: Eleanor Roosevelt and the Universal Declaration of Human Rights*, by Mary Ann Glendon, *First Things* 114 (2001): 43–45.

31. Oxfam Community Aid Abroad, "An Agenda for Human Rights," Briefing Paper, 1998, http://www.oxfam.org (accessed November 21, 2005).

32. Michael Ignatieff, "The Attack on Human Rights," *Foreign Affairs* 80, no. 6 (2001): 103–16, esp. 110.

33. Ibid., 114.

34. Ibid., 115.

35. Huntington, *Clash of Civilization*, 194.

36. Ibid., 196.

37. "Suppression, China and Oil," *Economist*, July 9, 2005, 51–52.

38. John A. Gentry, "The Cancer of Human Rights," *Washington Quarterly* 22, no. 4 (1999): 95–112.

39. Haughey, "Responsibility for Human Rights," 764.

40. Ignatieff, "Attack on Human Rights."

41. Peter Berger, "Are Human Rights Universal?" *Commentary* 64, no. 3 (September 1977): 60–63. "The deepest of these roots is I believe the biblical vision of man as created in the image and likeness of God, as a moral agent with intelligence and free will and thus endowed (to adopt Mr. Jefferson's language) with a certain 'inalienable' dignity. This moral claim—that the individual has an irreducible value and dignity prior to his or her 'public' status (as citizen, or slave, or indentured servant, or freedman, or member of the aristocracy)—is the sturdiest possible foundation for any scheme of 'human rights' that seeks to protect human beings from arbitrary (and often brutal) state power."

42. Moltmann, *God for Secular Society*, 117.

43. See further, Philip Quinn, "Christian Ethics and Human Rights" in *Human Rights and Responsibility in the World Religions* (Oxford: Oneworld Publications, 2003), 235: "The Bible, (Louis Henkin) tells us, mandates a duty upon me to love my neighbor, but it does not present my neighbor as having the right to be loved by me; he/she, one might say, is only a third party beneficiary of my duty to God."

44. Jack Donnelly, *Universal Human Rights*, 22.

45. Ibid., 21.

46. N. T. Wright, *The Challenge of Jesus: Rediscovering Who Jesus Was and Is* (Downers Grove, IL: InterVarsity, 1999), 53.

47. Max L. Stackhouse, "Sources of Basic Human Rights Ideas: A Christian Perspective," (paper presented at the University of Chicago Divinity School, Chicago, IL, January 27, 2003).

48. David Novak, "Human Rights in a Secular Society," in *Does Human Rights Need God?* ed. Elizabeth M. Bucar and Barbra Barnett (Grand Rapids: Eerdmans, 2005), 51.

Chapter 5 Between City and Steeple

1. John N. Vaughan, *Megachurches and America's Cities: How Churches Grow* (Grand Rapids: Baker, 1993), 53.

2. Vaughan calls this the "megaministry principle," by which "the size of the church in relation to its city or ministry area is the significant factor rather than church size alone" (*Megachurches*, 29–47, esp. 42).

3. Bishop Arthur Brazier of the Apostolic Church of God, quoted in Anne C. Loveland and Otis B. Wheeler, *From Meetinghouse to Megachurch: A Material and Cultural History* (Columbia: University of Missouri Press, 2003), 181.

4. Debora Vrana, "Religion: Designing a Mall-like Ambience for Worship," *Los Angeles Times*, November 8, 1997.

5. Loveland and Wheeler, *Meetinghouse to Megachurch*, 130.

6. Gregory A. Pritchard, *Willow Creek Seeker Services: Evaluating a New Way of Doing Church* (Grand Rapids: Baker, 1996), 81.

7. Ibid.

8. Not to forget the African thatch, or Chinese tier, or Asian terrace.

9. Michael L. White, *The Social Origins of Christian Architecture*, vol. 2, *Texts and Monuments for the Christian Domus Ecclesiae in Its Environment*, Harvard Theological Studies 42 (Valley Forge, PA: Trinity Press International, 1997), 19–20.

10. Per Gustaf Hamberg, *Temples for Protestants: Studies in the Architectural Milieu of the Early Reformed Church and the Lutheran Church*, trans. Nancy Adler (Gothenburg: University of Gothenburg, 2002), 36. The force of this comment is underscored by the fact that the author is referring to a utopian model.

11. Circular churches are more established in the Eastern Orthodox Church and were experimented with by the early Reformed Church.

12. See Jeanne H. Kilde, *When Church Became Theater: The Transformation of Evangelical Architecture and Worship in Nineteenth-Century America* (Oxford: Oxford University Press, 2002).

13. Ibid., 36. While Kilde is interested in the social dynamics affected by architectural space, one must not forget the movement and power of the Spirit in stirring the church to revival.

14. Ibid., 132, 149.

15. Ibid., 132.

16. The suburb is easy to stereotype, but Kenneth Jackson offers four basic characteristics: population density, home ownership, residential status, and journey to work (*Crabgrass Frontier: The Suburbanization of the United States* [New York: Oxford University Press, 1985], 6–11).

17. Vaughan, *Megachurches*, 63.

18. Joshua Olsen, *Better Places, Better Lives—A Biography of James Rouse* (Washington, DC: The Urban Land Institute, 2003), 55.

19. Peter Wagner differentiates between social services ("ministry geared to meet the needs of . . . persons in a direct and immediate way") and social action ("ministry geared toward changing social structures"). *Church Growth and the Whole Gospel: A Biblical Mandate* (New York: Harper and Row, 1981), 36.

20. William S. Kowinski, *The Malling of America: Travels in the United States of Shopping*, 2nd ed. (USA: Xlibris Corp., 2002), 90.

21. Ibid., 93.

22. Pritchard notes that in one church with two worship services, the preacher's second message was identical to the first and he used "not only the same script and gestures, but even the pregnant emotional pauses were identical. His messages are scripted and honed to a razor edge of excellence" (Pritchard, *Willow Creek Seeker Services*, 214). The danger is not so much the self-conscious evaluation that goes into honing one's skills, but the temptation to use these skills merely at the drop of a hat, to pretend so as to manipulate and achieve the desired result. A pastor at a megachurch resigned over this issue and wrote in a letter that his "talents and

gifts [had] created opportunities to do which exceeded" his "capacity to be. Such a discrepancy between doing and being is dangerous at best and destructive at worst, because it often leads to pretending" (Ibid., 217).

23. One must admit that many older churches are no less enclosed, and the questions asked here of the megachurch can be asked of other types of churches as well.

24. Mark Gottdiener, "Recapturing the Center: A Semiotic Analysis of Shopping Malls," in *The City and the Sign: An Introduction to Urban Semiotics*, ed. Mark Gottdiener and Alexandros Ph. Lagopoulos (New York: Columbia University Press, 1986), 288–303.

25. Ibid., 299.

26. Even if they were celebrating this in a house, as is likely, the activity makes it no longer a house for eating and drinking, but a place for remembrance and communion.

27. It is not easy to determine what makes a place theologically expressive. I have attempted to do so in my doctoral thesis and direct the interested reader there (see unnumbered note on p. 115). For other relevant works, see the suggested readings.

28. If effective communion entails a smaller group consisting of members who know each other, I am not sure what megachurch communion space should look like. Celebrating communion in homogenous cell groups is not the best option.

29. Carol Flake, *Redemptorama: Culture, Politics, and the New Evangelicalism* (Garden City, NY: Anchor, 1984), 55.

30. Verla Gillmor, "Community Is Their Middle Name," *Christianity Today*, November 13, 2000, 49.

31. Philip H. Towner, "Households and Household Codes," in *Dictionary of Paul and His Letters*, ed. Gerald F. Hawthorne and Ralph P. Martin (Downers Grove: InterVarsity, 1993), 417.

32. Derek Tidball, "Social Setting of Mission Churches," in *Dictionary of Paul*, 884.

33. Towner, "Households."

34. I owe this phrasing to Jon Pahl, *Shopping Malls and Other Sacred Spaces: Putting God in Place* (Grand Rapids: Brazos, 2003), 52.

35. Richard Kieckhefer, *Theology in Stone: Church Architecture from Byzantium to Berkeley* (New York: Oxford University Press, 2004), 136.

36. The choice of building material and age of the structure helps influence the symbolic atmosphere of the place. Older buildings might carry more memories, and earthy materials can invite more reflection.

37. One must acknowledge that much of Protestant/evangelical architecture has broken with historical practice and shied away from considering such spaces as sacred as opposed to profane. Kieckhefer proposes a more useful understanding of sacred space, suggesting: "what makes a building sacred is not its detachment from the profane (although this may be a secondary effect of sacrality, often mistaken for an essential factor) but the richness of its symbolic associations, its connectedness to images and narratives that bear on the deepest questions of human life" (Kieckhefer, *Theology in Stone*, 18). The manner and degree of this connectedness will vary with confession and culture, but its usefulness for theological community cannot be denied.

38. "Vernacular" is a difficult term to define. See William S. W. Lim and Tan Hock Beng, eds., *The New Asian Architecture: Vernacular Traditions and Contemporary Styles* (Hong Kong: Periplus, 1998); original edition entitled *Contemporary Vernacular: Evoking Traditions in Asian Architecture* (Singapore: Select Books, 1998), 11.

39. The cover picture for Gillmor's article on Willow Creek—titled "Community Is Their Middle Name"—is that of the church's audience/congregation gathered around a stage.

Chapter 6 Swords, Sandals, and Saviors

1. For instance, see the Center for Bioethics and Human Dignity's website, which frequently addresses bioethical issues in film and literature (www.cbhd.org) or *Christianity Today*'s publication *Books and Culture* and website (www.Christianitytoday.com/movies/).

2. Film critic David Ansen has suggested Russell Crowe is one of the few recent actors with staying power. David Ansen, "Is Anybody Making Movies We'll Actually Watch in 50 Years?" *Newsweek*, July 11, 2005, 62–64.

3. These deep structures are divided into at least two categories: root metaphors and deep symbols. Root metaphors are construals of the world as one thing or another (e.g., the world as machine). Stephen Peppers, *World Hypotheses* (Los Angeles: University of California Press, 1972), esp. 84–114. Beyond Peppers, I suggest that cultures may, and most likely do, have numerous root metaphors that guide and create boundaries for the society. At times, root metaphors may come into conflict with one another, and this creates tension within the very identity of the people. A closely related concept is a deep symbol: those concepts or ideals that are at the heart of a culture. Edward Farley defines deep symbols as "the values by which a community understands itself, from which it takes its aims, and to which it appeals as canons of cultural criticism" (*Deep Symbols: Their Postmodern Effacement and Reclamation* [Valley Forge, PA: Trinity Press International, 1996], 1–8, esp. 3). In addition to these two categories, I propose a third category of cultural existentials. Here I am directly referencing aspects of shared humanity such as are discussed in Martin Heidegger's *Being and Time*.

4. Todd McCarthy, "Gladiator Prevails," *Variety*, April 24–30, 2000, 27. A recent monograph by Monica Cyrino (*Big Screen Rome* [Malden, MA: Blackwell, 2005]) explores a number of films in this genre, including *Gladiator*, as well as others centered thematically on Roman civilization. While this book emerged too late in the publication cycle for me to include in this essay, I direct the interested reader to this worthwhile volume and particularly chap. 9 on *Gladiator*.

5. Leslie Felperin, "Decline and Brawl," *Sight & Sound* 10, no. 6 (2000): 34–35.

6. Thomas Doherty, "Of Swords and Sandals," National Forum 81, no. 2 (2001): 26; Felperin, "Decline and Brawl," 34–35.

7. Douglas Bankston, "Veni, vidi, vici," *American Cinematographer* 81, no. 5 (2000): 46–53. His most famous commercial was the popular 1984 Apple Super Bowl ad.

8. Ibid., 46.

9. Berys Gaut, "Film Authorship and Collaboration," in *Film Theory and Philosophy*, ed. Richard Allen and Murray Smith (New York: Oxford University Press, 1999), 149–72.

10. Felperin, "Decline and Brawl," 35.

11. McCarthy, "Gladiator Prevails," 27; John Simon, "What, No Orgy?" *National Review* 52, no. 10 (2000): 58–60.

12. Bankston, "Veni, vidi, vici," 48. In both, the final scene depicts Commodus and a general fighting gladiator-style for the throne, with the general winning.

13. Michael Grant, *The Roman Emperors: A Biographical Guide to the Rulers of Imperial Rome, 31 BC–AD 476* (New York: Scribners, 1985), 88–99; Dio Cassius, *Roman History*, trans. Earnest Cary, 9 vols., Loeb Classical Library (Cambridge, MA: Harvard University Press, 1961), 73.73–121. Cf. Martin Winkler, ed., *Gladiator: Film and History* (Malden, MA: Blackwell, 2004), which is a series of essays that explores historical background, cinematic influences, and the contemporary relevance of this film. I regret that I was unaware of this volume until too late in the manuscript process.

14. Dio Cassius, *Roman History* 73.105–17.

15. Ibid. 73.81.

16. Grant, *Roman Emperors*, 70–95, esp. 70–71.

17. Bankston, "Veni, vidi, vici," 46.

18. By the re-creation of the Roman aesthetic, I am referring to a later culture's appropriation and interpretation of Roman architecture, art, etc.

19. Ron Magid, "Rebuilding Ancient Rome," *American Cinematographer* 81, no. 5 (2000): 54–59; and film commentary on the DVD.

20. The advancement of a farmer to the role of leader is a story common to Roman culture. There is an interesting historical parallel with the story of Cincinnatus, which promotes the

Roman ideal of a farmer turned general who refuses the offer of tyranny and returns to farming. I am indebted to Charles Anderson for making me aware of this historical connection.

21. See the extended-length version available on DVD, along with the edited scenes plus commentary included in the bonus material.

22. Cf. Doherty, "Of Swords and Sandals," 28; McCarthy, "Gladiator Prevails," 27.

23. See the DVD film commentary.

24. It goes without comment that coherent speech acts or even cultural texts can produce unintended meanings, a possibility that resides in the surplus of meaning that is generated by texts of any kind.

25. Matt McEver, "Film Review: *Gladiator*," *Journal of Religion and Film* 4, no. 2 (2000), http://www.unomaha.edu/jrf/gladiatorart.htm (accessed August 12, 2005).

26. Ibid.

27. See the DVD film commentary.

28. Doherty, "Of Swords and Sandals," 28.

29. See the DVD film commentary.

30. Samuel Wells, a former student of Kevin Vanhoozer, wrote an unpublished B.D. honors thesis on precisely this topic at the University of Edinburgh. I am indebted to Kevin for pointing this out.

31. Ernst Bloch, *The Principle of Hope*, 3 vols., trans. Neville Plaice, Stephen Plaice, and Paul Knight (Cambridge, MA: MIT Press, 1986), 1:408–9.

32. Richard Bauckham and Trevor Hart, *Hope against Hope: Christian Eschatology in Contemporary Context* (Grand Rapids: Eerdmans, 1999), 1–25.

33. I am indebted to C. Ben Mitchell for this phrase.

34. This would include the work of Moltmann, Wolfhart Pannenberg, James McClendon, Thomas Finger, Stanley Grenz, and Gregory Beale.

35. See for instance Gen. 9:1–17; 12:1–3; 15:1–21; 17:1–22; Deut. 11:26–28; 2 Sam. 7; 1 Chron. 17.

36. Augustine explicates hope by examining the Lord's Prayer in his *Enchiridion*, which seeks to unpack the theological virtues of faith, hope, and love as the core of Christian life. A similar tradition is evidenced in the Orthodox confession of Peter Mogila. Karl Barth focused the attention of his theological formulation of ethics upon the Lord's Prayer in his unfinished volume (4.4: *The Christian Life*) of the *Church Dogmatics*.

37. See for instance Rev. 2:7, 11, 17, 26–29; 3:5–6, 11–13, 19–22; 21:7.

38. Bauckham and Hart, *Hope against Hope*, 201–10.

39. Ibid., 202.

40. Craig Gay, *The Way of the (Modern) World, or, Why It's Tempting to Live as if God Doesn't Exist* (Grand Rapids: Eerdmans, 1998), 73–74.

41. Ibid., 75.

42. Ibid., 75–76.

43. Farley suggests, "Ours is a largely secular society in which remnants of religious and ethical traditions somehow survive. Something like words of power still haunt the major institutions of our society" (*Deep Symbols*, 2).

Chapter 7 The Business of Busyness

1. Richard A. Swenson, *Margin: How to Create Emotional, Physical, Financial, and Time Reserves You Need* (Colorado Springs: NavPress, 1992), 145.

2. John P. Robinson and Geoffrey Godbey, "Busyness as Usual," *Social Research* 72 (2005): 417–20.

3. "New Page-Turner Bible is Launched," BBC News Online, http://news.bbc.co.uk/1/hi/england/4266564.stm (accessed September 21, 2005).

4. David Brooks, "The Organization Kid," *The Atlantic Monthly* (April 2001): 40.

5. F. Thomas Juster, Hiromi Ono, Frank P. Stafford, "Changing Times of American Youth: 1981–2003," Institute for Social Research, University of Michigan, http://www.umich.edu/news/Releases/2004/Nov04/teen_time_report.pdf (accessed September 20, 2005). Time spent on school and study per week has increased from just under 29 hours in 1981 to over 36 hours in 2003. Media and game time have also risen. What has declined is time in sports and outdoor activities.

6. Barbara Kantrowitz, "Busy Around the Clock," *Newsweek* (July 17, 2000): 49–50.

7. The ATUS homepage is http://www.bls.gov/tus/home.htm (accessed September 23, 2005). These ATUS figures are from Haley Frazis and Jay Stewart, "What Can Time-Use Data Tell Us About Hours of Work?" *Monthly Labor Review* 127.12 (2004): 6, http://www.bls.gov/opub/mlr/2004/12/art1full.pdf (accessed September 23, 2005).

8. John P. Robinson and Geoffrey Godbey, *Time for Life: The Surprising Ways Americans Use Their Time* (University Park: Pennsylvania State University Press, 1997), 95. They and the ATUS use the time-diary method, which tracks reports of how people spent a 24-hour period, and ensures greater accuracy than estimate surveys.

9. The average time for housework and family care has also declined, which is likely attributable to demographic shifts away from marriage and child-bearing (Robinson and Godbey, *Time for Life*, 107). Free time has increased to nearly 40 hours a week (124–35).

10. Jerry A. Jacobs, "Changing Hours of American Employment" (paper presented at Workplace/Workforce Mismatch: Work, Family, Health, and Well-Being Conference, Washington, DC, June 16–18, 2003), http://www.popcenter.umd.edu/events/nichd/papers/jacobs.pdf (accessed September 21, 2005), 26, 7.

11. Harriet B. Presser, "Toward a 24-Hour Economy," *Science* 284 (1999): 1778–79.

12. Jeffrey J. Mayer, *Time Management for Dummies* (Foster City, CA: IDG, 1995), 3.

13. Charles N. Darrah, "Anthropology and the Workplace/Workforce Mismatch" (paper presented at Workplace/Workforce Mismatch: Work, Family, Health, and Well-Being Conference, Washington, DC, June 16–18, 2003), http://www.popcenter.umd.edu/events/nichd/papers/darrah.pdf (accessed September 21, 2005), 15.

14. See, for example, Jeff Davidson, *The Complete Idiot's Guide to Managing Your Time*, 3rd ed. (Indianapolis: Alpha, 2002); Stephen R. Covey, et al., *First Things First: To Live, to Love, to Learn, to Leave a Legacy* (New York: Fireside, 1995).

15. See their homepage at http://www.simpleliving.net/timeday/ (accessed September 23, 2005), or their official book edited by John De Graaf, *Take Back Your Time: Fighting Overwork and Time Poverty in America* (San Francisco: Berrett-Koehler, 2003).

16. Robinson and Godbey, *Time for Life*, 38–42.

17. "Slowing Down to Look at Busyness: Interview with Charles Darrah," Sloan Work and Family Research Network 6 (October 2004): 2, http://wfnetwork.bc.edu/The_Network_News/04/The_Network_News_Interview04.pdf (accessed September 20, 2005).

18. Cf. William E. Scheuerman, "Busyness and Citizenship," *Social Research* 72 (2005): 451–53.

19. Alvin Toffler coined the term. See Davidson, *Idiot's Guide*, 39.

20. Charles N. Darrah, "Family Models, Model Families" (paper presented at the annual meeting of the American Anthropological Association, Chicago, November 23, 2003), http://www2.sjsu.edu/depts/anthropology/svcp/pdfs/svcpfmmf.pdf (accessed September 20, 2005).

21. Liah Greenfeld, "When the Sky Is the Limit: Busyness in Contemporary American Society," *Social Research* 72 (2005): 330–33.

22. Juliet B. Schor, *The Overworked American: The Unexpected Decline of Leisure* (New York: Basic Books, 1991), 22–24.

23. Associated Press, "Strained Life of the Nonstop American Family," http://www.msnbc.msn.com/id/7184763/page/2/ (accessed March 21, 2005).

24. Darrah, "Slowing Down," 1.

25. Gary Cross, "A Right to Be Lazy? Busyness in Retrospective," *Social Research* 72 (2005): 282.

26. Robinson and Godbey, *Time for Life*, 33.

27. Paul Mills, "A Brief Theology of Time. Part 2: Resisting the Tyranny of Time," *Cambridge Papers* 11, no. 2 (2002): 2.

28. See Robert Banks, *The Tyranny of Time: When 24 Hours Is Not Enough* (Downers Grove, IL: InterVarsity, 1983), 101–18.

29. Malcolm Waters, *Globalization*, 2nd ed. (London: Routledge, 2001), 65.

30. Both views come from David F. Ford, *The Shape of Living* (Grand Rapids: Baker, 1997), 137.

31. Banks, *Tyranny of Time*, 68.

32. Robert Levine, "A Geography of Busyness," *Social Research* 72 (2005): 356.

33. Darrah, "Family Models," 3.

34. It is also helpful here to introduce a distinction between busyness and hurry. "Busyness" focuses on activity and how it is approached, whereas "hurry" is an internal state, characterized by haste and concern that time is too short. See John Ortberg, "Taking Care of Busyness," *Leadership Journal* 19, no. 3 (1998): 28–34, http://www.christianitytoday.com/le/814.814028 .html (accessed February 28, 2003).

35. AP, "Strained Life."

36. Phil Lancaster, "Say 'No' to Busyness," http://www.patriarch.com/article.php?sid=42 (accessed September 12, 2005).

37. An earlier version of this chapter did not recognize this. I am indebted to Dr. D. A. Carson for this insight.

38. Robinson and Godbey, *Time for Life*, 305.

39. Barbara Moses, "The Busyness Trap," *Training* 35 (November 1998): 38–40.

40. Robert Banks, "Time," in *New Dictionary of Biblical Theology*, ed. T. Desmond Alexander and Brian Rosner (Downers Grove, IL: InterVarsity, 2000), 821. See also Karl Barth, *Church Dogmatics*, III/2: *The Doctrine of Creation*, trans. Harold Knight et al. (Edinburgh: T&T Clark, 1960), 438.

41. Banks, *Tyranny of Time*, 179–82.

42. I follow here Tremper Longman III, *The Book of Ecclesiastes*, New International Commentary on the Old Testament (Grand Rapids: Eerdmans, 1998), 111–25, who argues for a pessimistic view of this passage from the viewpoint of Qoheleth.

43. My translation. The participle *exagorazomenoi* should be translated as an adverbial participle of means (i.e., how the Colossians live wisely). So Peter O'Brien, *Colossians, Philemon*, Word Biblical Commentary (Waco: Word, 1982), 241.

44. Colin Gunton, "Time and Providence," in *Theology Through Preaching: Sermons for Brentwood* (Edinburgh: T&T Clark, 2001), 47.

45. Moses, "The Busyness Trap," 40.

46. Ford, *Shape of Living*, 131–32.

47. Banks, *Tyranny of Time*, 195–96.

48. 2 Cor. 11:23–29; 1 Thess. 2:9; 2 Thess. 3:8. See Banks, *Tyranny of Time*, 191–93, for Paul as an example of how to live in time. Banks rightly notes that some of these examples occur in the context of Paul defending himself or rebuking the idle. Still, he perhaps underplays the range of evidence for fear that some might read contemporary notions of busyness into Paul's life.

49. Leland Ryken, *Redeeming the Time: A Christian Approach to Work and Leisure* (Grand Rapids: Baker, 1995), 275.

50. For example, a Google search showed that more of the top 20 links for "busyness" (eight of them) were from a Christian perspective than from any other category (accessed September 22, 2005).

51. Jonathan Edwards, "The Preciousness of Time, and the Importance of Redeeming It," in *The Works of Jonathan Edwards*, rev. Edward Hickman (Carlisle: Banner of Truth Trust, 1974), 233.

52. Anonymous, *Time: How to Make the Most of It* (London: SPCK, 1856), 9, item no. 5 in volume SPCK.3.1856.2.

53. Edwards, "Time," 235.

54. Anonymous, *Time*, 4.

55. See Lauren F. Winner, "Sleep Therapy," *Books and Culture* 12 (January/February 2006): 7–8. Also, Drew Kaplan, "In Your Lying Down and in Your Rising Up: A Biblical Sleep Ethic," *Jewish Bible Quarterly* 34 (2006): 47–50.

56. I am indebted to Dr. Graham Cole for this phrasing.

57. Beverly Hamilton, "Is Busyness Affecting Your Business?" http://www.ezinearticles .com/?Is-Busyness-Affecting-Your-Business?&id=65114 (accessed September 12, 2005). See also, "Beating Busyness," http://www.regent.edu/acad/schbus/maz/busyness.html (accessed February 28, 2003).

58. U.S. Department of Labor, Bureau of Labor Statistics, "American Time Use Survey— 2004 Results Announced by BLS," USDL 05-1766, September 2005, http://www.bls.gov/news .release/pdf/atus.pdf (accessed September 30, 2005). See also, Robinson and Godbey, *Time for Life*, 124–25.

59. Quoted in Davidson, *Idiot's Guide*, 25.

60. Darrah, "Family Models," 6.

61. Gunton, "Time," 44–45.

62. On the question of whether the Sabbath is binding on Christians, see on the one side, Roger T. Beckwith and Wilfrid Stott, *This Is the Day: The Biblical Doctrine of the Christian Sunday in Its Jewish and Early Christian Setting* (London: Marshall, Morgan & Scott, 1978), and on the other, D. A. Carson, ed., *From Sabbath to Lord's Day: A Biblical, Historical, and Theological Investigation* (Grand Rapids: Zondervan, 1982).

63. Cf. Judith Shulevitz, "The View from Saturday: Secular Israelis Try to Rescue the Sabbath," *Slate*, July 29, 2005, http://www.slate.com/id/2123283/ (accessed July 29, 2005).

64. Ford, *Shape of Living*, 136.

65. Darrell L. Bock, *Luke, Vol. 2: 9:51–24:53*, Baker Exegetical Commentary on the New Testament (Grand Rapids: Baker, 1996), 1038.

66. Bock, *Luke, Vol. 2*, 1039; Joseph A. Fitzmyer, SJ, *The Gospel According to Luke (X– XXIV)*, Anchor Bible (Garden City, NJ: Doubleday, 1985), 892.

Chapter 8 Welcome to the Blogosphere

1. Trudy Tynan, "'Blog' Most Popular Word on Web Dictionary," *Globe Technology*, December 2, 2004, http://www.globetechnology.com/servlet/story/RTGAM.20041202.gtbloggdec2/ BNStory/Technology/ (accessed December 3, 2004).

2. L. J. Gurak, S. Antonijevic, L. Johnson, C. Ratliff, and J. Reyman, "Introduction: Weblogs, Rhetoric, Community and Culture," in *Into the Blogosphere*, July 1, 2004, http://blog.lib.umn .edu/blogosphere/introduction (accessed July 8, 2004).

3. Rebecca Blood, "Weblogs: A History and Perspective," Rebecca's Pocket, September 7, 2000, http://www.rebeccablood.net/essays/weblog_history.html (accessed November 8, 2004). While Blood's piece is a bit dated, her analysis is still insightful, and has been cited both by Gurak et al. ("Introduction"), and Rebecca Mackinnion ("Blogging, Journalism and Credibility" Conference Summary, Harvard University, January 21–22, 2005, http://cyber.law.harvard.edu/webcred [accessed July 11, 2005]) in their more recent assessments of the blogosphere.

4. Mallory Jensen, "A Brief History of Weblogs," *Contemporary Journalism Review* (September–October 2003): 22.

5. Rebecca Mead, "You've Got Blog," originally published in *New Yorker*, November 13, 2000, www.rebeccamead.com/2000_11_13_art_blog.html (accessed November 8, 2004).

6. Jeffrey Henning, "The Blogging Geyser," Perseus Development Corp, April 8, 2005, http://www.perseus.com/blogsurvey/geyser.html (accessed July 14, 2005).

7. Leila Fast, Little Bear, November 6, 2003, http://littlekermode.com/2003_11_02_archive.htm (accessed November 5, 2004).

8. April Witt, "Blog Interrupted," *Washington Post*, August 15, 2004, http://www.washingtonpost.com/wp-dyn/articles/A54736–2004Aug10.html (accessed August 10, 2005).

9. Fernanda B. Viegas, "Bloggers' Expectations of Privacy and Accountability," *Journal of Computer-Mediated Communication*, April 2005, http://jcmc.indiana.edu/vol10/issue3/viegas.html (accessed July 20, 2005).

10. See Gurak et al., "Introduction."

11. Blood, "Weblogs," 5.

12. Jennifer Howard, "It's a Little Too Cozy in the Blogosphere," *Washington Post*, November 16, 2003, www.washingtonpost.com/ac2/wp_dyn/A43254–2003Nov14 (accessed November 5, 2004).

13. Ibid.

14. Jason Kottke, "Doing kottke.org as a Full-Time Job," Kottke.org, February 22, 2005, http://www.kottke.org/05/02/kottke-micropatron (accessed July 11, 2005).

15. Mead, "You've Got Blog."

16. http://www.technorati.com

17. Anonymous, "BLOGMA 2001," Grudnuk Creations, November 14, 2000, http://grudnuk.com/blogma2001/ (accessed November 12, 2004).

18. Steven Levy, "Blogging Beyond the Men's Club," *Newsweek*, March 21, 2005, http://msnbc.msn.com/id/7160264/site/newsweek/ (accessed July 11, 2005). See also MacKinnion, "Blogging," 4.

19. Henning, "The Blogging Iceberg," Perseus Development Corp, October 4, 2003, http://www.perseus.com/blogsurvey/iceberg.html (accessed July 14, 2005).

20. Ibid.

21. J. D. Lasica, "Random Acts of Journalism," New Media Musings, March 12, 2003, http://www.jdlasica.com/blog/archives/2003_03_12.html (accessed August 11, 2005).

22. J. Richard Stevens, "Bloggergate: How the CBS National Guard Story Affected Coverage of Webloggers," International Symposium on Online Journalism, April 8–9, 2005, http://journalism.utexas.edu/onlinejournalism/2005/papers/JRSBloggergate.pdf (accessed August 11, 2005).

23. See Mackinnion's summary of the Harvard conference.

24. Terry Heaton, "News is a Conversation," Donata Communications, January 13, 2004, http://donatacom.com/papers/pomo16.htm (accessed August 11, 2005).

25. Blood, "Weblogs," 4.

26. Steven Johnson, "Mind Share: Blog Space," *Wired*, June 2003, http://www.wired.com/wired/archive/11.06/blog_spc.html (accessed November 8, 2004).

27. Ann Meyer, "Blogs Giving Firms a Human Voice," *Chicago Tribune*, August 1, 2005, http://www.chicagotribune.com/technology/chi-0508010079aug01,1,3827292.story?coll=chi-technology-hed (accessed August 11, 2005).

28. http://blogs4god.com.

29. Ganns Deen, "Superblessed Christian Blog Award Nominees 2004," Superblessed, October 14, 2004, http://superblessed.blogspot.com/2004/10/one-with-nominees-for-superblessed.html (accessed November 2004).

30. http://www.beliefnet.com/blogheaven/.

31. Robert Moll, "Blogger Predicts Revival via Web," *Leadership Journal*, April 13, 2004, http://www.christianitytoday.com/le/2004/004/4.13.html (accessed November 4, 2004).

32. Tim Bednar, "We Know More Than Our Pastors," E-Church.com, April 22, 2004, http://www.e-church.com/Downloads/We%20Know%20More%20Than%20Our%20Pastors .pdf (accessed November 12, 2004), 39.

33. Bednar, "We Know More," 3. See also Michael Spencer, "Prepare to be Blogged," Internet Monk, May 20, 2005, http://www.internetmonk.com/archives/2005/05/019916.html (accessed July 28, 2005).

34. Bednar, "We Know More," 7–8.

35. Ibid., 3.

36. Bednar's manifesto is well researched and intriguing, and warrants much more consideration than I can give it in this paper. In particular, Bednar's idea of "participatory church" is worth exploring as a way of interacting theologically with blogging.

37. Comment on Spencer, "Prepare."

38. Bednar, "We Know More," 14, emphasis mine.

39. Ibid., 29.

40. Ibid., 24.

41. Ibid., 42–44.

42. Timothy George, "The Priesthood of All Believers and the Quest for Theological Integrity," *Criswell Theological Journal*, Spring 1989, http://www.founders.org/FJ03/article1_fr.html (accessed November 20, 2004).

43. Johnson, "Mind Share," 1.

44. Jensen, "Brief History," 22.

45. See Quentin Schultze, *Habits of the High-Tech Heart* (Grand Rapids: Baker, 2002), 165–88.

46. Hubert L. Dreyfuss, "Kierkegaard on the Internet," University of California at Berkeley, 2004, http://ist-socrates.Berkeley.edu/~hdreyfus/html/paper_kierkegaard.html (accessed November 20, 2005).

47. Doug Groothuis, "Why Matter Matters: The Challenge of Cyberspace to Christian Doctrine and Ethics," Doug Groothuis.com, June 4, 2002, http://ivpress.gospelcom.net/groothuis/doug/archives/000135.php (accessed July 17, 2005).

48. This language is from Jay Rosen, quoted in Mackinnion, "Blogging," 77–78.

Chapter 9 Human 2.0

1. Kevin Warwick, *I, Cyborg* (London: Century, 2002), 1.

2. Christopher West, "The New Language: A Crash Course in the Theology of the Body," *Crisis* 22 (December 2004), http://www.catholiceducation.org/articles/sexuality/se0108.html (accessed August 16, 2005).

3. Biotechnology Industry Organization, "Biotechnology Industry Facts," http://www.bio .org/speeches/pubs/er/statistics.asp (accessed August 10, 2005).

4. See Jeremy Rifkin, *The Biotech Century: Harnessing the Gene and Remaking the World* (New York: Jeremy P. Tarcher/Putnam, 1998).

5. See National Center for Biotechnology Information, "Genome Sequencing," http://www .ncbi.nlm.nih.gov/genome/seq/ (accessed August 10, 2005).

6. See Biotechnology Industry Organization, "Approved Biotechnology Drugs," http://www .bio.org/ataglance/bio/200407drugs.asp?p=yes (accessed August 10, 2005), and Biotechnology Industry Organization, "Biotechnology Industry Facts."

7. KYW, "Anti-Biotech Protesters Disrupt Traffic," CBS3 Philadelphia, June 21, 2005, http:// kyw.com/Local%20News/local_story_172124333.html (accessed August 10, 2005).

8. Jim Wasserman, "Biotech Crops Get Backing in Poll: But 30 Percent Want State to Ban Them," *Sacramento Bee*, August 10, 2005, http://www.sacbee.com/content/business/story/ 13387079p-14228596c.html (accessed August 10, 2005).

9. Siri Steiner, "Better . . . Stronger . . . Faster . . ." *Popular Science*, September 2005, 49.

10. See President's Council on Bioethics, *Beyond Therapy: Biotechnology and the Pursuit of Happiness* (Washington, DC: President's Council on Bioethics, 2003). Also available at http://www .bioethics.gov/reports/beyondtherapy/index.html (accessed September 21, 2005).

11. Carl Elliott, *Better Than Well: American Medicine Meets the American Dream* (New York: Norton, 2003).

12. Nick Bostrom, "The Transhumanist FAQ: A General Introduction," World Transhumanist Association, http://www.transhumanism.org/resources/faq.html (accessed August 8, 2005). Note that due to the lack of page numbers and the length of this online document I am citing the subsection.

13. Max More, "Lextropicon: Extropian Neologisms," Extropy Institute, http://spock.extropy .org/ideas/lextropicon.html (accessed September 27, 2005).

14. Bostrom, "Transhumanist FAQ," 1.3.

15. James J. Hughes, email message to author, January 9, 2004.

16. Bostrom, "Transhumanist FAQ," 5.1.

17. Leon R. Kass, *The Beginning of Wisdom: Reading Genesis* (New York: Free Press, 2003), 243.

18. Bostrom, "Transhumanist FAQ," 1.1, 5.3.

19. "Humanism," *The Columbia Encyclopedia*, 6th ed. (New York: Columbia University Press, 2003), http://www.bartleby.com/65/hu/humanism.html (accessed December 6, 2003).

20. Bostrom, "Transhumanist FAQ," 1.2, 2.6.

21. Ibid., 1.2.

22. Ibid.

23. Ibid., 2.3.

24. Ibid., 2.7.

25. Ray Kurzweil, *The Singularity Is Near: When Humans Transcend Biology* (New York: Penguin, 2005).

26. Bostrom, "Transhumanist FAQ," 1.1.

27. Ibid., 1.2.

28. Ibid., 2.2.

29. Ibid., 2.6.

30. Ibid.

31. See Advanced Fertility Center of Chicago, http://www.advancedfertility.com/ (accessed September 27, 2005).

32. Bostrom, "Transhumanist FAQ," 1.1.

33. Ibid., 3.2.

34. Ibid.

35. Ibid., 4.1.

36. Ibid., 4.4.

37. Ibid., 4.2.

38. Ibid., 3.3–3.4.

39. Ibid., 2.7.

40. Ibid., 3.5.

41. Leon R. Kass, "*L'Chaim* and Its Limits: Why Not Immortality?" *First Things* 113 (May 2001), http://print.firstthings.com/ftissues/ft0105/articles/kass.html (accessed January 12, 2004).

42. C. Christopher Hook, "Cybernetics and Nanotechnology," in *Cutting-Edge Bioethics: A Christian Exploration of Technologies and Trends*, ed. John F. Kilner, C. Christopher Hook, and Diane B. Uustal (Grand Rapids: Eerdmans, 2002), 60.

43. Ibid.

44. Bostrom, "Transhumanist FAQ," 5.5.

45. Hook, "Cybernetics and Nanotechnology," 60.

46. Bostrom, "Transhumanist FAQ," 4.4.

47. Craig Detweiler and Barry Taylor, *A Matrix of Meanings: Finding God in Pop Culture* (Grand Rapids: Baker, 2003), 48.

48. Bostrom, "Transhumanist FAQ," 5.3.

49. Ibid.

50. U2/Bono, "The Wanderer," *Zooropa,* © 1993 Island Records.

51. Bostrom, "Transhumanist FAQ," 1.2.

52. Rom. 8:21–23; 1 Cor. 15; 2 Cor. 4:14–5:5. See also Randy Alcorn, *Heaven* (Wheaton: Tyndale, 2004), and N. T. Wright, *The Resurrection of the Son of God: Christian Origins and the Question of God*, vol. 3 (Minneapolis: Fortress, 2003).

53. Bostrom, "Transhumanist FAQ," 6.6.

54. Ibid.

55. 1 Pet. 1:1. See also Heb. 11.

56. 2 Cor. 5:5.

57. Graham Houston, *Virtual Morality: Christian Ethics in the Computer Age* (Leicester, UK: Apollos, 1998), 126.

58. Gerald P. McKenny, *To Relieve the Human Condition: Bioethics, Technology, and the Body* (Albany: State University of New York Press, 1997), 19.

59. Ibid., 9.

60. Ibid., 185.

61. Ibid., 210.

62. See David Pullinger, *Information Technology and Cyberspace: Extra-connected Living* (Cleveland: Pilgrim, 2001).

63. McKenny, *Relieve the Human Condition*, 5.

64. Houston, *Virtual Morality*, 126.

Chapter 10 Fantasy Funerals and Other Designer Ways of Going Out in Style

1. Lisa Takeuchi Cullen, "What a Way to Go," *Time*, July 7, 2003, 88.

2. Gina Gallo, "What a Way to Go!" *TheColumnist.com*, 2003, http://www.thecolumnists .com/gallo/gallo53.html (accessed January 6, 2006).

3. Jeanie Lerche Davis, "Designer Funerals: The Final Getaway," WebMD, October 29, 2003, http://www.webmd.com/content/article/76/90035.html (accessed January 3, 2006).

4. Adam Goldman, "Funeral Home Adds That Special Vegas Touch," *SFGate.com*, September 24, 2003, http://sfgate.com/cgi-bin/article.cgi?f=/n/a/2003/09/24/national0231EDT0446 .DTL&nl=fix (accessed January 6, 2006).

5. Wayne Alan Brenner, "Fashion Gets Grave," *Austin Chronicle*, October 29, 1999, http:// www.austinchronicle.com/issues/dispatch/1999–10–29/xtra_feature4.html (accessed January 3, 2006).

6. Cremation Association of North America, "Confirmed 2003 Statistics: 2003–2025," http://www.cremationassociation.org/html/statistics.html (accessed January 5, 2006).

7. Figures taken from Cullen, "What a Way to Go," 91.

8. LifeGem, http://www.lifegem.com/secondary/LGProcess2006.aspx (accessed January 3, 2006). See also Cullen, "What a Way to Go," 88.

9. Eternally Yours, http://www.eternally-yours.org (accessed January 3, 2006).

10. Space Services Inc., http://www.memorialspaceflights.com/services.asp (accessed January 3, 2006).

11. Davis, "Designer Funerals"; Eternal Reefs, http://www.eternalreefs.com/reefs/products .html (accessed January 6, 2006).

12. Jessica Mitford, *The American Way of Death Revisited* (New York: Vintage Books, 2000), 140.

13. Ibid., 148.

14. Gary Laderman, *Rest in Peace* (New York: Oxford University Press, 2003), 45–82.

15. Mitford, *American Way of Death*, 138–49.

16. Ibid., 148. Church leaders have often opposed the giving of flowers at funerals on merely pragmatic grounds, suggesting instead charitable donations in honor of the deceased.

17. Ibid., 138–49.

18. Cullen, "What a Way to Go," 88.

19. Eagle Custom Caskets, Inc., http://www.eaglecaskets.com/mission.html (accessed January 3, 2006).

20. Cullen, "What a Way to Go," 91.

21. Laderman, *Rest in Peace*, 45–82.

22. Davis, "Designer Funerals."

23. The television show "Boston Legal" had an episode ("Breast in Show") where a character hosted his own pre-death funeral (see http://www.tv.com/breast-in-show/episode/580523/summary.html [accessed March 31, 2006]). This trend is especially popular in other countries: for the United Kingdom, see Sarah Nelson, "Man Hosts His Own Funeral Party," *This Is Local London*, March 15, 2006, http://www.thisislocallondon.co.uk/search/display.var.706225.0.man_hosts_his_own_funeral_party.php (accessed March 31, 2006); for Australia, see Sue Hardy, "Renewing Your Vows," *Peace of Mind*, Winter 2003, http://www.forpeaceofmind.com.au/Vol3/funeral directors.cfm (accessed March 31, 2006); and for Japan, see Satsuki Kawano, "Pre-Funerals in Contemporary Japan: the Making of a New Ceremony of Later Life among Aging Japanese," http://www.funeralwire.com/modules.php?name=News&file=print&sid=13683 (accessed March 31, 2006).

24. Hollywood Forever Cemetery, http://www.hollywoodforever.com/Cemetery.htm (accessed January 3, 2006). See also Cullen, "What a Way to Go," 89.

25. Ray A. Smith, "Mausoleums Get Livelier, Adding Museums and Cafes; Voice Messages from Beyond," *Funeralwire.com*, September 24, 2003, http://www.funeralwire.com/modules.php?name=News&file=article&sid=10201 (accessed January 6, 2006).

26. Brenner, "Fashion Gets Grave."

27. Cullen, "What a Way to Go," 88.

28. Davis, "Designer Funerals."

29. As summarized from L. R. Bailey Sr., *Biblical Perspectives on Death* (Philadelphia: OBT, 1992), 97–101.

30. Information in this paragraph was taken from Kent Harold Richard, "Death in the Old Testament," in *The Anchor Bible Dictionary*, ed. David Noel Freedman (New York: Doubleday, 1992), 2:108–10.

31. Enoch (Gen. 5:24) and Elijah (2 Kings 2:11). P. S. Johnston, "Death and Resurrection," in *New Dictionary of Biblical Theology*, ed. T. Desmond Alexander and Brian S. Rosner (Downers Grove, IL: InterVarsity, 2000), 444.

32. Richard, "Death in the Old Testament," 2:109.

33. Ibid., 2:110.

34. J. E. Means, "Funerals," in *Dictionary of Christianity in America*, ed. Daniel G. Reid (Downers Grove, IL: InterVarsity, 1990), 469.

35. Typically early Christians were buried in communal burial grounds or catacombs, while occasionally, wealthier Christians were buried in private and often more elaborate tombs with monuments. Jeff Childers, "Funerary Practices" in *Encyclopedia of Early Christianity*, 2nd ed., ed. Everett Ferguson (New York: Garland, 1997), 1:443.

36. Charles H. Spurgeon, "Preparing to Depart," The C. H. Spurgeon Collection, October 8, 1865, http://www.biblebb.com/files/spurgeon/3116.htm (accessed January 3, 2006).

37. Kate Berridge, "Coffin Fits," *The Spectator*, November 9, 2002, http://www.findarticles.com/p/articles/mi_qa3724/is_200211/ai_n9158472 (accessed January 6, 2006).

38. Art Caskets, http://www.artcaskets.com/codepages/fish.html (accessed January 3, 2006).

Chapter 11 Putting It into Practice

1. *Wired*, http://www.wired.com/wired/; *Arts and Letters Daily*, http://www.aldaily.com/ (accessed January 12, 2006).

2. *The Knot*, http://www.theknot.com/au_industrystats.shtml (accessed January 5, 2006).

3. E.g. Lauren F. Winner, "Wedding Nights—and Daze," *Books & Culture* (January/February 2000): 26–27; Caitlin Flanagan, "The Wedding Merchants," *The Atlantic Monthly* (February 2001): 112–18; Flanagan, "Let's Call the Whole Thing Off," *The Atlantic Monthly* (November 2003): 153–55.

4. Northwestern University, http://nucat.library.northwestern.edu/ (accessed January 9, 2006).

5. Cele C. Otnes and Elizabeth H. Pleck, *Cinderella Dreams: The Allure of the Lavish Wedding* (Berkeley: University of California Press, 2003); Carol McD. Wallace, *All Dressed in White: The Irresistible Rise of the American Wedding* (New York: Penguin, 2004).

6. Winner, "Wedding Nights," 27.

7. Note the humorous comments about the sovereignty of the wedding photographer in L. Penseur, "Wedding Fever," *Re:generation Quarterly* 6 (Summer 2000): 44.

8. David Noel Freedman, ed., *Anchor Bible Dictionary*, 6 vols. (New York: Doubleday, 1992); Walter A. Elwell, ed., *Evangelical Dictionary of Theology* (Grand Rapids: Baker, 2001); I. Howard Marshall et al., *New Bible Dictionary*, 3rd ed. (Downers Grove, IL: InterVarsity, 1996). The latter is available, along with many other IVP dictionaries, on CD-ROM. For theological interpretation of Scripture, particularly useful volumes are Kevin J. Vanhoozer, *Dictionary for Theological Interpretation of the Bible* (Grand Rapids: Baker, 2005), and T. Desmond Alexander and Brian S. Rosner, eds., *New Dictionary of Biblical Theology* (Downers Grove, IL: InterVarsity, 2000).

9. Rolfing Library, Trinity International University, http://library.tiu.edu/ (accessed Jan. 17, 2006).

10. Christopher Ash, *Marriage: Sex in the Service of God* (Vancouver: Regent College, 2005); Geoffrey Bromiley, *God and Marriage* (Grand Rapids: Eerdmans, 1980).

11. Other important texts include Deut. 24:1–4; Ezek. 24:15–18; Hosea 1–3; Mal. 2:10–16; Matt. 22:1–14; Luke 14:25–27; 18:29–30; John 2:1–11; 1 Cor. 7:1–16; Col. 3:18–19; 1 Thess. 4:3–8; 1 Pet. 3:1–7.

12. See, for example, Craig Bartholomew and Michael W. Goheen, *The Drama of Scripture: Finding Our Place in the Biblical Story* (Grand Rapids: Baker, 2004). Albert M. Wolters, *Creation Regained: Biblical Basics for a Reformational Worldview* (Grand Rapids: Eerdmans, 1985), utilizes a similar schema as the basis for a Christian worldview.

13. *The Knot*, http://www.theknot.com/au_industrystats.shtml (accessed January 20, 2006).

14. Helpful in this regard is Daniel M. Doriani, *Putting the Truth to Work: The Theory and Practice of Biblical Application* (Phillipsburg, NJ: P & R, 2001). He focuses on holistic application in preaching, but his approach is relevant for cultural agency too.

Glossary

1. Albert M. Wolters, *Creation Regained: Biblical Basics for a Reformational Worldview* (Grand Rapids: Eerdmans, 1985), 2.

Everyday Theologians Information

Charles A. Anderson is working on a PhD in New Testament at the University of Cambridge.

Justin A. Bailey is youth pastor at Antioch Bible Church in Wheeling, IL and working on an MDiv at Trinity Evangelical Divinity School.

Matthew Eppinette is director of research and analysis at the Center for Bioethics and Human Dignity in Bannockburn, IL.

Jeremy D. Lawson teaches world history at St. Paul Christian Academy in Nashville, TN.

Ben Peays is working on a PhD in systematic theology at Trinity Evangelical Divinity School.

Darren Sarisky is working on a PhD in systematic theology at the University of Aberdeen.

Michael J. Sleasman is finishing a PhD in systematic theology at Trinity Evangelical Divinity School and has served as adjunct instructor at Trinity International University and tutor in the Distance Education program.

David G. Thompson works for Samaritan's Purse as regional director for Eastern Europe and Central Asia, where he focuses on the Operation Christmas Child Project and religious liberties.

Kevin J. Vanhoozer is research professor of systematic theology at Trinity Evangelical Divinity School.

Premkumar D. Williams is instructor in theology at Baptist Seminary of South India in Bangalore, India.

Subject Index

"high" vs. "low," 27, 250
industry, 38
and language, 34–35, 260n125
as lived worldview, 26
as means of spiritual formation, 31
nature vs., 21–22
as "objectification of spirit," 22
semantics vs. semiotics of, 44
society and, 23, 27
spiritual dimension of, 33, 257n66
as "system" and "practice," 26
theology of, 41, 149
as "web of significance," 25, 248
as works and worlds of meaning, 26, 28, 44
See also popular culture

Dark, David, 41
de Certeau, Michel, 56
deep structures, 133, 134, 139, 143, 270n3
Dilthey, Wilhelm, 22, 31, 249
discourse, 44–45, 248. *See also* cultural discourse
drama of redemption, 34, 113, 123, 127, 145, 150, 166, 242

Eliot, T. S., 18, 56
eschatology, 143, 163, 166, 194, 218
evolutionary biology, 38
excorporation, 56–57, 249
exegesis, 40, 140, 249
explanation, 17, 22, 140

fall, 41, 43, 110, 160, 192, 200–201, 202, 234, 240–41
Feuerbach, Ludwig, 37
Fiske, John, 56, 249
focal practices, 57
Frankfurt School, 38, 46, 50, 258n85
freedom, 21, 99, 100, 103, 138
Freud, Sigmund, 37

Geertz, Clifford, 24–25, 248, 251
general revelation. *See* revelation, general
genre, 50, 83, 85, 87–88, 93, 97, 134, 135–36, 139, 234–35
God, 29, 41, 43, 47, 53, 56, 103, 109, 126, 128, 161–62
good, the, 36, 45, 53, 65, 66, 70, 71–78, 109, 121, 129, 132, 160, 189, 217

gospel, 7, 53, 55, 59, 71–78, 82, 109, 111, 121, 192, 200, 238
Gramsci, Antonio, 39, 57, 249
Grenz, Stanley, 42, 259n104

health, 68, 73–74, 194, 197–98
hegemony, 39, 57–58, 249
Heidegger, Martin, 19, 24, 144, 147, 270n3
Herder, Johann, 24
hermeneutic(s)
    definition, 36, 45, 249
    general, 48
    of charity, 233–34
    of suspicion, 37, 39–40, 50, 225, 241, 249
history, 22, 127, 128, 165
holiness, 71, 93–94, 163
Holy Spirit, 42–44, 54, 117, 122, 126, 163, 259n104
hope, 91–92, 101, 108, 126, 128, 132, 134, 139, 141, 142–50, 197–98, 202, 222, 224, 271n36
human being, 48, 99, 103–7, 109–10, 112, 192, 195, 202, 224
human sciences, 22, 36, 38, 255n16

ideology, 38, 54, 107, 123, 241, 250
idolatry, 54, 164
illocutions, 31, 45, 48, 50–51, 56, 250. *See also* locutions; perlocutions
imagination, 29, 32, 52, 242
imago Dei, 43, 54, 109, 110, 112, 200, 201, 224, 263n22
incarnation, 42, 110, 111, 188, 206. *See also* Jesus
interpretation, 36–40, 45, 140, 148, 234, 236, 250

Jesus, 17, 53, 57, 73–74, 75–77, 109, 110, 126–27, 128, 145–46, 166. *See also* incarnation
Johnson, Mark, 52

Kant, Immanuel, 21, 169

Lakoff, George, 52
language, 24
life, the good, 36, 45, 53, 65, 66, 70, 71–78, 132, 189, 217
locutions, 45, 48, 50, 56, 250. *See also* illocutions; perlocutions

Scripture Index

Ezekiel

24:15–18 280n11
28:12 73
28:17 73

Hosea

1–3 280n11

Joel

2:28–32 163

Amos

3:15 75
5:18 162

Zephaniah

3:9–20 162

Malachi

2:10–16 280n11

Matthew

4:1–11 76
6:24 75
6:26 122
6:26–27 128
7:16 53
8:16–17 73
8:26 20
10:24–25 263n22
11:30 75
13:44–46 76
16 21
16:1–3 17
16:18 58
19:1–12 72
19:26 58
22:1–14 240, 280n11
22:23–33 239
22:31–32 220
22:39 19
26:12 220
28:19–20 120

Mark

1:15 163
1:35 166

1:38–39 77
2:8–12 74
6:31 157
8:31–34 263n22
10:1–12 239
12:26–27 76
12:28–34 109

Luke

Book of 92–93
4:18 92
5:16 166
6:20 92
7:4–5 75
7:11–17 220
7:22 92
8:1–3 77
9:10 166
9:57–58 77
10:25–37 109
10:30–37 171
10:38–42 171
12:1–13 171
12:16–20 161
14:13 92
14:21 92
14:25–27 280n11
16:20 92
16:22 92
18:29–30 280n11
23:42–43 222
23:56 220

John

Book of 94–95
1:1 94
1:14 57, 93
2:1–11 240, 280n11
3:16 200, 221
10:35 74
11:25–26 221
11:44 220
13 127
13:4–5 263n22
14:8–9 263n22

Acts

1:20 122
2 124

2:17 163
2:33–34 163
4:36–37 75
5:6 220
7:30 167
8:30–31 35
9:37 220
23:8 219

Romans

1:18 200
5:12 220
6:23 220
8:21–23 278n52
8:29 72
12 206
12:2 35
13:11–14 163

1 Corinthians

6:19 206
7:1–16 280n11
7:4 72
10:11 163
10:31 165
11:1 263n22
11:17–30 127
11:22 123
15 146, 202, 278n52
15:3 200
15:10 165
15:20–28 163
15:26 221
15:42–44 224
15:49 263n22
15:52 224

2 Corinthians

3:17–4:16 71
4:4 200
4:14–5:5 278n52
4:16 72
5:5 278n56
5:16 74
5:19 78
6 94
8:9 76, 77
10:5 58, 74